Praise for Tim Br

The Groundwater Diaries

'Quite brilliant' *Bookseller*

'Very funny' *Independent*

'Brilliantly crackers' *Word*

'Rapier wit' *Herald*

'Anarchic, hilarious, inspired' *Northern Echo*

Is Shane MacGowan Still Alive?

'Bizarre, funny, brash' *Sunday Times*

'Sly and funny' *Irish Post*

'An absolute must... hilarious' *Scotsman*

'Laugh-out-loud funny' *Herald*

'A superb and positively hilarious book'
Manchester Evening News

Author's Note

Apart from the obvious fictionalising of my adventures in France, the events in this book are true, at least in the sense that all of my recollections and memories are true. There is the odd factual inaccuracy, but these are authentic inaccuracies (i.e. true to my own version of events and not deliberate fabrications). Of course, it's real life and therefore there is not really much of a plot.

All names have been changed, apart from one or two who were more than happy to be revealed.

About the author

Tim Bradford was born and brought up in Lincolnshire. He has written two other non-fiction books, *The Groundwater Diaries* and *Is Shane MacGowan Still Alive?* Tim has been a cartoonist/illustrator for the football magazine *When Saturday Comes* since 1990 and is a regular illustrator for the *Guardian*. He also wrote and illustrated *Learn to Speak Capello*. He is married with three children and lives in a quiet North London valley.

In a parallel universe he is a tree-planter and artist based in the west of Ireland.

www.smalltownengland.co.uk

Small Town England

and how I survived it

Tim Bradford

EBURY
PRESS

For Louble, Flipflop, Sherbert and Tubman

1 3 5 7 9 10 8 6 4 2

Published in 2010 by Ebury Press, an imprint of Ebury Publishing
A Random House Group Company

Copyright © Tim Bradford 2010

Tim Bradford has asserted his right to be identified as the author of this Work
in accordance with the Copyright, Designs and Patents Act 1988

The Random House Group Limited Reg. No. 954009

Addresses for companies within the Random House Group can be found at
www.randomhouse.co.uk

A CIP catalogue record for this book is available from the British Library

The Random House Group Limited supports The Forest Stewardship
Council (FSC), the leading international forest certification organisation.
All our titles that are printed on Greenpeace approved FSC certified paper
carry the FSC logo. Our paper procurement policy can be found at
www.rbooks.co.uk/environment

Mixed Sources
Product group from well-managed
forests and other controlled sources
www.fsc.org Cert no. TT-COC-2139
© 1996 Forest Stewardship Council

FSC

Designed and set by seagulls.net

Printed in the UK by CPI Mackays, Chatham, ME5 8TD

ISBN 9780091928773

To buy books by your favourite authors and register for offers visit
www.rbooks.co.uk

This book is a work of non-fiction based on the life, experiences and
recollections of the author. In some cases names of people/places/dates
or sequences of the detail of events have been changed.

Contents

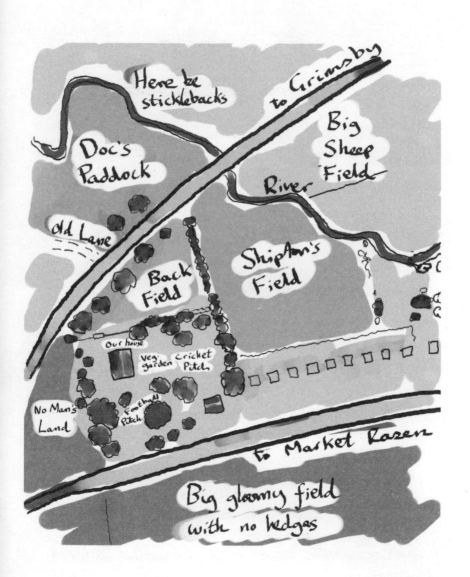

Prologue

Who Will Save the Elephant Seal?

'To myself I am only a child playing on the beach, while vast oceans of truth lie undiscovered before me.' – *Sir Isaac Newton* *

Like most things within the county of Lincolnshire in the 1970s, apart from the size of the county itself, Cleethorpes Zoo was small and slightly dog-eared.

The one thing it had that I will always remember was the elephant seal. The pool for the elephant seal was also small and inadequate. And the elephant seal itself was huge. Over twelve feet long, with a small square head and a huge nose, this ugly creature would swim round and round, round and round, in a way that, even as a small child, suggested to me the futility of life. I had a desire to jump into the pool and comfort it, swim with it.

Back home 1 had a friend whose dad was a milkman. He was famous in our town for three things. He'd never been out of Lincolnshire and he'd never had a day off sick in his life. And he was always really happy. He was like the anti-elephant seal, doing his round. Going round and round the town every day, picking up bottles, dropping them off. But he was happy doing this. It was his journey by choice. It was the repetition and the predictability that probably made him so happy. It's really a mistaken comparison

---

* Born Grantham, Lincolnshire. He's referring to his attempts to unlock the mechanisms of the universe, but really describing the experience of finding yourself being brought up in the rural suburbs.

Elephant seal.

because for the milkman this was his natural habitat, this small town in a big small-minded county. The elephant seal should have been diving for fish in some frozen seascape in Antarctica, not confined to a kids' swimming pool in a fading resort in the East Midlands. But I was still confused by the milkman, partly because we were different. I was always ill. I hated repetition. It was me and the elephant seal against the milkman.

Why has the memory of the poor ugly elephant seal stayed with me all these years? It has probably something to do with its being confined. Going round in circles. I always felt there was something claustrophobic about the experience of living in Lincolnshire. There was something about that huge expanse of land and the repetitive mundane nature of small-town life that would eventually lead me to the conclusion that escape and travel to somewhere else would be a very necessary part of growing up. Even now when I think of the elephant seal I feel melancholy and a little breathless, the same sensation I get when I accidentally stray into the suburbs.

A Brief Introduction to 'The Sleepiest Town in England'

Market Rasen. Hearing those two words can bring on various symptoms ranging from warm fuzziness to anxiety and a desire to escape from wherever I am. Those two powerful words make me think of hard, cold winds blowing down quiet streets on a Saturday afternoon. Situated in a geographical wind tunnel, with gusts blowing up from the south west and north east and meeting in vicious swirls on the municipal playing fields of mid-North Lincolnshire (just as clogging midfielders, i.e. me, are about to take a shot on goal), Market Rasen lies at the eastern side of a great flat plain that stretches up from the Fens as far north as Brigg. It's not the Fens but it's not hilly either. It isn't meadowland but it's not all arable either. About three miles down the road was the start of the Lincolnshire

This is a hill - honest.

Wolds. 'They're not wolds, they're nipples!' my Yorkshire grandad would say, laughing and nudging me in the ribs before being glared at by Yorkshire Granny.

My daily walks through Market Rasen in the early 70s, accompanied by my brother Toby as we sauntered slowly back from school, took me from one end to the other of our compact, not quite attractive, redbrick Victorian town. We would pass four butchers, five sweetshops, two toyshops, two newsagents, countless greengrocers and grocers and seven pubs, all for around 2,000 people. As we headed down Queen Street, the main thoroughfare, I can remember the chocolatey rush of Garnett's sweetshop, the smell of singed hair from Johnny Richards' barbershop where we all used to get our short back and sides. I can smell the petrol pumps from the little Cleveland garage in the middle of the town and the warm shampoo wafts from Audrey's Hairdressers across the road. A little further down would be the gentle coffee aroma of East-wood's café, a leftover from a more elegant age where mothers and middle-aged ladies congregated, and kids tried to catch the fish in the big goldfish pond. A glance down a side street towards the Liberal Club reminds me of where I would later do brass band practice in a thick fug of cigarette smoke and cleaning fluid. And Wilson's, the other sweetshop, where more adventurous souls than I would nick 1p bubblegums.

Into the market place and the wafts of brown-beer breath from nearby pubs, The Aston Arms and The Chase, the soapy blandness of the shiny new Co-op at the corner of the square, where until the 1960s a fine nineteenth-century town hall and corn exchange had stood. Then into King Street, towards the end of the town, and the thrillingly claustrophobic (and slightly damp) rooms of the little lending library where I learned to read from books about WW1, planes and battleships and then, a few doors down from there, the meths-like mustiness of the doctor's waiting room in a little Victorian terraced house.

Charles Dickens is supposed to have once said that Market Rasen was the sleepiest town in England (and that was in its high-octane, nineteenth-century heyday). We used to hear that a lot when we were kids. Maybe Dickens passed through while he was researching *Bleak House*, as in the novel he writes that 'there is no gainsaying the fact that Lincolnshire at its worst is hard to beat for utter dreariness'. Although this quote might have started as a rumour, it has now spread to become an acknowledged fact.

The ancient history of Market Rasen is a little vague. People have been coming to Rasen for centuries but only on their way to somewhere else. Caistor, ten miles up the road – the village we loved to hate, simply because it was the same size as Rasen and had more attractive old buildings – was once a Roman camp called Castra. It lies close to Ermine Street, the early Great North Road, which runs north all the way from Bishopsgate in London up to Lincoln and on to the Humber (now, in various places, the A10, A17, A1 and random farm tracks). The Saxons named our town East Rasen, the smallest of three settlements, the others being Middle Rasen and West Rasen, and from that time on it officially existed. The name 'Rasen' comes from the Old English *roesn*, 'plank', used for a plank bridge across the river – the river in question is called the Rase. Fast-forward 1400 years (where little or nothing appears to have happened, apart from the appearance of a market in the Middle Ages), and although much of the town is Georgian, it was the Victorians who really put the place on the map by building a railway line through the area. For a while it was the most sophisticated place for miles around with its racecourse, markets, cattle fairs, processions and parties. In the fading black and white prints in the local newspaper offices, you can just make out the contented expressions of our great-great-grandfathers' generation.

With exciting smells, cheap sweets, fat goldfish, garages that gave away football-related freebies and copious military books, Market Rasen had been a great place to be a young child.

1. Great! My Girlfriend's Moved to Scunthorpe and I Can See a Terrifying Shining Skull

This is the story of my teenage years in the rural suburbs. In 1977, I was twelve years old – The Clash had their debut album, the Sex Pistols were sacked by their label EMI, *Star Wars* first opened in the UK, *Abba: The Movie* came out and Britain went royalty-mad for the Queen's Silver Jubilee. I, however, had an unforgettably forgettable year – it was a strange bridge-time between childhood and adolescence.

1976-77 was my first year at De Aston, the local secondary school, and so life was, of course, rife with anxieties and change, and anxiety about change. I'd started the year being off school for a few weeks due to a mystery illness which was first diagnosed as flu, then glandular fever, but eventually came to be seen as some sort of minor nervous breakdown caused by too much close filmatic analysis of *Frankenstein: The True Story*, starring Michael Sarrazin. One theory I had at the time was that it was brought on by my eleven-year-old girlfriend, Debbie White, moving to Scunthorpe and leaving me forever just nine months earlier.

What had I been doing with a girlfriend at eleven years old? Had I been 'in love'? We used to kiss by stretching out our necks and touching our lips together with our bodies about two feet apart. Then I'd usually run off in the other direction and play British Bulldog or something similarly manly to feel better about it all.

Then, in the summer term before primary school, Debbie hit me with a bombshell. Her family were moving to Scunthorpe. It's not that far away, she'd said. We'd still see each other.

It was twenty miles, for God's sake – the far side of the moon as far as I was concerned.

I dealt with slow-burning heartbreak – and the anxiety of moving to secondary school – by throwing myself full on into lots of different activities: Scouts, church choir, piano lessons, football, rugby, school orchestra, the town brass band, supporting Leeds United, building Airfix models, becoming a full-time Christian (well, getting confirmed) and cross-country running.

At secondary school I started to become really fit. This was partly to do with avoiding the hard-nuts around the woodwork classrooms, but mostly down to my surprising ability at cross-country running. It wasn't that I was fast – God, no – it was

more down to the positive motivation techniques of Mr Minting, our burly PE teacher who, in the traditional English sporting style, believed effort was at least as important as natural
ability. And, unlike other teachers, he had the potential weapon
of a jog around the track or field to focus unfocused young
minds. When we weren't running, Mr Minting was a good
bloke, but when we were in PE kit he was the Most Sadistic PE
Teacher In The East Midlands.

Cross-country was one of those staples left over from the
muscular Christian ethos of the Victorian era. It was also a good
way for PE teachers to get tabloid/porn-mag reading time. I
foolishly got myself into the cross-country team because my
asthma meant I never stopped for fag breaks but instead ran
quite slowly at a steady pace and refused to give up. One
windswept day we were due to run in the fields around Lincoln
for an inter-schools race but I'd forgotten my plimsolls. Mr
Minting generously managed to borrow a pair of moulded football boots and made me run in them, through mud and roads,
for six miles.

The true start of my rather Jane Austen-type malaise had
nothing to do with Debbie White or sadistic PE teachers, in fact,
but can more likely be traced to the terrifying sighting of a ghost
– the figure of an old woman in a shawl holding a candle –
outside my bedroom one night, as I lay in bed looking out at the
partly open door. She stood outside the door briefly, seemingly
'looking' in (though being a ghost she didn't have eyes, just a
dark shadowy bit where her face should have been) before
moving down the corridor to my younger brothers' room. In a
just world she would have frightened the living shit out of them,
too, but Tobe and Snake, the bastards, never had problems
sleeping at night.

There are two ways of reacting to stuff like this. You can
either tell yourself that you had an interesting experience, or
you can go completely apeshit and become terrified of the dark

and start screaming things like, 'Argh! I can see dead people!'
I took the latter, more pleasingly melodramatic, route. Next I
started to see a grinning shining skull in my dreams, and sometimes when I just had my eyes closed. It was not that dissimilar
to the diamond one produced by Damien Hirst recently, except
rather than resting on a plinth with slavering people from the
art world fawning all around it, it just sort of floated in the air
above the bed. I was certainly seen as a bit of a headcase (I
prefer to think I was just sensitive) and the doctor put me on
sleeping pills for a short while.

Everybody – because 'everybody' is usually an expert on
these things – told me I must have dreamed the ghost or else I
had a 'vivid imagination'. One explanation could be the influence on my early life of Brooke Bond Tea collectors' cards. In
the early 70s I had collected Fashion Through the Ages – how
else could my subconscious brain know about bustles? The other,
far more plausible theory, to my twelve-year-old mind, at least,
was that at the edge of my bedroom door was a gateway to a
parallel universe where the people lived about one hundred years
in the past. And didn't have eyes.

Anyway, as you can see I was worried about stuff. There was
a lot to be worried about. There was a lot in the papers about
serial killers, or more specifically serial kidnappers. Thanks to
the influence of superhero comics and spotty sub-editors, all
notorious criminals had nicknames in those days, like the Black
Panther or the Lincolnshire Throttler. They were on the TV
and in the papers. I was so worried I worked out an escape plan
if I got kidnapped – I'd just have to leg it and run as fast as I
could, hoping that the killer was slower than me. My cross-
country running would be an unexpected advantage here. As
was not being a prostitute, of course.

Another worry was that, according to my *Guinness Book of
World Records*, the USSR had a bomb they called the Dooms-
day Device, that could kill every living thing on the earth. Of

course, the only time they'd use it was if they were losing a war and decided that to win they had to blow up all of the enemy really fast. Apparently even if their own side died of radiation poisoning it would be worth it to know that they had killed more people than the other side, and it would go down as a victory and the history books would say what geniuses all the Soviet generals were. So it would be up to the *Guinness Book of World Records* men, the McWhirter brothers Norris and Ross, to decide who had won a war. Possibly Roy Castle too. Roy used to appear on their spin-off *Record Breakers* series and he had smashed the tap-dancing-while-playing-the-trumpet record. Although looking back now it seems unlikely that this particular record pre-existed.

In July, the Silver Jubilee celebrations came and went – with me 200 miles away from the rest of my family. I missed the street party that was held in our garden because of a prior engagement – a week with my mum's sister Auntie Hazel and her family in Horsham, which my parents had arranged earlier in the year. While my brothers, cousins and mates were goose-stepping round our garden dressed in union jack outfits, and eating lots of red, white and blue cakes and sweets, I was being driven round the lanes of West Sussex in a Reliant Robin as we searched in vain for some kind of event we could tack on to, eventually giving up and going to the seaside to play ducks and drakes before returning to the flat where we watched Raquel Welch in *One Million Years B.C.* on the telly. I was a bit hacked off. But it was only later that I had to thank Mum. By missing the party I didn't appear in any of the photos of people cavorting around with union jacks and *I Heart Hereditary Monarchy* T-shirts. In years to come no-one would be able to blackmail me and say I was a closet monarchist. At the time, of course, everyone was a monarchist. Every kid, even hard-nuts like Kenny Groswin, Adey Whitehead and Martin Lebowsky, were thrilled when they were given a royal sovereign. And everyone got excited when watching soldiers Trooping the Colour on TV. We all whole-heartedly believed the Russian army would never dare invade us when we had expertly choreographed soldiers like these.

2. My Fantastic Record Collection

The scene is my bedroom. Use this map to help you around or you'll get lost amid the clutter. The room exists in a kind of thrilling chaos, thanks to there being stuff all over the floor. Pride of place in the room goes to my Beautiful Record Collection. My record collection is, I have to say, amazing, and for a twelve-year-old boy it was doubly so. Pieced together since I was six, it's a part of who I am. It charts the highs and lows of modern popular culture:

The Jungle Book

My first proper LP and for a while the only one in my 'collection', it was probably the first film I went to see as well. The most played track was the crazy dance number 'I Wanna Be Like You', especially the bit where Baloo comes in and starts bebop scat vocalising:

> *A wam bam zoni!*
> *Abba deeba dabba wap bam bone*
> *A doopa zap doob doppa doba daza bone*
> *A zey be zaw ba zapp dam doni!*

In the late 60s, when this came out, Bebop was just hitting Lincolnshire and this would have seemed really hot and contemporary.

I remember clearly the moment when I was told that all the adult helpers at Cubs and Scouts had names that came from *The Jungle Book*. Some kid mentioned it in passing and I thought he was joking – then it all fell into place. It was an enormous realisation. And why then, at Scouts, did we sing the boring National Anthem and not 'I Wanna Be Like You'?

Instant Replay (The Monkees)

I got *Instant Replay* from Father Christmas when I was six years old. I had written a letter to him then immediately put it into the fire, as you did in those days (not realising that the skill was in letting a grown-up do it for you so they could have a sneaky peek before it went up in flames), so it could speed to Greenland, and they could get to work at Father Christmas's workshop specially pressing my LP. My mum was shocked by this development and demanded to know what I'd put in the letter. 'Don't worry, Mum,' I said, 'Father Christmas will sort it all out.' 'Of course he will, darling, I'm just interested, that's all,' she'd replied, nonchalantly. I had also asked for a WW2 battlefield set, a 1972 *Beano* annual, a satsuma and a brazil nut.

Peter Tork was my favourite in The Monkees but to my disappointment he didn't appear on the front of this album. I didn't recognise any of the tracks and only the poppy 'Tear Drop City' was in any way reminiscent of the stuff from their TV show. What was Father Christmas thinking? Anybody would be mistaken for thinking he was a thirty-something suburban parent who didn't know anything about popular culture and had simply grabbed the first thing in view with 'Monkees' written on it.

The Monkees (The Monkees)

The fact that I had only three albums and two of them were by the same band suggested that my favourite act was The Monkees, a group that hadn't made a proper album for ten years. Of course, I had no idea how far from the zeitgeist I was surfing. I hadn't even made it to the beach. In fact, I was on holiday miles from said beach. But I liked their music, so who cared?

This album was acquired from my Auntie Hazel's record collection during the aforementioned Queen's Silver Jubilee celebrations in 1977. In a bitter response to not being able to bellow 'Land Of Hope And Glory' in our front garden, I had somehow persuaded her to give it to me.

'Help'/'I'm Down' (The Beatles)

Although I have this single in my possession, I'm sure it belongs to Tobe and was the first one he went to buy for himself. He'd recently been given *The Beatles: An Illustrated Record* by Roy Carr and Tony Tyler and was becoming a master of Beatle facts. My only comeback to this was that *I could remember The Beatles before they split*. I was born in 1965. In Beatles time, this was some time between *Help!* and *Rubber Soul*.

One of the prominent psychoanalysts of the early twentieth century was Alfred Adler, who believed that we are shaped by our earliest memories: *'The first memory will show the individual's fundamental view of life, his first satisfactory crystallization of his attitude... I would never investigate a personality without asking for the first memory.'*

Did The Beatles give me my first memory? The problem is I can't work out what my first memory was. I can recall seeing The Beatles on TV singing 'All You Need Is Love' on our black and white TV in 1967 (Ringo was my favourite). I can also remember seeing my Grandad Bradford, who died in 1967, being shaved while sitting up in bed, as 'Smoke Gets In Your Eyes' played on an old musical box, and I can also remember having the top of one of my fingers chopped off in a domestic accident involving a door and a clumsy friend (this would have a profound effect on my guitar-playing capabilities in later years).

I have no idea what I was doing before then. There must have been fragments of music and picture books. Ant and Bee lost their hats and journeyed to the Land of Lost Things to retrieve them. On the big wooden radiogram in the sitting room were songs like 'Lily The Pink' by The Scaffold and The Beatles' 'Yellow Submarine' and occasionally Dad's Benny Goodman and Dutch Swing College EPs.

My memories are like fishing boats which sometimes appear out of the mist.

The small details of my life are fish. Haddock mostly. They appear quickly and I write them down before they swim off in the other direction

Although those early scenes are quite clear in my mind, much of my childhood is a blank. I look back and squint to try to see and it's like looking out from Cleethorpes beach over the North Sea on a misty January morning. Everything is just a grey milky murk, no matter how hard I concentrate or try to focus. There are people and sounds and feelings in the mist but now I'll never find them. They've just wandered off into the mist like Captain Oates.

Sing Lofty (Don Estelle and Windsor Davies)

Multi-talented celebrity actors recording an album is no longer a particularly original concept, but back in the 70s it was shockingly exciting. This album was given to me by my Yorkshire gran and grandad. Don Estelle (Lofty) does his best at crooning an old song while Windsor Davies makes funny comments and asides. My brother Tobe had received the slightly more left-field *Jehosphat and Jones*, a country spoof by The Two Ronnies.

'The Ying Tong Song' (The Goons)

Also nabbed from Auntie Hazel's, to my shame (why didn't she resist?). One of my many side projects at that time was making homemade recordings of *Goon Show* scripts on my dad's Hitachi cassette player. We usually did it round at Roly Chesterfield's house. Roly was two years older than me and so was better at negotiating the plum parts for himself and his best mate, Rod Kitchen. Roly was always Eccles and Rod got to be Bluebottle and Seagoon. I usually had to make do with Major Bloodnok or Grytpype-Thynne. But my acquisition of 'The Ying Tong Song' meant that I now had some major leverage when it came to casting. Roly retaliated by upping the negotiations with the announcement that he had a porn-mag collection that he had found in a bin and that we could look at it if we wanted (as long as he could be Eccles).

'D.I.V.O.R.C.E.' (Billy Connolly)

I cried with laughter every time I put on this single, especially the bit where he says the Q.U.A.R.A.N.T.I.N.E. starts today. It would be another twenty years before I'd hear the Dolly Parton original. This was the first single I had bought myself, from the local record shop in Market Rasen. Langfords Records had a decent selection of albums but their speciality was singles. Mrs Langford kept a little exercise book with all their stock hand-written in the margin with the year of release. Although they didn't keep a lot of LPs, the section was nicely situated near the back of the shop which meant I had to walk past, and browse, the rock and pop section and – look, I'll be honest, my area of interest was the cover of Roxy Music's *Country Life* album, which showed two models in see-through underwear. I'd find myself staring at it for what seemed like hours until Mrs Langford asked if there was anything I wanted.

'Bohemian Rhapsody' (Queen)

What was I thinking? I only really liked the Sabbath-esque rocky-out bit at the end. Our neighbours, the Black brothers, had bought it for my eleventh birthday. But then they liked 00 gauge railways, Airfix models, prog and heavy rock.

The Benny Goodman EP (The Benny Goodman Quartet)

This was my dad's but I liked to keep it with my collection just to flesh it out. 'Have you seen my Benny Goodman EP?' my dad would say. I'd reluctantly give it back to him but it would always eventually make its way back into my collection. It was a good way for us to interact and talk about music without him shouting 'Turn it down!' or 'What's that racket?' The EP was also an early attempt at the chick-seducing record – you know, just in case an attractive girl happened to be passing my record collection she'd see the Benny

Goodman EP and think I was sophisticated with great taste. Then we could have walked hand in hand up to Top Field and had a snog.

At this stage my dad was still my main cultural influence. As a consequence, the only gig I'd been to was a performance of *The Mikado* by the D'Oily Carte group at Sadler's Wells. Although I loved *Top of the Pops*, I hadn't yet got to the stage of consuming pop products. Whenever I had saved enough pocket money for a single, I tended to see comedy songs as better value. No collection could have been complete without the hilarious 'Funky Gibbon'.

'Funky Gibbon' (The Goodies)

Blimey, this was what I thought was hard-edged dance music in the mid 70s. It would be another few months before I'd start worshipping at the altar of Monty Python (or, more specifically, Terry Gilliam). Up until then The Goodies would be my favourite TV comedy group.

The Railway Stories (read by Johnny Morris)

Reverend Awdry's train tales read by Johnny Morris, the bloke who did *Animal Magic*, complete with funny voices (well, he had about three voices and used them in rotation). We got a few of these when we were really little. They had great picture sleeves and the hole in the middle of the record was where the engine's nose should have been. '*I won't stop here, I'll run away. Shh shh shh shh shh shh shh shh.*' Brilliant.

'24 Hours From Tulsa' (Gene Pitney)

This was another disc purloined from Auntie Hazel's record collection, about being apart from the girl you loved. I had spent my entire life being apart from the girl I loved. Though it wasn't just one girl but two. Suzy Fry – our love lasted from 1970 to 1974, so long in fact, she gets her own chapter – and

Debbie White (don't want to talk about her because it's still too painful – 1975-76).

'Sun Arise'/'Six White Boomers' (Rolf Harris)

These two numbers made me see things from a world perspective and got me understanding indigenous cultures. I would have loved a stylophone but only one kid in our school was lucky enough to get one. Years later I would buy a didgeridoo from a bloke in Sheffield, of all places, and put it down to my love of this record.

3. Girls Girls Girls (Girls) 1: The Ineluctable Flower-Scented Beauty of Suzy Fry

I'd fancied Suzy Fry since I was five years old. But what does that mean? Can you fancy someone when you're five? She was very pretty, had long straight chestnut-brown hair and big eyes. I was smitten by her.

Our classroom was in an old school house built in the 1850s – in my first year we still used little chalkboards. In infant class, Suzy and I were put at a desk together and I used to get a fluttery feeling in my stomach every morning. We were a classic combination. I was a gawky swot with thick, albino, unstylable hair, bad asthma and a permanent snot problem while she was a hip, popular beauty. I constantly tried to impress Suzy – say with my reading ability or recall of *Pogles' Wood* episodes or statistical knowledge of League Division 1 and FA Cup winners since 1965, the specific roles of each Thunderbird craft, the time it takes to travel up the M1 to the West Riding of Yorkshire, how to tell Rotherham and Sheffield apart on a five-mile stretch of the M1.

I used to have dreams about Suzy Fry. In them, Suzy and I walked around the playground hand-in-hand in slow motion.

Here is Tim.
Tim is a lovesick 6 year old.
He writes a love poem
  for Suzy Fry.
Suzy tells Miss.
Miss tells Tim to go and
  sit somewhere else.

Here is Fang.
Fang is Suzy Fry's dog.
Suzy Fry tells Fang
  to bite Tim.
Fang chases Tim.
See Tim run.

Every time anybody tried to get near to us we would just float up into the sky together. I took this as a sign that Suzy and I were destined to be together for ever. Her strawberry-silky-smelled goodness intoxicated me and I often found it hard to concentrate. I would fluctuate between being very quiet and intense and becoming utterly exhibitionist. Nothing I seemed to do would impress her.

One awful day, the teacher, Miss Cross, decided to move us all around, and another girl was placed next to me; a girl whose name I can't recall and who didn't stay long in the school. She had blonde hair and, from what I can remember, wore flouncy dresses and frilly tops. The only recollection I have of any interaction between us is the time when I lay on the floor and stared up her skirt and described to the class the colour of her knickers. Miss Cross sent me to stand at the front of the class for the rest of the lesson, with the threat of being given the dreaded bat. Eventually I ended up next to Bacon Hawkins, a nice, simple lad who wasn't quite as pretty as Suzy.

A year and a half later I found myself once again sitting next to Suzy. I certainly wouldn't have come right out with it and told her I had been in love with her for over two years, but I must have made my feelings known to her in some way for her to have brushed me off with a ruthless rejection: 'You're a rich puff who lives in a big house.'

Being rather quick to take offence, the remark made me feel breathless with disgust at my parents' shortsightedness.

'It's not that big. It's only got four bedrooms. It is much smaller inside. It's nowhere near

Suzy is sad.
She wants Tim to stop following her.
She wants to sit next to the new boy with long hair.

as big as it looks from the outside,' I said, desperately.

'Danny is nicer and he's got long hair,' she replied, ending the discussion. Danny Coxon was a glamorous new boy who had arrived from London a few months earlier. He had what was called a feather cut, with his hair down over his ears and long at the back. I still sported my 1950s-style short back and sides. Danny actually came from Hatfield, but the fact that it was, he said, 'near London', was enough for Suzy, who imagined that he must know all the stars personally.

It's funny when I look back at certain key moments in my life and how they set me off on a certain trajectory. This was one of those moments, possibly the most seminal moment of my childhood and teenage years. Suzy was not to know it but she had set me off down a path which disdained affluence and wealth creation (because if you were a rich puff girls wouldn't fancy you) and gave me a hatred

Suzy explains to Tim about class consciousness.
"Come the revolution, you'll be up against a wall," she says. Miss laughs.

of having my hair cut (because if you had short hair, girls wouldn't fancy you).

That evening I went home and had it out with my parents. I told them we had to move back to the old bungalow on the other side of town (we had moved in the spring of 1971). It was a matter of some urgency, I told my mother, possibly while hurriedly packing my things. I felt sick. Actually, it wasn't sickness, it was like a heavy weight in my guts. Why did we have to live in a windy, slightly damp, former gentleman's residence at the edge of the town surrounded by loads of grass and trees? And would anyone ever love me while we still did?

4. An Intense Love of the Late Cretaceous

I loved dinosaurs. Almost as much as I loved Suzy Fry. In the early 1970s it would appear there were only five known dinosaurs (as far as school children knew, anyway): Brontosaurus, with its long neck and little head; Diplodocus, with its even longer neck and even smaller head; Stegosaurus, spiky plates down the spine; Tyrannosaurus Rex, the big meat-eater; and Triceratops, basically a rhino with a big Elizabethan-style ruff.

I liked Triceratops. I like the fact that he was a vegetarian and therefore peaceable in a slightly Buddhist way. I liked reading about him in my dinosaur book, about all the plants he would eat and all the adventures he would get up to like, erm, trying to escape from Tyrannosaurus. Every time I read about Triceratops the story would end with him either being eaten by Tyrannosaurus or being nearly eaten by Tyrannosaurus. In terms of the kind of man I wanted to become, Triceratops ticked all the boxes. Although quite peaceable, he was tough-looking so nobody messed with him. Nobody apart from Tyrannosaurus, of course.

My enjoyment of the film *One Million Years BC* was tempered by the fact that in the big dinosaur fight scene Triceratops was not fighting Tyrannosaurus but a less glamorous meat eater called Ceratosaurus, who he beat up relatively easily. The incongruity of men and dinosaurs co-existing was not that important, historical accuracy an irrelevancy compared to the sight of Raquel Welch in a fur bikini.

HERE'S A BIT MORE STUFF ABOUT...

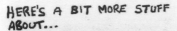

THE GIRLFRIEND WHO MOVED TO SCUNTHORPE

DEBBIE WHITE HAD BEEN A FRIEND OF SUZY FRY'S. SHE WASN'T SHY LIKE SUZY AND ALSO WASN'T AS ANTI-BOURGEOIS. SHE HAD OLIVE SKIN, BROWN EYES AND LIGHT BROWN HAIR THAT WAS THE COLOUR OF FRIED ONIONS.

DEBBIE WAS FUNNY AND SMELLED OF PEPPERMINT.

ONE SEPTEMBER AFTERNOON WE CROUCHED DOWN BEHIND THE BOOKCASE IN THE LIBRARY CORNER AND SHE KISSED ME.

1. SALTY
2. TOOTHPASTE
3. SWEET
4. WET

ALMOST IMMEDIATELY, THE SINGING STARTED...

How many times has Debbie had it off?

In an English country garden...

She's had it twice and thought it very nice

In an English country garden

Once in the flower bed... once in the potting shed...

Now she's having a BA-A-BY

♪ For that is BAD ♪ cos Tim is a DAD in an English country garden ♪

We used to play kiss chase.

Then one day she was gone...

I bought her an Easter egg. (but ate it myself.)

SCUNTHORPE

5. Philip Larkin Stamped my Father's Library Book (and Other Family Stories)

According to Philip Larkin, who was the librarian at the university my parents went to, 1963 was the true start of the 60s. My parents had moved to Market Rasen in 1963. Up until then they had been living for a few months in a little flat in Grimsby.

In his late teens my dad, according to him, was sad and drifting and nobody understood him. At least not at his isolated boarding school in the middle of a misty moor in Devon. The moor was *always* misty, apparently, like the 1930s version of *The Hound of the Baskervilles* starring Basil Rathbone. This was the 1950s and Britain badly needed scientific boys to build the next nuclear bomb/power station/jet rocket/hovertank/futuristic city of the future. Dad did really badly in his exams and he wasn't going to be able to go to Cambridge like his brother. At this point Dad could have gone off the rails and formed a bohemian art-beat jazz combo or written crazy poetry, but luckily an old family friend, Uncle Joe (who'd been friends with Grandad Bradford in Market Rasen during the war), came to the rescue and said to my dad that he'd give him a job as a solicitor in his practice in the town. So my father went to study law at a provincial university.

My dad admits it was the best thing that ever happened to him. For it was in Hull that he met my mum. My mum was very pretty and she wore a green paisley mini-dress and had dark brown hair in a long ponytail down her back. She had danced at Bradford Alhambra in her youth and she was also the first person in her entire large extended West Riding family to go to university. My mum has always been good at everything. To Yorkshire Grandad she was a special princess with superhuman powers. To Yorkshire Gran she was the one who would achieve all the things that she had not been able to. And so, after she got married in early '63, my mum became a German teacher at a nice girls' school in Grimsby. In the photo of her at the nice girls' school she looks pretty but very serious in her gown. But she didn't get much of a chance to turn the nice girls of Grimsby into special princesses with superhuman powers, because I came along about a year and a half later and she gave up her job and my parents went to live in a little suburban bungalow on the southern edge of the town.

Mum was always thinking about everybody. In a group she always wanted everyone to be at ease. She also taught ballet to generations of eager, pink-faced village girls, counting the

pennies up every Wednesday night then sending it all off to various charities. 'Why don't you keep the money – we could spend it ourselves?' I used to ask.

I also used to ask Mum, in all seriousness and on more than one occasion, whether my younger brother was a midget. Tobe is eighteen months younger than me but where I was a straw-haired, lanky child, Tobe was silken-haired, finer and more delicate looking. And very short. Like a jockey. He ate small portions, methodically cutting each item into neat squares then chewing slowly, staring into space, as if trying to solve complex mathematical problems. Which he probably was. I would look at my own plate, a mass of exploded food items and third helpings, and wonder if we really were related to each other.

Tobe was quiet and a little shy and didn't have a lot of friends, partly due to the fact that he was brilliant at maths. The friends he did have were quiet boffins like himself, kids who were on the school quiz team with Tobe and whose names you never remembered, names like Roger and Howard and Gordon. Whereas I never even knew the quiz tournament existed at junior school, a year later Tobe was a key member of the team, which had brain-size competitions against swots from other local schools.

He had been a Beatles fan since someone had bought him a copy of *The Beatles 1967–70* when he was six. 'Man, you are such a square,' I would say to him, advising him in big-brotherly fashion that he should be digging Rolf Harris and Benny Goodman. Tobe would then patiently take the time to explain why he loved The Beatles. He preferred Paul McCartney to John Lennon because for him Lennon's compositions involved mainly singing the same note in a whining northern drawl while a few chords changed in the background, whereas McCartney's songs fizzed with musical ideas and tightly built structure. I didn't really understand what Tobe was on about.

Tobe was a gentle kid but he could lose his rag if pushed. And usually it was me doing the pushing. If I copied what he said enough times he would blow. He once threw a cricket bat at my head for no reason, other than the fact that we were arguing about whose turn it was to bat and I possibly mimicked his voice a little. As usual, my folks sided with Tobe, reasoning that if I'd been hurt then it must have been my fault in some way. At some point Dad resorted to the method used by his father when he'd been young. He put a pair of boxing gloves on us and told us to fight it out according to the Marquis of Queensberry rules. In weight to age terms I was a light heavyweight and Tobe was bantam to flyweight. If he hadn't had such a temper he'd have been able to pick me off, despite the six-inch-reach difference, using his knowledge of geometry and angles. Instead, he'd just shout, 'Arrrrrggggggghhhhhhh.'

Despite his lack of success in the boxing ring, Tobe was on the whole very comfortable in his skin. You can see it in old photos of us. Tobe often holds a pose and looks cool, staring boldly at the camera, whereas I am just grinning goofily and slightly embarrassedly. Or doing rabbit ears.

My other brother Snake was four years younger than Tobe and came along in time to soften the blow following The Beatles' split in 1970. Because we now lived on the edge of town, when he was five my parents decided to send Snake to the village school in Middle Rasen and so he became a country boy, a Huck Finn, wandering the lanes with his country cronies, climbing trees, playing in streams, disappearing off down rivers on big inner tubes. He was a skinny kid with a big belly, a blond basin cut and massive ears, who walked around clutching his first love, a blanket bear called Snuggly. Tobe and I would regularly kidnap and torture Snuggly before Snake's earth-shattering scream would have adults come running from up to five miles away.

A change took place when my parents refused to buy Snake an airgun for his birthday one year. He'd wanted to spend his time shooting rabbits and living off the land. Thwarted, as he got older he became more and more of a serious tech-minded soul and formed the first computer-nerd gang in the area. They would sit around in his bedroom silently playing with their Rubik's Cubes.

Unusually for maths-brained geeks, Snake was a linguist, so much so that he had created his own language that only our family could understand. All vowel sounds would be replaced by the sound aaaaaa.

Snuggly
(the blanket bear)

Snake: Whaaaats faaa taaaa, Maaaaam? (What's for tea, Mum?)

Snake: Aaaaaxskaaaas maaa, haaas aaanaaawaaan saaaan maaa Raaaabaaaks Cyaaaaaab? (Excuse me, has anyone seen my Rubik's Cube?)

Snake: Maaaaaaaam! Taaaam and Taaaab are taaaacharaaan Snaaaaaglaaaa! (Mum! Tim and Tobe are torturing Snuggly!)

And for one heady autumn in 1974, it was as if I had four brothers. Our cousins Rob and Rich had come back to live in Market Rasen from Trinidad. I suppose it didn't occur to me how traumatic this might be for them, going from a smart modern house on a hill with palm trees around it and bananas growing in the garden to a wintry, windswept little town like ours. But Rob was so confident – spending the whole journey back from the airport talking about cricket statistics and footballers and pop stars and general trivia – that I presumed he must be delighted to be moving to the rubbish suburban backwater that was Market Rasen, and have kids shout abuse at him and Rich because they looked different. Rob was thoroughly normal in nearly every respect, apart from his total recall of County Cricket Championship statistics from 1971 to the present day. How had he come across this sort of information in the Port of Spain?

Rich was only six when they came back. He had always seemed like a crazy, happy-go-lucky free spirit but now spent his time shivering and at times seemed to disappear into his now permanent outfit of thick white Aran jumper (knitted by Gran). Rich's unique gift was the ability to get up in the early hours of the morning and his generous nature meant that he just had to share the new day with all of us.

Happy smiling face: Wake up Tim! Let's play!

Tired kid: It's half past five, Rich.

Happy smiling face: Woohoo!!

(Rich jumps on bed, laughing. Whole street wakes up.)

One strange quirk about my family was that we were allowed to paint on walls. Next to the kitchen was an old utility/breakfast room which became our playroom and my parents gave us carte blanche to cover it in our doodles, paintings and cartoons. Every year or so they would paint over it in white emulsion so we could start again. Eventually they gave us the paint pot and let us do it – well, the lower bits, anyway. I can't remember how many layers of artwork are now under the wallpaper. It'll be an interesting job for a house archaeologist one day. So I found it strange that none of my friends were allowed to paint on walls.

Just one of the wall drawings survives, a not-very-flattering cartoon I did of Snake when I was about ten. By rights Mum and Dad should have been telling me off but instead they put a wooden frame round it.

The Family Brain

(Trying to explain the family dynamic)

Mum
A West Riding lass.
Into ballet and yoga
and playing Scott
Joplin on the piano.
Changed our lives
when she purchased
Cordon Bleu Cookery
Course partworks.
Once danced at
Bradford Alhambra.

Auntie N
A midwife, originally from
Trinidad. Into Stones, Blood
Sweat & Tears, Roxy
Music. Outspoken on a
range of topics. Cooks
spicy chicken with big fat
chips. Plays the Cuatro.

LEFT BRAIN   RIGHT BRAIN

Cousin Rob
Great memory for
sports stats. Loves
cricket and salted
prunes and breeding
gerbils. Wants to be
an international fast
bowler.

Me
Big lazy pisstaker.
Addictive doodler and
reader of cereal
packets. Teases
Snake & Tobe.

Cousin Rich
Always wakes up too
early. Collects
Charlie Brown books.
Can play the drums
really fast.

Snake
Showed signs of
being a boffin from
an early age. Had a
desire to take things
apart to see how they
worked then put them
back together again.

Gran
A great gardening
genius. Makes stews
and big puddings.
Vicious with a
wooden spoon.
Feeds the birds.

Uncle T
Former amateur
boxer now lawyer,
with thespian
tendencies. Slow left
arm bowler and
gardener.

Dad
Into rugby, Dickens,
Schubert and
Guinness. A solicitor
but prefers to talk
about physics and
how to get rid of
moles.

Tobe
Had a secret desire
to do acting, but was
heading down the
road of being a pure
maths guru. Owns a
Leeds Utd replica kit.
In the school quiz
team.

6. The Sights, Sounds and Smells of the Lincolnshire Countryside

It seems strange now, when I describe myself as a country boy, that I had no real interest in nature when growing up. But at the time I was no different to most of my peers. Nature gave us grass so we could play football. It gave us shorter grass on a flat patch so we could play cricket. It gave us trees so we could climb them then hang upside down and read the latest issue of *Whizzer and Chips*. It gave us those really tiny little red spiders so we could pretend to be a giant from another planet and squash them then feel a bit guilty afterwards (though not that guilty).

When I do tell people I come from the country I think they might sometimes have a vision of me as having a DH Lawrence-style connectedness to nature, that there was something barefoot and elemental about my childhood. I didn't look *at* nature and wonder at its beauty. There wasn't that much to see apart from expanses of arable crops or grass and big, cloudy skies. In Market Rasen, nature was beautiful on a smaller scale: in churchyards, overgrown cottage gardens, beside railway lines, on the urban river bank – the forgotten places, rather than the manicured and factory farmed.

It is the sounds and smells of Lincolnshire that were more memorable. The constant drone of a lone fly buzzing around the kitchen trying to get at the plate of sliced hard-boiled egg and salad cream that my mum has covered. Rooks circling above the tall beech trees on Gainsborough Road, squawking around their chunky nests. The smell of a rotting animal by the side of the road as cars backed up along the A631 on their way to the racecourse or Skegness. The tractors in the big field across the road.

We were surrounded by fields but not of the pastoral picturesque kind. These were huge factory farm arable prairies, with a lot of the hedges grubbed up and only the occasional copse of trees to salve the eye. Think American Midwest without that environment's tolerance and culture. There was an illusion of space in Lincolnshire, but it wasn't space you could occupy. When you're a teenager, large fields and long, narrow country lanes offer nothing in the way of emotional succour.

Our world was the rook-infested, green-swathed, tractor-trundling area within a three-and-a-half-mile radius from our small town. We didn't really want to know the rest of Lincolnshire; we weren't curious in the slightest about these places that were four or five miles away. Travelling anywhere more than three and a half miles away in the car in summer was an ordeal. For some reason our Austin 1800 always smelt of

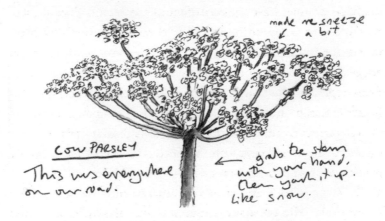

made me sneeze a bit

COW PARSLEY
This was everywhere on our road.

← grab the stem with your hand. Then yank it up. Like snow.

ham sandwiches, which made me feel sick. I could usually stop myself vomiting, instead spending half an hour in agony, staring out of the window and imagining specks on the glass were spaceships diving over the countryside and shooting up sheep and farmers. Snake was not so self-controlled. He'd regularly let it all fly out, only rarely opening the window in time to vomit down the side of the car. If you were ever out and about in Lincolnshire in the 70s and saw a green British Leyland car with a go-faster stripe of sick down the side, that was probably us.

Arriving home, with relief we'd drive down our road that was half rural, half countryside. On one side was a huge field, a dread expanse that I used to stare at from my bedroom window, the biggest field in Lincolnshire. On the other side was a long row of between twenty and twenty-five inter-war bungalows, with little gables over the front windows. Toby and I used to repeat their names like a mantra, seeing how many we could memorise. It was our nature poem to this liminal space between settlements. We'd close our eyes and chant: Ferndale, Ditchingham, Roseville, Rivelin, Green Gables, Heathcote, Lingmell, Partlin, Ambernell, Inglenook, The Willows.

Where we lived meant we weren't quite in open countryside, yet also weren't townies. There were loads of trees around our house. I suppose you could say we lived in the darkness on the edge of town, though actually it would be more accurate to describe it as the junction of the A46 bypass where it splits off and heads towards Grimsby. The bleak, uninspiring view from my bedroom window was of that grey field the size of Rutland, with no hedgerows, that disappeared into the distance on a gentle slope, with only a gnarled tree or two on the horizon.

I was never remotely interested in gardens when I was young. We had a big garden, most of it laid out as a rough field which was used for various weekly sporting events and games of army. The garden really only came into its own during autumn when our two main harvests took place. Firstly, conkers – I would collect big sacks of them which I'd store efficiently in the pantry until they went mouldy. Then a month or so later would come our big crop of leaves. We were successful leaf farmers, though most of the harvest immediately went on feeding Dad's dangerous bonfire habit, which was always accompanied by Radio 3 squawking out on his Roberts portable, and the all-too-familiar pall of smoke visible over the rear garden wall as he planned the next ground assault on the local mole population, which was forever digging up his garden.

When Gran came to live with us she did all the flower and herb gardening and kept a collection of sticks of various shapes and sizes to whack us with if we strayed onto her flowerbeds or criticised her beloved Kenneth Williams in any way (or perhaps failed to laugh at the vaguely amusing bits in *Round the Horne*).

Gran moved in with us in 1971, a few years after Grandad died, and became like a third parent to us. She was born in 1901 in a village in rural Buckinghamshire. Her dad was a coachbuilder with a penchant for cowboy hats who used to go AWOL to play the squeezebox in pubs around the Midlands. Gran left school in her mid teens and went into service at a big house, and eventually ended up running a hotel in Northampton, where she met my grandad in the 1930s. The family myth goes that he strode in wearing his WW1 major's uniform, arm in a sling, and offered her a cigarette. A great image, but it's unlikely that he was still wearing khaki fifteen years after he'd been demobbed.

Between the service job and meeting Grandad there were about fifteen years of Gran's life about which we knew nothing. If we asked she just scowled. But in a good way. Gran was from the old school of the old school: a wooden spoon for whacking and right-wing views – she would sometimes throw fox hunting into the conversation to try to flush out communist sympathisers in a subtle McCarthyite way, and it got me every time.

Apart from worshipping Kenneth Williams (*Round the Horne* was a weekly ritual), Gran's hobbies were drinking the odd G&T, having a crafty fag now and then, going to the races at the other end of town with her mates and Meals on Wheels. She did Meals on Wheels for old-age pensioners until she was well into her eighties. Though not on Wednesdays. That was when she fed the three of us to within an inch of our lives. And when we were very young she always read stories to us. *The Land of Green Ginger*, Spike Milligan poems and Christopher Robin's adventures.

Dad was the veggie gardener, and had rotovated a large chunk of field on the eastern side of the house and turned it into a beautiful vegetable patch. From his upstairs window he had a .22 rifle ready to be trained on the rabbits and wood pigeons that would attack his precious broad beans and lettuces. I sometimes wondered whether his first love wasn't actually wood pigeon and rabbit hunting, but he was too embarrassed to admit it to Mum, so kept up the vegetable plot as a front.

The Best Plants in the Whole of Nature

- **Sticky Willy** Hilariously named plant that appeared on the edges of the garden and ended up on your mate's jumper when he wasn't looking. He was too busy laughing at the name.

- **Those Arrow Things** You'd throw them and they'd stick to your jumper. Ended up on your mate's jumper if he was a cowboy and you were an Indian. Kept a stockpile in my school desk during times of conflict.

- **Nettles** Nettles are good teachers; grip them hard and they don't sting. I liked the strange tingle of nettle stings, like when you put your hand on an electric fence. Sometimes a

crowd of us would line up and do the electric fence thing – it
was in the pre-drug thrill days.

- **Asparagus** Tall elegant fronds
(good word, frond) waving in
the wind that grew on a raised
piece of soil near my dad's shed.
Made your wee smell (asparagus, not Dad's shed).

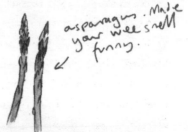

As for other people's gardens, they are just a blur, like trying
to recall the face of the friend of the girl you fancied at a disco
in the early 80s. For instance, try as I might I just cannot
picture the gardens of my mates. Gardens just never really
registered at all. Being surrounded by garden meant that I had
absolutely no motivation to do any gardening, unless it was
Bob a Job week. My wife has recently told me that she and
her best friend used to pretend to be Guides or Brownies and
do Bob a Job for people and keep the money. I like to think
of myself as a man of the world, but I was scandalised by this
confession.

Bob a Job was the nearest most East Midlands kids between
the ages of eight and ten got to being utterly selfless, like Jesus,
The Spiritual Head of the Cub Scout Movement Along with
the Queen. And God. We would weed old ladies' paths and get
paid the equivalent of 5p, of which we had to put a large
percentage (100 per cent) towards a local charity. I didn't like
gardening, it was suburban, old, slow, boring, post war and far
too earnest. And all those stupid Latin names! I'd sit there trow-
elling weeds with a scowl on my face, vowing to give up Latin
as soon as possible when I got to secondary school. The trouble with Bob a Job was that the concept meant you got a bob
for whatever you did. So whether the job was picking one
flower or redesigning and landscaping an entire large garden,
the pay was the same. A bob.

I had the Cubs to thank for such a sadistic concept. I'd joined Baden-Powell's right-wing child-army when I was eight and immediately I was pledging my loyalty to the two undemocratic figures of our time, God and the Queen. If Akela had asked me to shop my family, I'd probably have done it in exchange for a stitch-on badge.

A couple of years later I graduated to Scouts. It really was like getting promoted to a new division. Scouts was a lot more physical. Some of the kids were mature teenagers and it seemed that every other week there had to be a Greco-Roman wrestling session in which we'd push and pull each other in the middle of the Scout hut while Skip and Kim (the Scout leaders) looked on approvingly. We'd sometimes go down to the woods to make bivouacs from twigs and leaves and swap stories about the Warren Wogle. The Wogle was an ancient Lincolnshire beast, similar to the monster in the tale of Beowulf but not quite as celebrated (typical, even the Lincolnshire folklore is rubbish). If the Wogle had lived anywhere else in the country apart from Linwood Warren, he would have gone down into legend as a feared legendary creature, as opposed to a half-forgotten comedy animal brought up by bored Baden-Powellites on damp autumn weekends.

7. The Third Urinal From the Left

Get ahead
of fashion from

AUDREY'S

QUEEN STREET,
MARKET RASEN
TEL. 3454

The late 1970s were not good times for Market Rasen. There was a retrenchment after the recession of the mid 70s. The posh café with the fish pond had gone. There was now a supermarket on the main street which meant you had to walk around and put things in a basket, rather than rely on the man behind the counter to fetch things from his shelves. Old people were not happy. Paula's Patisserie had gone, as had Audrey's Hairdressers, the Wella Wine shop, Wilson's sweetshop, Charlie's Tuck Shop and the old library. Arthur's Tuck Shop had gone, to be replaced by Marwood's sweetshop. Marwood's sweetshop was identical in form to Arthur's shop, even down to the fact that it occupied exactly the same space in the town. But whereas Arthur was ninety, with no teeth, a wizened face, no hair and you couldn't understand a word he said, Marwood was ridiculously young to be running a sweetshop: he was in his mid fifties. Another difference was that it was much harder now to nick stuff. They called Marwood 'Hawkeye'. Actually, I don't know who *they* are. It's quite likely that Marwood himself coined the nickname to scare budding goody lifters. The confectionery trade must also have been linked to the dental profession: for 1p you could buy enough sweets to fill all the drawers in your bedroom. That couldn't be right. And if you were foolish enough to buy those cheap sweets – usually black-jacks and fruit salads – in winter when they were hard, they could pull your teeth out.

But shops were not that big a deal to us kids. What was a big deal was the Bell playing field. This patch of ground with the river on one side and the railway line on another, with a swing, a pulley and a strange wooden hut that smelt of wee, was on its last legs, vandalised to within an inch of its life. (The ethos seemed to be that anything 'good' had to be wrecked and made 'rubbish', as if to somehow validate everyone's idea that the town was shit.) The playing field had long been a magnet for gang activity. I had intermittently been able to penetrate the outer reaches of the main playground gang, last time a few years earlier as they congregated on the roof of the wooden hut to watch an eclipse and nothing had happened – it continued to be a grey, cold Saturday lunchtime. After that the hardest boy, actually the hardest boy in Market Rasen in the early 70s, Kid Jimmy McKay, outraged at the lack of amazing pyrotechnics in the sky, took it out on someone – he began baiting and teasing podgey Carwyn Lovehandles until he cried, and I suddenly realised how precarious life was when you were further down the food chain. Two years before that, Kid Jimmy McKay had won most of Dad's old 1940s marbles off me in a fixed encounter at the old junior school playground. Kid Jimmy sometimes used to star in Dougie Milligan's football team. The big football match took place every playtime at primary school, courtesy of Dougie who, for some unknown reason, was the only kid who had a decent ball (or whose parents would allow him to take it to school). Dougie always picked his team first – he'd stand beneath the monkey bars that acted as goalposts and choose a fiendishly gauged gang of skilful kids: fast kids, strong kids, hard kids and angry mentalist kids. Dougie's team was always a supergroup team: they were West Germany and the rest of us were also-rans like Wales. Or England (who never qualified for any tournaments).

I never got picked by Dougie. Funnily enough, Dougie's team didn't always win, but he'd make sure that whoever starred in an unexpected victory against him would be in his team next playtime. Or he'd get Kid Jimmy to 'explain' the rules to us. At some point Kid Jimmy McKay disappeared and everyone said that he had gone to borstal, which sounded like a grim seaside resort somewhere near Cleethorpes.

Just before I started De Aston, Dad had dropped a bomb-shell by stating that he wanted me to go off to a boarding school in Rutland. I liked Rutland Weekend Television, so that was quite promising, but I sensed that it wasn't going to be right for me. It was just another kind of borstal, except for rich kids. I had just wanted to be normal. To be like everyone else. (Thankfully Dad remembered in time that he'd hated boarding school, so I didn't go.)

Plus I had a best mate, which according to my rules exempted me from going away to boarding school. Tony Hopkins had been my best friend for a couple of years and going away to school would mean I'd have to get a new best mate, which was always hard work.

Tony lived a long way from town and was obsessed with Speedway. At that time Tony's Speedway stories – tales about races the great Speedway riders like Ivan Mauger and Ole Olsen had taken part in – seemed exciting and different.

Tony: What did you do at the weekend, Tim?

Tim: Er, played tig in the field with Tobe and Snake. What about you, Tony?

Tony: I went to King's Lynn to watch the Speedway and I got Ivan Mauger's autograph.

Along with most of my primary school mates, when I started secondary school I was hit by the massive culture shock of entering a school with 1,200 pupils. Most terrifying were the

crazed Neanderthals with grown-out feather cuts who roamed the playgrounds looking for young kids to beat up. Equally bizarre were the grammar school fossils, tweedy prefects with posh accents who patrolled the corridors testing people on Latin poetry. One such young fogey caught a friend of mine messing about in the lunch queue and ordered him to write an essay on the sex life of a ping-pong ball and hand it in the next day. You learned very quickly to stay in the shadows and hide in cloakrooms. I had spent much of the first year at De Aston standing near the temporary staff room with Tony and his cousin, Mike Green. (Mike Green was really into tractors, his favourite being John Deere, though he'd drive a Massey Ferguson for you if he wasn't too busy. But he wouldn't touch a Fordson with a barge-pole.) For some reason Tony and Mike never moved from their spot, as if this was the only place in the whole school they could be safe. Mike probably left school at sixteen having never set foot in most of the playground or the school field.

As time went on, things began to cool a bit between me and Tony. It wasn't that I didn't get on with him – we were still friends – it's just that we had drifted apart; that natural state as kids start to grow up and differences become more marked. I was probably feeling a little bit left out from the normal talk of not just Speedway but the minutiae of farm machinery.

I started to roam round different areas of the school, and was especially fascinated with the new west entrance, through which you got to the woodwork classrooms. It was as if the woodwork class existed in another establishment. It was in a new building tacked onto the youth wing which, with its three doors, was one of the hubs from which to get anywhere else, if you didn't want to go through the main entrance of the school to the bike sheds, which was only really there for kids who were experimenting with cigarettes. (This was where Bacon Hawkins and I tried to get our lungs around some Embassys I'd nicked from Gran, but after a few goes my post-asthmatic chest was not up to it.)

If you carried on going, you were round the back of the sports hall, which was an eerily quiet dead zone, with invisible miasmas of fag smoke hanging in the breeze. You always knew if you went down that way that Kenny Groswin or Martin Lebowsky would come swaggering round the corner and yell, 'What are you starin' at?'

The woodwork teachers, Mr Preston and Mr Walbrook, had come from the old modern school (after it had merged with De Aston in 1974 to become a comprehensive). Mr Preston had been a sportsman of some repute and played in the local football and cricket teams. His nickname was 'Gammy Leg' because of an old football injury to his knee. Impressions of him involved walking behind him with a dead straight leg and making a sloshing, splat sound each time the bad foot hit the floor. Mr Walbrook was short and bald with a pair of eyebrows like small birds.

Woodwork was where the natural order of things was reversed. That is, if you were near the top of the class normally, you would be shit at woodwork. Those that struggled with normal lessons seemed to thrive in woodwork. I put every ounce of effort and concentration into making a very average flip-top box with a finger hole. The box was not perfect; one of the dovetail joints showed a 3mm gap, and the flip-top lid was not put in quite straight. And while most of the class sanded and polished their boxes, or painted them, I opted to use a dark woodstain.

The big new woodwork toilets were a particularly dangerous place to be and Preston and Walbrook were always too busy
to bother patrolling them. If you got caught in this neck of the
woods you were a long way from safety, as this part of the
school was 'owned' by a collection of self-styled hard lads from
the villages. I began to develop a system. I would always use
the same urinal. The third urinal from the left. This was my
lucky urinal and as long as I had a leak there no-one could
threaten me. If for some reason I had to use the second or the
fourth from the left – if the third was already taken – there could
be repercussions.

Martin Lebowsky, Snowey Ginfisten, Billy Black, Frank
Bruntwood, Mickey Whitehead and Reg Chupman were older
kids whose attitude was that the sooner they could get kicked
out of school the better. Most of them wore denim jackets at all
times and still wore big galumphing Oxford bags with Dr
Marten boots. Basically they just looked harder than everyone
else. This gang once (according to school lore) hung maths
teacher Mr Lambert out of the classroom window by his ankles
– that's after they'd lifted him up against the blackboard and
threatened to beat him up.

Now that I had left the warm, machine-loving embrace of
Tony and Mike I had become isolated, and had started to
spend lonely lunchtimes on my own in the library, in my
favourite sections – sports and science fiction. Even when it
was sheeting it down outside, the library was usually empty,
quiet except for the nervous fidgeting of the librarians themselves. The librarians were kids who loved libraries and lived

for libraries, pale-faced spot merchants with flat, greasy hair and spectacles.

It was during my lunchtime browsing that I realised I could have a problem. In the sports biography books, someone had been graffitying graphic pictures: a sex artist had been scribbling willies all over the pages. I remember flicking through Brian Close's autobiography – it was a very quiet lunchtime – and finding a picture of him heading out to bat with Geoff Boycott, with the now-infamous willy suddenly appearing in the foreground. Quite why the artist had chosen Brian Close as the background to his erotic art was beyond me. Perhaps the artist himself was an avid Yorkshireman and was trying to somehow portray his love for the county.

There had to be more than one penis artist because as you went through the sports biography section – David Hemery, the rugby player Danny Hearn, a book about the 1970 All Blacks tour of South Africa – the willy seemed to be everywhere. I then began to wonder if people thought I was the Penis Artist. After all, I frequented the library all the time. And the willy was always in the books I was looking at. I started to worry that maybe I was the Penis Artist and I didn't realise it, like Jekyll and Hyde.

Life improved dramatically at the start of my second year with the arrival of the Figurine Panini Football 78 sticker album. Although I had been confirmed by the Bishop of Lincoln in 1977, I quickly swapped my Church of England religion for a discipline of obsessive collecting.

The spicy chemical smell as you opened a new packet of Football 78 stickers was like a blissful drug, and the cost, 5p per packet, was worth it just for that. Your heart would start to beat faster as first you'd see the curly, permed 70s hair – you still had no idea who it was – then a moustache or beard. You had to watch out for duplicates, though. It seemed that the manufacturers had flooded the system with players that nobody

would want, in a fiendish bid to test the entrepreneurial trad-
ing powers of the kids in Labour-controlled, debt-ridden
Britain. Colin Suggett of Norwich City, 'Big' Dave Watson of
Manchester City, Terry Curran of Nottingham Forest and
Willie Pettigrew of Motherwell. A system of bartering and
swaps took place in the school playground and my album
slowly began to fill up. My confidence, too, seemed to be
building with each new sticker.

You never got to completely fill up your album, unless you
were loaded and could buy all the spares and swaps on the
market. That was just the way of the world. It was expecting
too much to be able to get every sticker you wanted. The in-
built disappointment was part of the beauty of it. Some people
have subsequently completed their collections using eBay but to
me those gaps are part of the story: those little failures that are
uniquely yours. Just like the 3mm gaps in the joints of wooden
flip-top boxes.

8. The Kid On the Pink Chopper

At this time I started to hang out more and more with Michael Rioch, the skinny kid everyone called Bandy. I had always liked him and had already noted that he was a bit of a loner, like me. Bandy lived three miles away in a tiny village called Linwood so we started biking round to each other's house to listen to the football on the radio, or play Subbuteo.

'Nice pink bike,' I said to Bandy as he wobbled down our drive the first time.

'It's not pink,' said Bandy. 'It's sort of purple.'

'Looks pink to me, mate.'

'Well, maybe it's faded red.'

I wasn't allowed to have a Chopper. They were too dangerous, said Mum, though secretly I felt they were too subversively popular culture. Would Lord Reith have ridden a Chopper? Would he hell. She had probably seen *Easy Rider* and that would have been enough. And *John Craven's Newsround* probably had reports about their safety issues.

Before we discovered music, the only other thing to do to keep yourself entertained was to cycle around aimlessly, lost in space. We'd cycle round the local lanes, back and forth to each other's houses, stand on bridges waiting for a train to go past, watch the train go past and cycle off again.

It turned out Bandy and I had gone to the same pre-school playgroup, but our paths had diverged sharply at five. Bandy and his older sister, Julia, went to a local private school. He

wore a black old-fashioned uniform with a cap and was taught French and public speaking in a big Victorian house by a strict headmistress, whereas I went to the local primary school and got swindled out of all my marbles by the school bully. We'd see each other at the odd birthday party. At one bash, when I was seven or eight, Bandy regaled us all with tales of his favourite bands and the singles he had. Gary Glitter, Slade, T-Rex. I stayed quiet, as my collection still only amounted to stuff of my dad's.

We had also met one other time. Bandy used to walk back from his school to get a lift home from his father, whose office was near our junior school. One day he had the misfortune to run into Kid Jimmy McKay, Pip Podland, Douglas Webb and the rest of the gang, with me tagging along behind. Someone had nicked Bandy's hat and I had laughed, not because it was funny but out of relief that I wasn't him and that I was in the background while someone else took the heat of the jeering big kids.

'You were with your mates, Pip and that crowd, and you nicked my cap,' Bandy said, matter-of-factly. He never forgot anything, especially if he'd been crossed. I'd better keep an eye on him, I thought to myself.

The pink Chopper aside, Bandy was utterly normal in nearly every respect. Except one – he had an alter-ego, or imaginary friend, I'm not sure which – called Rubble Man. Rubble Man meant Trouble Man. Rubble would get up to mischief then say 'Tricky me!' when he'd been found out. You never knew when he would appear. In stressful situations Bandy might disappear completely and you were left to deal with Rubble, who was some kind of channelled sprite from the medieval era, I reckon.

Like me, Bandy hated the tough-guy culture of De Aston. On our own we were just weedy kids who weren't very popular. But together we were a successful magazine publishing company. Our first production was designed to combat bullying by highlighting the ridiculousness of trying to be hard. *Hardo Mag* consisted of fictional interviews with and profiles of the school's toughest hardmen. So there was *How to Smoke* with Big Reg; *Bullying the Easy Way* with Snowy Ginfisten; *The Top Ten Hardos of the School*; tips on how to beat up a little kid and lots more. Naturally we couldn't use real photos of the hardos so instead we used spares from our Football 78 sticker album. Brain Talbot became Mickey White, John Hawley became Derek Gripper, and so on, with leather jackets and cigarettes drawn on for added authenticity. Sadly the original of *Hardo Mag* has long since disappeared so this is a recreation:

9. When Did You Last Copy Your Father?

'I just owe almost everything to my father and it's passionately interesting for me... things that I learned in a small town...'
– Margaret Thatcher*

It's 1978. Dad is in the back field, overseeing a grade-three bonfire (leaves with the odd mole corpse) and, as usual, staring at it in silence. If quizzed on his favourite hobbies, Dad would probably say that they were (in no particular order): listening to Schubert, reading Dickens, drinking good wine, reading Dickens Society newsletters, playing rugby, drinking Guinness, writing imaginary letters in his head about *Martin Chuzzlewit* to the Dickens Society newsletter and gardening. But his favourite hobby, by a country mile, has always been lighting, overseeing and standing next to bonfires. Especially bonfires made of leaves.

The nippy breeze carries the lovely leaf smoke off along the A46 bypass towards Market Rasen. Dad has his pint mug of tea nestled in the long grass. Years before, this field had apparently been a hockey pitch. We never really played sport in it that much, it being too uneven and cloddy, so it was reserved for more obscure games, such as 'Colditz Jailbreak', 'Tread In The Sheep Poo', 'Boiling Hot River With Spiders'

---

* Born in Grantham. It's south Lincolnshire, a long way from Market Rasen. But it still counts (I wouldn't be quoting her otherwise).

or 'Destroy And Tickle' – the last game involved a crowd of us chasing after Snake while pretending to be Cybermen or zombies and chanting 'Destroy and tickle'. Not really a game so much as codified bullying.

Dad is probably communicating with other fathers several miles away using smoke signals (this was a time before fathers' support networks) – he's probably saying to them, 'If you don't like rugby or Dickens or Schubert or drinking lots of beer then I have no wish to be your friend.' (Since then he has softened to a woolly liberal state in which mates can now take on three, two, one or even none of the required interests.)

Dad was a double Marxist in the sense that he had the won't-suffer-fools-gladly stern outlook and steely gaze of Karl, and the neat hair and spiky charm of Groucho. Most of my friends only saw the former and were, as a result, dead scared of him, a feeling compounded on a Saturday night when he'd come home from the rugby club with a gallon of beer inside him and attack any friend of mine with his outsize, stubbly chin. 'Argh, he's going to chin us!' I'd cry and it would put the fear of God into any male under twenty-one, but especially Bandy and Chris Hines. Hinesy, my new mate from one of the villages, was tall but no match for Dad's chin.

Dad had also talked of a terrifying game that involved 'nurdling' poles. This was a game using eight-foot metal rods with large spikes in the end. The contestants waved them around in a Kendo-type way, and injuries were common. If you got injured by a spike you had been 'dwile flonked'. Dad claimed he had once accidentally killed a fellow pupil in a nurdling pole tournament at his school. Naturally, we believed all this because it seemed entirely plausible. There was even a nurdling pole song that all nurdling polers sang before a contest:

I will dwile flonk you with my nurdling pole.
I will dwile flonk you with my nurdling pole.

I will dwile, I will dwile flonk you
I will dwile flonk you with my nurdling pole.

The song seemed strangely familiar. But when, at the start of a France v England rugby match on telly, I turned to Dad and said, 'They've nicked that dwile flonk tune for the French National Anthem!', he seemed unconcerned.

Dad also had a story in which he said he used to spar with a boxer who went on to become British middleweight champion, which I was rather dubious about (and which was, of course, true – though was not the cause of his bent nose).

What a man! All I wanted was to be like Dad. If I'd been more like him I'd have known where that Market Rasen Dickens quote came from. In an essay at school around this time we had to describe what we wanted to be when we grew up – I said I wanted to go to Cambridge University (er, not like Dad), become a lawyer (like Dad) and be captain of the England rugby team (ahem, also not like Dad). I guess these were all ambitions that second-guessed what I thought Dad wanted for me. How could I be more like Dad?

1) Be a giant

My dad wasn't like normal dads. He was a giant. At least he was until I was about fourteen. When he'd first been introduced to my mum's family in Yorkshire there were gasps of amazement.

'By heck – he's a ruddy giant!'

'What's it like up there?'

'Ee by gum, get that lad some oxygen!'

At his most elastic, my dad measured five foot nine and a half. That was a full two and a half inches above the average height for a UK male in the 1970s. The tallest living member of my mum's family was her dad at a massive five foot six. He'd reached that height by the age of eleven or twelve, replete with moustache and hairy chest. At a different time his schoolfriends would have expected him to become captain of the England rugby team. I mean, if you're five foot six when you're eleven, what'll you be when you're twenty-one?

2) Be a fitness fanatic

My dad, although slightly injury prone, was a dedicated fitness fanatic. He had various publications about different kinds of strength and fitness routines. There was a Ray Williams book about Welsh Rugby Union fitness training, which involved lots of bouncing up and down on the spot until you lost the feeling in your thighs, your kneecaps exploded, and you vomited all over the carpet. Still, it worked for the Welsh rugby team in the 1970s. Then there was the Canadian flying squad fitness programme, with about twenty different levels of fitness exercises. I never seemed to manage to get beyond level two, due to my pathetic strength and endurance.

And there was a classic book, *Isometrics For You, Middle Class Businessman*, which suffered because the bloke in the photos looked like someone in a normal 'before' picture, a bald businessman with a slightly flabby middle and man breasts (though in the 1970s these terrific appendages were referred to as 'relaxed pectorals').

And of course there was the mighty Bullworker. This was two steel tubes held together by a single internal spring with steel plastic-covered cables holding it all together. It came with an indepth colour pamphlet showing the different exercises, which involved a stern-faced German basically pulverising the Bullworker in every exercise. It had been developed at the Max Planck Institute, so you got the impression that the Bullworker was an associated technology by-product of World War II Messerschmitt jet research. At the front of the booklet was a testimonial by Britain's most muscular man ever, a bodybuilder called Dave Prowse. As well as showing off his muscles, Dave gave his spindly readers diet tips, like eat loads of meat and

cheese and drink gallons of milk. Not long after this he became the 1978 version of an A-list celebrity by becoming the Green Cross Code man, who took over all road safety duties from Tufty, the giant red squirrel who presumably had been forced to move to the Highlands and Lake District due to the ever-encroaching American grey squirrel. I don't really know what Tufty did wrong, but perhaps the authorities thought that nobody would trust a giant red squirrel, whereas they would trust a West Country bodybuilder in a tight white outfit with a green cross painted on his chest. Dave was also Darth Vader in the first *Star Wars* film, though his Bristol accent didn't make the final cut, and was replaced by the deep honeyed tones of James Earl Jones (more's the pity).

There was no doubt that I was skinny and weedy, and not in a lean, athletic way. My childhood asthma had left me with a lanky body with very ill-defined muscles. Why did I need muscle? Was I going to have to lift some heavy objects? No. It was girls, of course. Girls liked blokes with muscle-bound bodies. It had to be true, I had seen those adverts for Charles Atlas booklets in the back of my superhero comics and while I laughed at them, the part of my brain that dealt with sex *truly believed* them. I never actually asked a girl what she thought of muscly blokes – girls didn't tell you what they really thought.

3) Be good at rugby

I dreamed of playing rugby. Many of the books I read were rugby biographies, my favourites being about Willie John McBride, Gerald Davies and, of course, the story of the 1970 All Black tour of South Africa which included sketches by the De Aston penis artist. I had been in the schoolboy club of *Rugby World* since 1976 and devoured the magazines. I'd started playing rugby at secondary school. Due to my innate lack of speed and finesse and my slightly-tall-for-his-age gangliness, I was put in the second row. This, for the ninety-nine per cent of readers who have no interest in or knowledge of rugby, is the position for towering, beefy Neanderthals with superhuman strength. I ended up doing my back in so badly that even now, over thirty years later, it still affects me. This didn't make me give up rugby, of course, but I knew deep down that captaining England, or even playing for my local club first team, might be a bit of a stretch.

4) Become a lawyer
That's what I wanted to be. Yep. Except, on closer scrutiny, I had for a while realised that at times Dad didn't actually seem to like his job that much. And he'd stare off into space and say things to me like 'make sure you do a job you love'. Which was a bit confusing. Plus you had to be able to concentrate and read lots of boring books from cover to cover. That sort of thing always sent me to sleep within minutes.

5) Go to boarding school
My dad had suggested that I should go to a boarding school, presumably to stop me becoming a father before the age of fourteen, but also due to acknowledging my drift downwards academically in an effort to keep up (or, rather, down) with everybody else. Some smart people at school just kept their heads down and worked hard, so nobody noticed them beavering away in the corner of the library. But they were all called Swotty Tomkins or Four-Eyes Fortesque. I didn't want to be one of them because they would never have a girlfriend and they weren't cool. My God, there's the stark truth. Never mind a pretty girlfriend. To get a pretty girlfriend you needed to be cool and slightly dangerous, funny, anti-authoritarian and slightly rebellious, like a cross between James Dean and Arthur Scargill. And to be cool you really needed to be part of a cool set, so you had to have cool mates who would treat you like a

cool person, a tough, hard man, with disdain for intellectual achievement.

Cool kid: 'Got an F in my report!'

All his friends (with thumbs held aloft): 'Well done, mate!'

6) Get into classical music

Tough one, this. I obviously wanted to be a complete and utter carbon copy of my father but, you know, classical music was, basically, unlistenable rubbish with absolutely no beat and the lyrics, when there were lyrics, were invariably shit. Though I quite liked *Pictures at an Exhibition* by Mussorgsky and *Finlandia* by Sibelius because we had studied them at school with Mr Hair, and learned something about the composers. So, in fact, I said I hated classical music but on closer inspection it wasn't that bad. The stuff I really didn't like were the pieces I had to learn for my trombone and piano lessons. The point of being able to play an instrument was obviously to impress girls, but what girl in her right mind would get excited by trombone versions of classical hits?

7) Love reading Dickens

Dad's favourite novels were *Catch 22* and *The Pickwick Papers*, the latter being, in his view, the funniest book in the English language. He had two complete works of Dickens, as well, to keep him going.

Apart from *Rugby World* and rugby biographies, I also liked reading books about WW1 battleships, Greek mythology, Brian Aldiss *Space Opera* stuff and comics. Our pretty new English teacher, Miss Cornhill, had recently got us reading *Oliver Twist*, but because I was in love with her I found it very hard to concentrate during class and so didn't really take in much of the book. Like most serious literature, it had me dropping off after a couple of pages.

8) *Consume 'everything in moderation'*

This was Dad's mantra. Or one of them. Don't eat until you're sick. Don't overdo things. I was more addictive and couldn't stick to this eminently sensible advice. Fourth helpings of banana custard? Yes, please.

9) *Get a bent nose*

Even trickier than getting into classical music, this one. Dad's nose had actually got smashed playing rugby. I tried squashing and bending my nose but to no avail. I then began taking the piss out of older, tougher kids, in the hope that they would smash me in the face and break it for me (I only achieved this feat several years later, by which time I no longer wanted a bent nose).

10) *Wear tweedy stuff*

According to Mum, Dad had had the same clothes style since 1957. Tweedy sports jacket, cavalry twills, square. Not a cravat, a square. (A square is like a cravat, except it's square.)

On my eleventh birthday I went to the golf club to have a steak dinner with my parents. I was dressed, very proudly, in my brand-new tweed sports jacket. 'Thanks for my new

Tweed sports jacket

child's-size tweed jacket, Mum and Dad. It's exactly the same as Dad's!'

Trying to be an identikit version of my dad seemed like the most natural thing in the world. I was the oldest son, after all. But I wasn't him. Look in a mirror and you can see your parents; they're there behind your skin, looking back at you. I realised I was similar to Dad in many ways but the differences were becoming more apparent.

Dad took an intense interest in our sporting development. If possible he would always try and watch the rugby matches in which we played. That was, until the infamous game against King's Grantham in 1978, also known as The Game With The Gent's Secret Penalty Move.

How did 'The Gent' get to be our secret weapon? The person in question was a well-spoken young man of Hong Kong descent whose family had moved to the area in 1976. At that time we were all high on kung fu TV trickery, with *The Water Margin* and *Monkey* being two of our favourite programmes. When we first saw The Gent's family's shop, the Silver Lantern, open for business on the main street, we all burst into high-pitched Chinese kung fu-style voices, attacking each other with karate chops while simultaneously singing the *Hong Kong Phooey* theme tune. Seeing it written down like this over thirty years later, one can't help feel slightly queasy at the unthinking casual racism of it all. But casual racist idiocy soon gave way to genuine wonder, surprise and eventually devotion to the take-away food cooking talents of The Gent's parents. The first time we got home with tinfoil cartons of piping-hot Chinese food from the Silver Lantern, it was like reaching a new stage of personal enlightenment. Crunchy bamboo shoots, chalky water chestnuts. You didn't need to eat pork as a roasted joint – you could roll it into balls, cover it in batter and serve with an orange sweet and sour sauce that had the consistency of hot molten lava.

Over the next couple of years I became good friends with The Gent. He was a cheeky, smart, slightly shy, chubby little boy whose green snorkel parka pockets were always stuffed with various kinds of sweets. His typical playtime activity was shouting 'Goodies!' at big kids from about fifty yards away, then running as fast as he could in the other direction, knowing that his stout little legs would not get him far before the big kid caught him, turned him upside down, and relieved him of all his wares. It was like something out of a rather surreal *Beano* story.

The Gent's goodie-based weight had somehow earned him a place in Mr McTavish's under-13 school rugby team. Although The Gent was stocky, none of his girth was muscle. 'It's all just loose skin,' he would say sadly, inspecting his physique in the changing-room mirrors. But Mr McTavish seemed impressed with The Gent and picked him as hooker, tasked with tapping the ball back in the scrums and throwing the ball in at line-outs. The Gent had pretty good hands and, with the biggest game of the season coming up against the county's best, and most evil, under-13 team, King's School Grantham, McTavish started to discuss game-breaking new moves with us. At that stage of the season, in early 1978, we had played four games and lost four, with twelve points scored but with 106 points against. McTavish was determined that the rot would stop here. And with this in mind he devised a complex and quite brilliant attacking penalty move with which we would take apart the King's Grantham defence, and thoroughly demoralise them in the process. We called it The Gent's Secret Penalty Move.

It was a tapped penalty move. Our scrum-half, Tony Hopkins, would stop talking about Speedway for five minutes and take the penalty. Then he'd pass back to the onrushing Gent. Various diversionary fast runners would attack the ball to seemingly make themselves available for the pass and thus draw in defenders, then the loose forwards would bind onto The Gent

Top secret running angles

and drive him forwards, while a second wave of runners ran diagonals behind him, one of whom, Sean Striker, our most elusive runner, would take the ball and run unimpeded through the middle of the pitch and the dumbfounded defenders, scoring just under the posts. (The plan, unofficially, continued in that we'd then jump in the air and hug each other and chair Scan Striker around the pitch, then go on to win by a huge score and all get a massive confidence boost from the game and all suddenly become really popular at school and the best-looking sixth-form girls would fight over us and we would all get great exam results and go on to achieve great things in arts, politics, music, finance, law, farming, Speedway, rugby, etc., and we'd all look back to the epiphany of The Gent's great penalty move (top secret) and marvel at the impact it had on all of our lives and every ten years we would meet up at a hotel in a secret mountain location (owned by one of us) to celebrate The Gent and his subsequent brilliant international rugby career.)

On the day of the match, the ball went, as planned, to The Gent and various runners set off in different directions just as McTavish had told them to. The worrying thing at this point was the fact that several of the onrushing hulking Grantham defenders were smiling. Just as they reached the oblivious Gent, and before our forwards, including myself, had had a chance to bind on and protect him, they piled into him and he was unceremoniously flattened. King's Grantham took the ball, ran up the pitch and scored under the posts. Poor McTavish was going crazy (and he was the ref). They had stolen the try. More than that, they had stolen our lives. They had stolen our secret gentlemen's club and The Gent's 103 England caps.

During the second half, with us being completely overrun, somebody pointed out that my dad, who was on the touchline, had started shouting something at us.

'What's he saying – fluted?'

'Pewter. He's saying pewter.'

'Why is your Dad shouting "pewter" at us, Tim?'

It wasn't 'pewter' but 'putrid'.

'*Putrid*! Absolutely *putrid*!'

He was furious. Going red in the face and shaking his head.

I hoped McTavish would send my dad off, though this would probably have been more embarrassing than his outburst. Dad was the only parent who ever turned up to these games; he sometimes even refereed them when there was no teacher available, and occasionally helped out with coaching. Rugby was his passion so I know he was heartbroken to have to watch me take part in such a rugby comedy cabaret. But I decided that I'd have to have a word with him afterwards.

At the end of the game the final score was 86-0.

'You can't say putrid at rugby, Dad.'

He shook his head, still livid.

'Putrid!'

At the end of that term I got a terrible school report. Keen to show how cool and 'one of the lads' I was, I had started mucking about in many of my lessons. Dad got mad with me and asked me what I thought I was doing. I got outraged too because I was thirteen and it felt like the correct response. I was officially misunderstood.

I had finally become a proper teenager.

There's a Radio Playing in the Background: 1978

10cc 'Dreadlock Holiday'

Crystal Gayle 'Don't It Make My Brown Eyes Blue'

Plastic Bertrand 'Ca Plane Pour Moi'

Clout 'Substitute'

ELO 'Mr Blue Sky'

Jackson Browne 'Stay'

Patti Smith 'Because The Night'

Blondie 'Denis'

Boney M 'Daddy Cool'

Althea & Donna 'Uptown Top Ranking'

Andrew Gold 'Never Let Her Slip Away'

10. A la Recherche des Vélomoteurs Perdus

Some of this is vivid in my memory. Other parts of the trip have disappeared completely and I've sort of made them up – bits where the French girl is in a swimsuit, for example. And also any bits where I am shown to be understanding French easily. And I've exaggerated some bits and completely ignored others (such as the many lost hours I spent trying to play pinball and babyfoot properly and the antics and characteristics of The French Family). Apart from that it's all kosher, just about. Nearly. Maybe. So this is a semi-remembered account – with help from my 1978 diary – of a French exchange visit, as portrayed by members of the North Lincolnshire Rude Film Society (who usually make vampire erotica* in the woods outside Market Rasen, so cut them some slack).

TIM sits at the table at home. His DAD reads a
newspaper. MUM is busying herself. The phone
rings. MUM goes to answer it.

      DAD
What are you reading?

---

* All their videos got confiscated by the police after a *Rasen Mail* exposé so they were available for work.

                TIM
        The cereal packet.

                DAD
        But you're only reading the side of it.

                TIM
        Yeah, I know. I've read the back
        already.

                DAD
        (Sighs) Idiot.

        MUM returns.

                MUM
        Tim, I have some very exciting
        news for you.

                TIM
        The school's fallen down?

                MUM
        No, don't be silly.

                TIM
        All the *Blue Peter* presenters
        have been kidnapped?

                MUM
        No. That was Mr Gladwold, your
        French teacher. It's the French
        exchange on at the moment.

TIM

Yeah, I know. A load of swots
from England visiting a load
of swots in France.

MUM

Well, one of the boys from your
school, has, erm, dropped out,
so they have a spare boy.

TIM

Wow. That's interesting, Mum. Cheers.

MUM

(Smiling strangely and staring at TIM)

TIM

(Suspicious)
You'd better not have done…

MUM

What?

TIM

You've volunteered me, haven't
you?

MUM

I thought you'd be excited.

TIM

What, about the prospect of
trying to speak French for
a week?

MUM

Um, ten days to be precise.

TIM

Ten days?! Bloody hell.

DAD

Don't swear!

TIM

But, Dad…

DAD

If you've volunteered for something,
you have to see it through.

TIM

But I didn't volunteer!

DAD

Well, now you know how soldiers in the
First World War felt.

1. Voici la famille Bertillon–papa, maman et les trois
enfants, Philippe, Marie-Claude et Alain.

                    TIM
          Eh?

                                                  CUT TO:

EXT. DAY
A bus waits in the market square. Kids climb
onto it. A bossy teacher with a clipboard orders
people around. Then he gets on the bus and takes
the register.

               MR SAVAGE
          Now remember, you are all ambassadors
          for the school.

               SMART KID
          What, like Henry Kissinger, sir?

               MR SAVAGE
          Yes, I suppose so. A bit like
          Henry Kissinger.

               SMART KID
          So will we be destroying the village
          we're going to visit in order to
          save it?

He looks around. Other kids with glasses laugh.

               MR SAVAGE
          (Clips smart kid around the ears)
          Henry Kissinger won the Nobel Peace
          Prize, you idiot.

SASSY GIRL
Yes, but he was instrumental in
the policy of bombing Cambodia.

MR SAVAGE
You have no idea what you're talking
about.

SASSY GIRL
Miss Cornhill showed us a documentary
about Cambodia, sir. It said that
Henry Kissinger could get done for
war crimes.

MR GLADWOLD
Mr Savage. Do you think we could
tie up this conversation and head
off? Remember, we have a ferry to
catch.

MR SAVAGE
It's all under control.

The bus pulls off. Kids cheer. Shots of bus on
motorway. Kids looking out of it. Chatting.
Throwing things at each other. TIM and his mate
PAUL are seated behind two older girls called
LILY FLINT and her friend ANNA CHRISTIE.

LILY
(Laughing)
Hey, boys. Bet you can't guess
what my bra size is.

>   PAUL
> (Goes quiet)

>   TIM
> (Goes very quiet)

>   LILY
> No?

>   TIM
> (After taking deep breaths)
> What are you on about? What's a 'bra size'?

>   LILY
> Ha ha. It's how big your bosoms are.
> I'm a 34C.

>   TIM
> (Goes quiet again)

>   PAUL
> (Hyperventilating)

>   CUT TO:

Back of the coach. Middle-aged female teacher is talking about verbs.

>   FEMALE TEACHER
> Does anyone know what the verb 'venir' means?

There is tittering. A few of the boys look around at each other and giggle. A smart-looking girl puts her hand up.

                    GIRL
    Is it 'to come', miss?

                    FEMALE TEACHER
    Yes, well done.

                    RED-FACED BOY
    Fwah haaa! She said 'come'!

    The other boys laugh.

                    FEMALE TEACHER
    Come here, you idiot.

                    RED-FACED BOY
    Miss, you said 'come' again! Fwah haaaa!

                                        CUT TO:

    Montage of bus, ferry, train and bus. The bus
    pulls in to a typical French small town square,
    not unlike the one they left, except the church,
    most of the buildings and the cars are a
    different shape. There are lots of people
    standing around, including a large family, all
    with big hair, waving madly. The kids file off
    the bus.

                    PAUL
    I hope my penpal has an attractive sister.

                    TIM
    (Looking at crowd.)
    Paul...

                    PAUL
What's up?

                    TIM
Remember I'm filling in for a
kid who dropped out?

                    PAUL
Yeah, what about it?

                    TIM
Well, I bet you any money I'm
staying with the big haired waving
family.

                                        CUT TO:

The kids file off the bus to their hosts until
only TIM is left. The smiling family wave and
hold up signs saying 'Tim Bradford'.

They all pile into a really battered old Citroen
DS and the dad drives really really fast out of
town, into country lanes, turns his lights off
and laughs. The rest of the family laugh. They
are all talking French very quickly.

                    TIM
Er, I don't speak French.

                   FATHER
(French, with subtitles)
What did the English boy say?

     ALAIN

(FWS)

He says 'What the fuck are you
French going on about?

All the family laugh again.

     FATHER

(FWS)

Alain, just do that bad French
thing again. It kills me.

     ALAIN

C'est the jambes de grenouille
avec the gendarme dans le piscine?
[Are the frogs' legs with the policeman
in the swimming pool?]

The family are in hysterics. TIM, earnestly,
tries to answer.

     TIM

OK, I think I understood a bit of that.
Something about the ham from Grenoble
being served at swimming pools?

     FATHER

(FWS)

What did he say? What did he say?

     ALAIN

(FWS)

Something about the ham from Grenoble
being served at swimming pools?

They laugh again. The father is laughing and
crying so much that he swerves off the road,
through a hedge and ends up in a field,
surrounded by cows. They all look at each other
then start laughing again.

                              CUT TO:

A farmer on a tractor pulls the car out of the
field. The family all wave and the girls kiss
him.

                              CUT TO:

The car pulls into a little farmyard.

        ALAIN
    Tim, this is our home.

        TIM
    Hey, I understood that!

        ALAIN
    That's because I said it in English.

        TIM
    But you were all talking French
    before.

        ALAIN
    Er, that's because we *are* French.

The family all sit around a huge kitchen table.
The father takes out a bottle of Calvados and

lots of glasses. He then takes out a packet of
drinking straws and places one next to each
glass. He pours a glassful of Calvados for TIM
and offers him the straw, then makes a sucking
noise with his lips. TIM picks up the straw and
drinks some Calvados, then he falls backwards
off his chair, coughing. The whole family laugh
but the mother scolds the father.

        ALAIN
(Lifts TIM up)
Sorry, Tim. My father has what's
called a 'French sense of humour'.

                             CUT TO:

ALAIN and TIM walking around the farmyard,
investigating the buildings.

        TIM
What's all this stuff?

        ALAIN
My father is a farmer, but his real
passion is taking things apart and
putting them back together again.
During his National Service he
specialised in taking tanks apart
and putting them back together again
really quickly. It was the happiest time
of his life. He now spends his time
trying to recreate that buzz.

They walk into a huge barn where various
motorbikes of different sizes and stages of
completeness lie around.

>   ALAIN
> (Pointing at a moped)
> Come on, let's go into town.

>   TIM
> Don't we need helmets?

>   ALAIN
> Ha ha! It's no wonder you
> English guys are hopeless with women.

They climb onto a tiny orange Puch 50cc moped and
tear off down the country lane to the main road.
The wind blows TIM's hair and he is happy. The
wind also blows ALAIN's crazy wavy hair and it
gets in TIM's face. The heavy metal music from
Easy Rider starts to play, and TIM isn't sure
what to do with his hands, and is still trying
to get the hair out of his eyes and mouth. ALAIN
toots his little horn at various passers-by and
a crowd of old men playing boules.

>   OLD MAN 1
> (FWS)
> I don't think much of Alain's new bird.

>   OLD MAN 2
> (FWS)
> Yeah, pretty ugly. She looks like
> an English schoolboy.

CUT TO:

There's a deafening sound of grasshoppers.
A farmland scene of small fields, some with
maize, others with young wheat. On each side,
the fields are bordered by thick hedgerows.
The next field along is a large meadow and at
the end of that is a pond. All around is the
sound of birds. And flying insects. The sound of
a tractor toiling uphill can be heard along a
distant field. Then there is a faint buzzing in
the distance. It's now more of a clanging
grinding moan. This is not just a motorbike.
It's a motorbike put together from old parts by
teenage French people.

CUT TO:

The motorbike. Riding it is ALAIN, waving
manically. He stops in the middle of the lane and
Tim jumps on. As they set off, the opening bars to
'Ca Plane Pour Moi' by Plastic Bertrand plays in
the background. The old brown motorbike shoots up
the old lane towards the village, with dust flying
up behind it, the two boys shouting wildly.

TIM
Woooooooeeeeeoooo!!

ALAIN
Yaaaaaaaaeeeeee!!

CAMERA follows bike up a low hill. Music still
plays. Camera shows POV of riders.

FREEZE FRAME on rider grinning manically, wind
in his hair.

>   TIM (V.O.)
>   This is Alain. Alain
>   was my penpal. Although I never used
>   to write to him so technically he
>   was just a pal. That's *copine*. Or
>   does that mean girlfriend? God, it's
>   still so confusing.

The motorbike approaches an idyllic-looking
village.

>   TIM (V.O.)
>   Actually, maybe *copine* means
>   prostitute.

                                    CUT TO:

A BUSTLING CAFE. Lots of cigarette smoke. Young
people playing pinball.

ATTRACTIVE INTENSE-LOOKING TEENAGE BRUNETTE
holds cigarette stylishly and talks to camera.

>   BRUNETTE
>   Do I have bad faith? Sartre would
>   say that the epistemological truth
>   was unverifiable.

BRUNETTE blows smoke in camera.

Keywords

La baguette

Le singe

Le viande

Le chien

L' Orangina

Le chewing gūm

Le pinball

Le bidet

Le French moped

Le bar-tabac

Le Johnny Halliday

La French chick

        TIM (V.O.)
    It was an exciting time.

                                    CUT TO:

ATTRACTIVE INTENSE-LOOKING TEENAGE REDHEAD holds
cigarette stylishly and talks to camera.

        REDHEAD
    As Rousseau said: 'How frightful are
    the illusions of human life!'

TIM sits grinning embarrassedly between the two girls, who sit smoking stylishly and staring off into the distance intensely.

                                        CUT TO:

CLOSE-UP of TIM taking a drag on a cigarette and coughing his guts up. He falls onto his hands and knees, still coughing.

          TIM (V.O.)
     I met so many interesting people.

                                        CUT TO:

THE MARKET SQUARE. A GANG OF OLDER TEENS - THE PATTI SMITH-LOVING BIKERS with shaggy hair, mirror shades and big scarves sit with their parked motorbikes and mopeds, all smoking and talking.

          PSL BIKER 1
     We love Patti Smith.

          PSL BIKER 2
     And we love cinema. Ha ha - Jerry
     Lewis is a film comedy genius!

                                        CUT TO:

OLD MEN PLAYING BOULE and drinking pastis. ALAIN and TIM stroll up.

TIM (V.O.)
Everyone was so friendly.

ALAIN
Hello - this is my friend Tim. He's
from England.

One by one the OLD MEN all spit on the floor and
scowl at Tim. He grins sheepishly and does a
little wave.

TIM
Hi there!

OLD MAN 1
(FWS)
Fucking English.

CUT TO:

ALAIN and TIM on the motorbike riding along a
road, past neat suburban houses. The bike stops.
They get off. ALAIN parks it at side of road. They
walk down a small drive and ring the doorbell.
A tall handsome woman, Mme LISIERE, answers.

Mme LISIERE
Alain! How are you?

They do that triple cheek-kissing thing.

ALAIN
Fine, thanks. This is my English
penpal, Tim Bradford.

    Mme LISIERE
Pleased to meet you, Timbradford.

They do that triple cheek-kissing thing but TIM
is confused as to how many times he should kiss.
He grabs Mme Lisiere and hugs her tightly. She
looks at Alain, and shrugs.

    ALAIN
Is Madeleine here?

    Mme LISIERE
(Shouts in the door)
Madeleine! Alain is here to see you.

    TIM (V.O.)
This is the girl.

A beautiful dark-haired girl appears at the
door. FREEZE FRAME of her in the doorway. She
looks like a young Jane Birkin. Or maybe a
young, tanned Glenda Jackson from around 1968.

                          CUT TO:

FREEZE FRAME of TIM looking completely
gobsmacked.

MADELEINE moves forward in slow motion, lightly
touches TIM'S arms and presses two kisses, one
on each cheek.

(The opening bars of 'Je T'aime' play as she
moves.)

CUT TO:

DIAGRAM of blood pumping increasingly faster
through blood vessels. A swingometer marked
'Blood pressure' swings about wildly. Echoing
harp music plays.

CUT TO:

A field of tall grass and flowers blows gently
in the breeze. Then loud music. ALAIN, TIM and
MADELEINE running and laughing through the
field.

CUT TO:

Café scene. MADELEINE showing TIM how to play
pinball. Holding his hands over the buttons.

CUT TO:

Outdoor swimming pool, fast motion like silent
film. MADELEINE, in pale blue swimsuit,
splashing TIM, while ALAIN looks on, laughing.

      TIM (V.O.)
    Madeleine Lisiere. Even the sound
    of her name makes me come out in
    a sweat. She was fifteen, two years
    older than me. For a week in 1978 I was
    in paradise. But it couldn't last.

Dejected film people put their cameras away and
walk off.

> TIM (V.O.)
> Wait. There's a bit left.

The film people look happy and set their gear up
again.

> CUT TO:

A COACH pulling out of the market square. TIM
looking miserable, staring out of the window.
ALAIN is waving happily with his huge family
alongside him. As the bus waits to turn into the
main road, MADELEINE, in a summer dress, comes
cycling alongside the bus and waves to TIM,
laughing. Bus drives into the distance.
MADELEINE stops her bike and stares after it.

> CUT TO:

INT. COACH
TIM sits on his own looking glum. 'Supernature'
by Cerrone plays on bus tape machine as all
around him kids are laughing and joking.

> TIM (V.O.)
> Would I ever see her again? I
> couldn't be sure of that, so I'd
> written her a letter.

> CUT TO:

INT. BEDROOM - EVENING
MADELEINE sits on her bed, reading letter.

     TIM (V.O.)
Dear Madeleine. I really enjoyed
my time with you this last week
or so. Thanks for a great time in the
kitchen when you talked with Alain
and I just stared. I will never forget
your beautiful eyes and sweet smile.
I would love to see you again.
Maybe you can write to me.
Love Tim

                                    CUT TO:

EXT. FARMYARD
ALAIN talks to camera.

          ALAIN
The thing is, Tim's French wasn't
very good, so he dictated the letter
to me and asked me to write it in
French. So me and my brothers - well,
we thought Tim was a great guy, and
we were only trying to help…

                                    CUT TO:

INT. BEDROOM - EVENING
MADELEINE sits on her bed, reading letter.

          TIM (V.O.)
Dear Madeleine
You are a very sexy bird. I really
would very much like to have it off
with you.
Love Tim

                                              CUT TO:

INT. SCHOOLROOM
TIM in school. Walking between classes. Hanging
around with his mates.

          TIM (V.O.)
     So I went back to normal life.
     Except that it wasn't normal any more.
     I started writing to Alain, mostly
     to try and get news of Madeleine. But
     his letters were full of stuff about
     mopeds and farm machinery, Patti Smith
     and pinball.

                                              CUT TO:

MADELEINE sitting with her friends in a cafe,
reading Tim's letter, and looking really
annoyed.

'Because The Night' by Patti Smith comes on.

          TIM (V.O.)
     Madeleine Lisiere was everything I
     wanted in a woman. She was older.
     She was beautiful. I didn't understand
     a word she said. She was utterly
     unattainable. Like having all the stars
     in alignment, this meant that I couldn't
     help falling instantly in love with her.
     I would never see her again.

'Because The Night' plays out then stops
suddenly as the needle is taken off the record.
The film crew walk away, shaking their heads.

11. Girls Girls Girls (Girls) 2: Tim's Sex File

'Tim's Sex File' was a pink (pink!) foolscap legal folder that would normally have carried the files of clients at Dad's office but instead had been customised to reflect my thirteen-year-old interests. Carefully glued onto each of its sides were pictures of models from the copies of *Playboy* and *Knave* that I had nicked from Roly Chesterfield's bedroom (possibly as revenge for him stealing all the best parts in our *Goon Show* recording sessions).

I used to think that my sex file was a snapshot of my early teenage desires and fears but in fact it was really just a collection of available erotic material. The most bizarre thing about it was not its idiosyncratic montage of large-breasted nudes, and small ads for sex toys, along with my own notes and annotations about the various women (with speech bubbles making them say things like 'Wow, Tim, you are great!' and 'Sex... Mmmm!!'), but the fact that after a few months of keeping it hidden under the socks and underpants of my top drawer I then hid it away for ever, folded neatly into a small cube, on a ledge in the old chicken shed in the back field where it was not discovered until my dad found it while clearing out the shed in 2001. (Naturally, the whole family found out about this turn of events before I did.) In some ways it was a missed opportunity. I could have created an ongoing reference point for sex as my teen years progressed, jotting down ideas and thoughts about girls I fancied, plus the sporadic advice I got from my elders about sex. And, of course, more stuff cut out from stolen porn mags. But my decision to hide it away was a sign that I was embarrassed and a little guilty about my feelings towards girls, English teachers and stroppy film actresses. Somehow, possibly through a combination of Mum's religious morality and the feminist political theories I was picking up at school, I had sort of taken on the view that sex should not be manipulative, but should be taken part in, in the context of a consensual relationship. So as far as the sexual fantasies in my head went, one minute I would be seducing a woman in the style of 007 or Terence Stamp, then as soon as I opened my mouth I would become a combination of *Viz*'s Student Grant and Rick from *The Young Ones* (worryingly, these characters didn't even exist then). Which just confused me all the more. If, say, Glenda Jackson or Anna Karina, feeling frisky and at a loose end in the East Midlands, suddenly turned up at the house one afternoon when everyone else was out, would I go for it, or first try and get to know them better?

One other, rather more alarming, aspect of Tim's Sex File is that in the top right-hand corner of the first page are written the words 'Leeds United Rule OK'.

12. Plastic, Glue and War

Marcus Black has come round with my Airfix model of the SS *Tirpitz*. I am happy yet sad. Happy because it looks so amazing – if you squint you could almost think it was the real SS *Tirpitz*, just far away. Except that the *Tirpitz* was sunk by Lancaster bombers in 1944, which somehow doesn't seem fair because what was the point of having a ship if it's going to be attacked by big planes? They might as well have just made it a plane in the first place. But they were the Nazis, so we were allowed to be unfair, I think is the reasoning.

But although I'm happy with how it looks, I'm not happy deep inside. I'm sad that I didn't do it myself. So it's only *mine* in the sense that I personally, not Marcus Black, bought it from the little model shop in the town. Marcus Black is brilliant at making models, as is his younger brother, Simon. They both seem to lose themselves in the making, disappearing into their own concentration.

The *Tirpitz* is one of the last models I will buy. I've been into them since I was seven, but the thrill is wearing off. Not just the thrill of buying and making them, but the thrill of war and war machines. I always loved the chase, the sniffing out and buying of models when you've a few pennies in your pocket. Down Waterloo Street, a long narrow lane with tiny terraced houses, just near the bridge, was a little Jet petrol station with one pump and a shop, with patchy grass outside. Next to it was a specialist shop devoted entirely to Airfix and Revell models. As you entered the shop, the smell of Humbrol paint, new plastic and cardboard plus engine odours from the corrugated steel garage next door was like the bouquet of a fine wine. The owner, the silvery-coifed Mr Peatfield, would observe you quietly, then let you get on with your browsing. British or Jerries? Yanks or Japs? Maybe go crazy and get something Italian or Australian?

Dad had built a lot of models. He'd done a Junkers 88, a Lancaster, a Spitfire, a Lysander and various ships including the *QE2*, HMS *Hood*, the *Bismarck*, HMS *Nelson*, and various little destroyers. Once finished, they went upstairs into a cupboard which left me with the sneaking suspicion that the only reason for their existence was in the making of them. Years later, they would come out again to take part in death-or-glory battles involving Action Men, the late 70s West Bromwich Albion Subbuteo team and cigarette lighters. Many were reduced to twisted, smouldering plastic or were smashed to pieces (most of the West Brom side survived – in fact Cyrille Regis single-handedly sank the *Bismarck*).

The Blacks, who lived on our road, were at once handsome and nerdy. Their house was a fascinating place. Simon Black had been chucked out of his bedroom so that Mr Black could build a massive model railway complete with landscaping and various

buildings, I remember once sitting in the 'railway room' watching a train go round and round as Marcus Black, who was three years older than me, operated the signal box. We were listening to the radio and 'Lucy In The Sky With Diamonds' came on. 'That song's about LSD,' said Marcus, very seriously. What the fuck was he talking about? It was about a girl who lives in the sky and has a lot of diamonds, you fool.

And so it was the Blacks and their perfect modelling of the SS *Tirpitz* who finally ended my model-making career. After having made half the Royal Air Force, several tanks and a fair proportion of the British and German navies, I had found myself now with too many model kits and not enough time. Marcus and Simon Black volunteered to make one for me. The *Tirpitz* was sister ship to the *Bismarck* (the one sunk in the famous battle involving Cyrille Regis). I agreed, and even said they could paint it for me. A few days later the ship was ready.

It used to take me ages to finish my models. But it wasn't just speed with the Blacks. This ship was perfect in every detail. They'd even painted little finishing touches to the smallest bits of decking stuff. For a brief period I gave them my backlog of unmade models. They didn't want payment, they just wanted the thrill of exquisite craftsmanship, a concept I had obviously forgotten or, more likely, never had. While they made the models I'd loll about nearby in their sitting room, staring at their tropical fish or listening to the sound of their mum hoovering. She was always hoovering. Eventually it got to the point where I'd just drop the model off and pick it up a few days later. After a while I tired of the relationship and decided to give up model-making completely. But it instilled in me the idea that proper model makers were serious, intelligent young men who didn't get out much.

13. God in the Radiators

Punk music may have been bubbling away for a while in the nation's consciousness but it was another crazy 'new' idea, which I had only just cottoned on to, that was fascinating me. Espoused by Charles Darwin, the theory of evolution turned everything I had been told in stories upside down and I started to realise that Adam and Eve *weren't* the first humans. Crazy! Up until then we hadn't been taught creationism. We didn't need to be. Everyone seemed to be a creationist. (Except Dad, of course.)

To some kids, the beginning of the teenage years is when the world starts to seem different. But to me, 1978 was turning out to be quite similar in some ways to 1968. Most of my time was taken up with playing games of one sort or another: football, cricket, tig, Blocky 123, Destroy and Tickle, Go to Wembley, Spot and climbing trees, building dens or playing with toys.

And going to church. We'd go to church (C of E) twice every Sunday, for morning service and evensong. I still had a highish-pitched voice and still sung in the church choir, as my dad and uncle had done. I was in denial. (Luckily I didn't know about being in denial – I was in denial about being in denial. So in a sense my double denial cancelled itself out and I was actually very well adjusted.) The choirmaster and organist was the same man who'd watched over my dad and uncle in the late 1940s.

Mr Robinson, now in his 80s, had legs cartoonishly bowed due to rickets as a child. He lived in the oldest house in Market Rasen, a late-seventeeth-century townhouse with gas lighting and a tin bath in front of the fire in the kitchen. Clocks ticking. The smell of wood polish and musty old carpet. Mr Robinson's one item of luxury was a one-bar electric fire that he'd put on when we went round for piano lessons. Relief from boredom came in trying to melt the soles of our black school shoes.

Now and then Mr Robinson would take me aside and try to explain the intricacies of musical notation using his best Tempo pen on musical paper. But, as ever, my eyes would start to feel heavy, like they would always do in any maths or physics lesson. I was a pretty useless pupil of his.

The church vestry was cold, colder than usual. Possibly the heating system had packed up but I was never really sure if the church had a heating system. I got changed into my 'work' clothes, the long black cassock that made me look like a Catholic priest or monk, then the girly white cotton surplus over the top that I always thought ruined the look and made us look a bit effeminate, and I sat down, like a footballer before a

game, to gather my thoughts. No-one else had turned up yet. The vestry was from the Victorian age, built within a stone church that had been there since Norman times. We each had our own peg that sort of reflected our pecking order in the choir. The choir depended on its pecking order. At this stage I was the head chorister. It's a lonely job: you're the go-between between the vicar and choirmaster, and the rest of the choir.

The vicar came out of his little room in his finery, carrying a big pile of books, which he dumped on the old wooden table in the middle of the vestry. He had the foresight to always have a big stash of paperbacks that he'd dish out every morning and evening. This was so that we wouldn't mess about during his long sermons. The books were mostly CS Lewis novels. *The Lion, the Witch and the Wardrobe*, *The Horse and His Boy*, *Prince Caspian*, *The Last Battle* and those others that I can't remember. We had to carry the books under our cassocks as we filed in – with our hands on our chests we looked very saintly. Naturally, if it was the evening, I had also been to Marwood's Tuck Shop beforehand to stock up on Victory Vs. At six o'clock it was time to file in, just me and the vicar. Sitting in the congregation were just three people, in a church that probably had the capacity to hold over 500. 1 opened *Prince Caspian* on page 135 and placed it on the pew next to the psalm book.

Religion had been part of my life since I was tiny. Now the choir was a way of earning money. We had once been (we reckoned) the greatest choir in North Lincolnshire. Mickey Miner, Stuart and Ian Quinsworth, Rodney Kitchen, Roly Chesterfield. They were legends. But now 1 was the last of this old order. The others had gone: balls and voices and religious observance dropped, God all but forgotten. In the glory days we had had a football team and we were dirty; we had had a cricket team and we were good. Now there was me, my two brothers, my two cousins and a few really young kids whose names I could never remember.

And then there was our new star singer. Carmen Williams. Carmen was the first girl in the choir's history. I think Mr Robinson had had to do some serious arm-twisting and probably said to the reluctant vicar, 'Those Bradford lads are bloody awful, we need some new talent.' Not long after that another girl joined and the two of them hung out together and it changed the atmosphere completely. Rather than concentrate on the important things, like how Prince Caspian was going to get his kingdom back, or what psalm we were doing next, I used to catch myself staring at Carmen Williams. Carmen was dark-haired and pretty, with an encyclopaedic knowledge of Bible stories and catechism facts.

Although at the time I didn't think I really believed in God, I'm certain that I was quite religious. I didn't pray to Him much or believe He had any influence over world affairs. God, to me, had always been like a stern father figure watching over everything and giving a sort of thumbs up or down depending on your behaviour, in the style of the film critic Roger Ebert.

If I did sometimes talk to God, I never talked to Him in church. The only place He appeared was when I was in my

bedroom, alone, in the quiet. He lived in the radiators. In 1978 I moved into the big room next to my parents, the slightly damp and spooky spare bedroom where guests stayed. It was cold and creaky and at night the central heating system made strange noises. Did God live in the radiators? Or was that the spirits of people who used to live in this house? Is that where Bustle Lady called home most of the time? Or was it my dead relatives and pets trying to communicate with me? I had started to get into ghosts when I was eight and by the time I was nine I wished I hadn't, because I started to see and imagine ghosts everywhere. In the patterns on carpets, wallpaper or curtains, in the houses outside, in the shadows. In the dark at night, after my parents had gone to bed and the comforting sounds of Radio 4 could no longer be heard.

In the summer one of the ex-choirboys, Rodney Kitchen, had started lending me records, obviously under the mistaken impression that my record collection was not well stocked enough to enhance my spiritual development. One of the first was The Clash's '(White Man) In Hammersmith Palais'. I had never heard anything like it. It wasn't cartoony punk like I heard on *Top of the Pops*. This evoked an atmosphere of harsh, witty aggression and a vital claustrophobia. The singer sort of talk-shouted the lyrics, half of which were completely unintelligible. I played the single over and over again until, in my imagination, I began to enter the scene. As well as being a kind of 'state of the nation' piece, the song was also about singer Joe Strummer's disdain for groups who 'sold out'. Selling out! I would never do that. I looked at myself. I was thirteen years old. I still sang in the choir, did piano lessons. It was as if I had held a new lens up to my eye and was, for the first time, seeing the world as it really was. I wanted to be a proper teenager and not the *Boy's Own* version envisioned by my parents.

As a result I decided I had had enough of cassocks and surplices and especially Peter, Edmund, Susan and Lucy and that useless puff of wind Prince Caspian. It was tough because I enjoyed the money the choir brought in (£20 a year) and felt bad at leaving Mr Robinson without a head chorister. And I wouldn't be hanging out with Carmen Williams any more. Within a couple of weeks I had told Mr Robinson that my voice had broken (it hadn't, so I had to put on a husky voice) and that I had to leave the choir immediately. I also gave up piano lessons. What if The Clash came round and found me sitting in front of a grand piano? They'd laugh. Or beat me up. Or not invite me to be the fifth member of their band. I kept on with the trombone – after all, you could get a job in a dub punky reggae act if you played the trombone. From now on, though, it was no sell-out all the way. The revolution had begun. And it meant lie-ins on a Sunday morning for the first time in years.

Punk epiphany

14. Tales of the Unexpected (Bandy's Conceptual Art Pranks)

It's late 1978 and surprisingly, perhaps, for a nearly fourteen-year-old, I was starting to get into politics, beginning with a regular deconstruction of Dad's *Daily Telegraph*.

'It's so right-wing!' (Said in whiny, self-righteous voice.)

Dad would counter with 'I only read it for the sport' without looking up. True enough, half the paper seemed to be rugby reports from minor public schools.

Miss Cornhill, my greatly worshipped English teacher, was a left-wing feminist so, in my innocence, I believed that I must become a left-wing feminist too. Then Miss Cornhill would fancy me and all the other girls would follow her lead. It seemed like a foolproof plan. It felt good to be a progressive thirteen-year-old. In 1978 we had a Labour government and really we'd never had it so good. The IMF had given us lots of money. The unions were strong. The Tories had a squeaky-voiced woman as leader so would be out of power for at least a generation.

But it was a difficult time for me in one sense because I had just started wearing glasses. Unlike today, where glasses are trendy, sexy, a sign of attractive intellectualism, and with images of good-looking bespectacled people plastered over billboards and magazine adverts, in 1978 the reaction to a kid in glasses was subtly different.

2009 comment: Hey, cool glasses.

1978 comment: Ha ha, look at four eyes! Tim has got four eyes, he used to have two eyes, but now he's got four eyes. Ha ha. Ha ha. Four eyes four eyes.

Four eyes four eyes.

Four eyes four eyes.

I don't blame them for this response. This is how teenage boys are programmed. Knowing that you might be feeling a bit sensitive and unsure about your new eyewear, the natural response is surely just to make you feel even worse, the delight, of course, really stemming from the fact that it is someone else rather than themselves who look different. OK, OK, not just different but like a daft, four-eyed swot.

I had a crush on a girl in our year, a quiet lass called Clarissa Bolt. I was confident, in the manner of a Jane Austen character, that my feelings for Clarissa were silently reciprocated. I wrote in my 1978 *Sunday Times* Rugby Union diary that we were going steady – a brazen lie, and I find it quite bizarre (and worrying) that I felt a need to lie to myself. But my mind was also elsewhere – much of the first half of that year's diary was a long-running love letter to the actress Barbara Bach, who played a Soviet agent in the film *The Spy Who Loved Me*.

Things then moved on apace thanks to a generous intervention by my so-called best mate, Bandy. For our religious education class, we were required to hand in our exercise books with essays every week to the RE pigeonhole in the staff room. One Tuesday morning, as Mrs Barnes the RE teacher was giving back exercise books with the marked essays inside, she asked me to stand up.

'Some people seem to think it's OK to scrawl about their love life all over their RE book. But I can tell them it isn't funny and it isn't clever.' Then she asked me to come and pick up the book. There, scribbled in the margins, and at the top and bottom of the page, all round the essay was Bandy's tiny spidery handwriting: 'Tim 4 Clarissa', 'Tim loves Clarissa', 'Clarissa 4 me'.

Possible response of class (1): 'Gosh, that's pretty open and honest, Tim.'

Possible response of class (2): 'Ha ha HAAAAAA. HA HA HA HA HA HA HA HA HA HA HA HA HA HA 'HAAAAAAAAAAAAAAAAAAAAAAAAAAAAAAAAAAAAAAAA AAAAAAAAAAAAAAAAAAAAAAAAAAAAAAAAAAAA Tim for Clarissa! Tim for Clarissa!' etc., etc.

Tim and Clarissa sitting in a tree
K.I.S.S.I.N.G.
How many times has Clarissa had it off in an English country garden? Etc., etc....

'You're dead, Bandy,' I said, pointing at him. Everybody giggled. Outside in the corridor after the lesson I grabbed him by the throat. 'You bastard,' I shouted and he sort of smiled, looking scared at the same time. I couldn't do anything. I just started to laugh, realising that Bandy didn't want me to have a girlfriend and was just being possessive.

And then I took a step back and thought to myself that I was thirteen – what did I need a girlfriend for? In actuality, all I wanted to do was write unrequited love poetry to her. Although that's not entirely true. Even though I was just thirteen I would have quite liked to have covered Clarissa's face with kisses but there was no way I would even admit that to myself, never mind to anyone else. I somehow had an innate understanding of Bandy's affection for me and need to have me all to himself. This didn't seem particularly strange. We had a good thing going. And imagine the pressure on Bandy if I had had a girlfriend… he would have had to get a girlfriend as well and I would have to listen to him banging on about some unattainable fifth-form girl that he was going to go out with and if the unimaginable had happened and we'd both gone out with girls at the same time, I was quite sure (and still am) that we would both have been thoroughly miserable after only a couple of days.

After the humiliation in front of the RE class, I don't think Clarissa Bolt spoke to me again for the rest of my school days.

I suppose Bandy's next prank was really all my fault. My cousin, Rob, had borrowed a copy of the Sex Pistols' *Never Mind the Bollocks* from Julie Winchelsea, the fifth-form girl who babysat for him and Rich, and I'd been going round to their house at the other side of town on a regular basis to listen to it. As was usual when I got together with Rob, we analysed the album after continuous plays, though after a while Rob was getting bored so I asked if I could borrow it. Sure, he said. The album came with a limited edition one-sided seven-inch single, 'Submission', and a blank B-side with a plain white label, and I borrowed that too.

I looked after the records properly but it was blatant negligence on my part to then let Bandy/Rubble Man be alone in

the same room as the limited edition seven-inch Sex Pistols single *with a plain white label on the B-side*. It was a red rag to a bull. Or, to be more exact, a pristine white collectors item rag to a writing-obsessed bull with a pen full of ink. It was as if I had said to Bandy: 'Here, take this seven-inch single that has a plain white label on the B-side and, please, fill the blank space with your own opinions of the Sex Pistols.' Of course I didn't say this but I might as well have done.

Bandy morphed into Rubble Man then scrawled his opinions on the Sex Pistols and their album all over the plain white label. My heart sank.

'Oooer. Tricky me!' said Rubble Man, showing me what he'd done. I was complicit. And I was torn between finding it incredibly funny and punkish, and realising that I would have to explain to Rob, and then to Julie Winchelsea, what had happened to her single.

Of course I dumped Bandy in it when I gave the album and single back to Rob and agreed that, yes, Bandy was a complete twat. I found out soon afterwards that Julie Winchelsea did not see the incident in any way as funny, and it was a fortunate thing that she had neither boyfriend nor older brother to come round and discuss the matter further with us.

In some ways punk was wasted on the urban sophisticates of the big cities. Looking back now, though I didn't understand it at the time, punk was a kind of plaintive, angry folk music. Stuck as we were in the middle of Lincolnshire, the music of punk spoke to us with an energy that we all seemed to lack. After the experience of *Never Mind the Bollocks*, Bandy and I started to tap into more and more punk music, thanks to his sister's record collection.

We started to gently take the piss out of various other kids at school, especially older lads with facial deformities, such as Julian 'Wang Eye' Bedingford, Eric 'Flatty Flatnose' Putney and Steven 'The Buck Tooth Rabbit' Draper, eventually creating Mike Yarwood-like characters out of their flaws. Oh, the godlike genius of Mike Yarwood! If the kids had been in our year or younger we'd have admitted it was psychological bullying but because they were older and bigger than us they were somehow fair game.

One Sunday evening in Bandy's living room, during the holidays, while we were sitting in front of the telly waiting for *Tales of the Unexpected* and messing about, we created our own 'band'. Bandy sang and I played guitar, except it wasn't actually a guitar. I didn't own a guitar. I had to make the sound of a guitar with my voice. I was pretty good. I could do a nice, slightly fuzzy sound of an old-fashioned Vox amp on overdrive while simultaneously throwing in a simple bass part and a high hat. While doing all this I'd bang the leather pouffes in Bandy's parents' living room. It was a total band sound. Sparse but adequate. The still-squeaky-voiced Bandy (his voice wouldn't break until later in the year) croaked, squealed and warbled over the top of it all.

Our first single, 'Slit My Gullet', was in a limited edition of one. I'd pinched one of my dad's boring (but now it would be limited edition – ha ha) Benny Goodman EPs, painted it olive green using Humbrol model paint and we had designed a label and sleeve. We were called Heart Attack. We were on our way.

'Have you seen my Benny Goodman EP?' said Dad.

We were, of course, a punk band. Punk was the perfect medium for adolescent songs, what with its infantile chord changes and shouty fake aggression. Bandy's parents were going through a rough patch, so he was much more punkish and angry than I was. This manifested itself particularly in our living-room performances. Bandy was able to push himself to the point where he looked disturbed and absurd. Bandy's group persona was Arnold Slitgullet, a misanthrope obsessed with VD, slitting wrists, being depressed and committing suicide. At the time I thought it was a great made-up character but, in retrospect, perhaps Bandy was trying to say a little bit more. My character, Johnny Faeces, was in the more orthodox British music-hall, toilet-humour tradition. I spelt the second name wrong on all artwork, sometimes Fisces, other times Fesces. And even then it was on my mind – that fear that I was Paul McCartney and Bandy was John Lennon. I think it must be a primal fear in any close relationship. This was of course more a structural thing, rather than our relative talents being similar to the Beatles duo. Yet there were times when I'd create a hummable melody for a verse and chorus and Bandy would steam in with strident vocals about sexual politics, death or simply that most people in the world were fucking wankers. At these times I reckoned Bandy was Frank Zappa and I was The Eagles. Sadly there didn't seem to be room in Bandy's life for both Arnold Slitgullet and Rubble Man, and Bandy's imaginary friend left for good.

We played our first gig in my bedroom a couple of weeks later. No-one else was there, but we were in the zone. I was now using my dad's Bullworker as a guitar, and we both wore pyjamas. Bandy bounced up and down on the bed. It was a great gig but then my dad banged on the door and said,

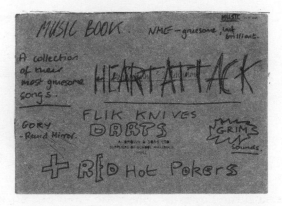

'Turn that racket down!' Wow. We must be real punks, we thought, the parents are getting pissed off with us.

Soon we graduated to real music, using the Bontempi air organ that stood in Bandy's dining room. I never understood why it was there, as nobody in the family could play it. And that is exactly what we attempted to do. Thanks to five years' worth of Mr Robinson's piano tuition, I could play 'Here Come The Farmer's Men' and the first four bars of Mozart's *Minuet in G*. But I could also play a few simple chords and that was enough for us.

The organ was about two feet off the ground and had brown plastic casing, big plastic keys and small white key chord buttons and rocker switches. After it was turned on it took ages for the sound to come out. An internal motor whirred for several seconds before the bellows unit kicked in. It made a surprisingly nice sound, if a little churchy.

I began saving up for an electric guitar. I had a lucrative babysitting job across the field at the doctor's house, earning as much as 50p for a night with as much instant coffee as I could drink, and loads of biscuits thrown in. The doctor had a big colour TV and I could watch my favourite programmes, such as David Attenborough's *Life on Earth*, and *Top of the Pops*.

At the rate I was going, I'd have enough for a guitar by the time I left university.

15. Goodbye,
Uncle Joe

As the year turned towards winter, we knew bad weather was coming. I had recently become aware of the term 'the Winter of Discontent'. On the news there were scenes with piles of black bin bags on the streets in the big cities. All of a sudden the Labour government appeared to be on its last legs. Then it snowed for ages, leaving big drifts in the main street. To add insult to injury, sweet Miss Cornhill announced she was going to marry the drama teacher, Mr Fountain. And my dad's business partner, Uncle Joe, died.

In my memory Uncle Joe's funeral was one of those cold, flinty East Midlands days when no matter what you're wearing, the wind somehow finds its way inside your clothes and makes you shudder. The old church was full. That didn't happen that much, even back in the late seventies. Mr Robinson, perhaps enjoying performing to a packed house for a change, was playing the ancient organ and filling the aisles with runs, swell and Procol Harum-style riffs and motifs. I hadn't been in the church for a few months since jacking in the choir and I was missing the money, which would now have come in handy. If I'd still been a choirboy I could have afforded to be a punk star but I couldn't be a punk star if I was still a choirboy. The irony.

Uncle Joe had been one of the most respected figures in the town. As both my dad and uncle were partners in the firm, we all sat in the front row with Uncle Joe's immediate family. I was squirming in my seat. I felt that I shouldn't have been there. I was now a rebellious punk rocker. At least in my head. In reality I was wearing a blazer and tie and a pair of smart school trousers. What did I feel? Was I upset?

I can't recall any 'different' music at this funeral. I'm sure it was the usual stuff, 'The Lord Is My Shepherd', 'Morning has Broken' (where half the congregation sang it the normal way and the other younger half sang like they heard Cat Stevens do it a few years earlier with that roll on 'like the first mo-o-orning'.

I could see people looking sad and crying but I didn't feel anything. Was there something wrong with me? I kept a furrowed brow expression so I looked concerned, just in case anyone might be looking in my direction to check I was in full mourning. I had met Uncle Joe many times but didn't know that much about him. He liked dripping sandwiches, and I'd join him after walking down to his house after brass band practice on a Monday night. He was also well known for cutting the legs shorter on his client chair so he would loom over them in his office and intimidate them.

Uncle Joe was the reason we were all there. I mean we as in my family. If he hadn't offered Dad a job all those years ago, God knows where we'd be. I certainly wouldn't be around.

Being an old family friend, Uncle Joe had been a father figure to my dad for many years. Now Dad was on his own and had to fill Joe's shoes. He suddenly had to work double time to clear all Uncle Joe's jobs and to get new business. In typical dad fashion, he was also captain of the golf club that year on top of other stuff he was obligated to. All of a sudden we stopped seeing him in the evenings and he was usually gone before we got up in the mornings. It felt like the symbolic end of the old world in some respects. Certainly the end of the gentle rhythms of my early childhood.

The knock-on effect for me was that suddenly, strangely, I was free. I didn't choose to be free, but I was. Free from Dad's regular guiding hand, his opinions and his advice. At first I

didn't really notice, but around this time I started to listen to John Peel, in the evenings on the old Bush radiogram, which had ended up in my bedroom after Dad had got a fancy new Hitachi deck. Normally, Dad would have been shouting, 'Turn that racket down!', but now he wasn't around, I could listen to Peely – a new father figure with a beard – in peace.

16. Newsprint Dreams

I had fallen in love with comics when I was six, after managing to persuade Yorkshire Grandad to buy me a copy of *Wizard* at the newsagents at Cleckheaton bus station. I was quite good at reading so didn't find it too difficult. It was a mixture of sports, wild west and WW2 stories so a lot of the speech balloons would have been 'Goal!', 'Arrgh!' or 'Look out!' I then 'progressed' to *Whizzer and Chips* and then, in 1972, the UK version of *The Mighty World of Marvel*. I loved them – the Marvel world was full of superheroes who'd got their power by accidentally getting a dose of some kind of radiation. I was Rural Kid, given superpowers by sniffing the petrol cap of Dad's lawnmower and able to draw daft pictures of my enemies.

A year later I was tired of the Marvel format, which seemed to just invent loads of new characters with big muscles and a tight outfit. Occasionally Grandad would buy me the *Avengers* comic, but my regular read changed to *Shiver and Shake* (you got loads of free gifts), then *Beano*, and then in 1975 I went back to war comics with *Warlord*. They had a great club you could join. It involved having a little plastic wallet with your Warlord Club membership card and a special code-breaker kit.

Through most of 1978 I was still making do with a reading diet of war and sport. My staples were two comics, *Tiger* and *Victor*. The latter was no different to the *Wizard* I'd been reading in 1971, suggesting I was stuck in a grenade-throwing, Jap-shooting, tank-exploding, commando-obsessed rut. *Tiger* had a bit more variety, with its mixture of stories taking in native

American wrestlers (Johnny Cougar), rally drivers (Martin's Marvellous Mini) and footballers (Roy of the Rovers). But I was no longer a comic addict.

One Thursday at the end of 1978, a different paper popped through our door. It was called *Record Mirror* and had been delivered by mistake by Bacon Hawkins, our new paperboy. I decided to read it, and in doing so entered a new world where people cared about and talked about music, with singles reviews, interviews, news and letters. I looked at my record collection, which all of a sudden didn't seem quite as amazing as it had a year earlier. It hadn't expanded much. The only new albums I'd bought were the *Grease* soundtrack, *Jazz* by Queen and *Plastic Letters* by Blondie, along with a couple of singles: 'Le Freak' by Chic and 'September' by Earth, Wind & Fire.

For the next few weeks I bought *Record Mirror* and a new paper called *Superpop*. Then, in February 1979, I bought my first *New Musical Express*. This was one of the key moments, as if I'd been looking through a prism and was now seeing

through clear glass for the first time in my life: punk was the most important thing to happen in Britain since the war. You should not 'sell out'. Right-wing people were evil. The Beat writers were cool. John Coltrane was God. The world view that I now still hold dear appeared pretty much fully formed to me in those first few months as I sat in the kitchen breathlessly reading through *NME* every Thursday evening after school, like an eager pilgrim happening upon the Dead Sea Scrolls. Thanks to Bacon Hawkins, for the next four and a half years, Thursday would be the best day of the week.

17. What Did 1979 Mean?

What was 1979 like? For some reason I always assume it's quite recent, but as my kids never fail to point out it is, in fact, the 'olden days'. In 1979, things weren't bright orange like they'd been for a lot of the 70s, but were becoming a sort of browny dark green with a hint of grey. Specifically, this was the colour of the car that my dad had been driving through the late 70s – an Austin 1800 painted a kind of army green. Its unique selling point was that it broke down at every opportunity. Its main feature, apart from its breakdown capabilities, was a cigarette lighter. My dad didn't smoke, but when he was younger he used to smoke a lot and the lighter obviously reminded him of how strong-willed he was.

1979 was a kind of in-between-eras year. The idea of a new decade was exciting. I couldn't really remember the thrill of moving from 1969 to 1970. Luckily, 1980 was coming up fast and it seemed racy and new and high tech. Something to do with

Austin 1800

the way the numbers 8 and 0 looked on a digital calculator. The number 1979 by comparison looked positively Victorian.

In 1979 things were changing around the world. It was the beginning of Islamic revolution in the Middle East, though my most vivid memory of the Iranian revolution is probably listening to 'Shah Shah A Go Go' by The Stranglers.

The Stranglers had mentioned in an interview about Nostradamus's prediction that Armageddon would come after a conflict in the Middle East and they pointed out that this referred to the overthrow of the Shah. I now realise they were just trying to plug their latest record, but at the time this seemed like a worrying new development.

In Market Rasen we had a revolution of our own – Langfords Records had put the prices of their singles up to £1.05, making a mockery of their oft-repeated catchy slogan '99 down from 1.15'. Controversially, Mrs Langford charged 16p extra for picture sleeves. This enraged Bandy so much that he wrote to *Sounds* magazine about it, after which 'Granny' Langford phoned Bandy's mother to complain.

'It's up to Michael what music newspaper consumer columns he writes to and on what issue,' Bandy's mum had replied. Bandy then garnered the huge kudos of being publicly congratulated by some of the coolest kids at the school. Git.

18. Hanging Around

I was in the third year at school. Messing about. Playing a lot of sport. And hanging around with mates. As well as Bandy I now had a few good friends at school. Chris Hines from Binbrook; Shorty Blackwell and Bramley Edwards from Faldingworth; and The Gent, Kev Coleman and Johnny Sidebottom from Rasen. I'd got to know some of them during lunch breaks, where I'd renounced the silent realm of the library and instead embraced the world of high-octane tennis-ball football matches on the all-weather pitch.

Hanging around was a big part of how we lived our lives. It wasn't boredom in the sense that we couldn't find anything to do, but boredom as a way of approaching life. We knew that there wasn't anything to do so we just hung around at each other's houses. Waiting. Listening to the radio. To relieve the

A Queen Victoria Jubilee bench, one of the local hotspots for intense hanging around

boredom we'd sometimes have a cup of instant coffee. (Instant coffee was the future. My favourite was Maxwell House but Mum usually bought Nescafé. Some families swore by Mellow Birds but it was so weak you had to put nearly half the jar in to make a decent cup of coffee.) Tea was just too old-fashioned, the sort of thing your granny drank. We'd drink coffee and sit around listening to football results coming through on the radio. We didn't despair of our boredom because we didn't really see any other options. It was only later that this boredom would manifest into an intense longing to escape. To *go* somewhere and *do* something.

Life was slow. Saturday afternoons were the slowest. You'd wake up on a Saturday morning all excited and watch a bit of TV (*Banana Splits*: good, *Swap Shop*: bad) then have your lunch and watch *Football Focus*. Then at around two o'clock you'd go to a friend's house and have a cup of instant coffee and stare at the clock and it'd still be two o'clock so you'd play a game of cards or Connect 4 or make smalltalk with their mum and it'd then be five past two. You'd be dying for teatime to come around, when the football results would start to come in. But you knew that was a whole two and a half hours away. Sometimes you'd walk to the sweetshop and buy some bubblegum and chew it at the playground. There was nothing at the playground that worked anymore. Apart from the swings, but they were for little kids. If it rained, the boredom increased. My God, it was almost exquisite.

At night we were starting to do what rural kids have always done – try and get off our faces on cheap/stolen alcohol. I got the ball rolling by nicking three-quarters of a bottle of VAT 19 rum from our pantry then topping it up with water, before doling it out to eager friends. A few weeks later Bandy followed suit, little realising that his mum ran a minutely accurate booze measurement system by marking lines on the bottle. Needless to say, the retribution wasn't pretty. We'd also started going to the pub, where we'd beg kindly older kids to buy us a half pint of beer or two.

The downside of this was the occasional violent hangover and a morning in bed wanting to die, while vowing never again to touch alcohol – more specifically never to mix Stones bitter and rum. My parents were strangely non-judgemental about these episodes, somehow seeing it as part of our rite of passage.

In those days, when we weren't busy sipping shandy or shooting up Nescafé, there was the odd programme on TV that was watchable. Mainly it was on Thursday night when both *Tomorrow's World* and *Top of the Pops* were on. *Tomorrow's World* showed us how we'd be living in the future – pills for food, shiny suits, jet cars, unimaginably well-built sexy blonde women. Sometimes to relieve the boredom of life I would immerse myself in *Tomorrow's World* and imagine myself somewhere off in the far distance – say, the year 2000 – with my (possibly alien) large-breasted wife and my interplanetary house with lots of fancy gadgets. Basically the world of the future combined the swanky designer house of George Best with the utopian shininess of *Blake's 7* – lots of tinfoil and serious expressions.

Obviously more important than *Tomorrow's World* was *Top of the Pops*. We would sit seething in outrage, like prematurely grumpy old men, as yet another rubbish song would sit at the top of the charts ahead of our favourites. The soundtrack to 1979 was a strange one, with 'Fat Bottomed Girls' by Queen, various songs from the soundtrack to *Grease*, the odd Wings number and about a thousand overproduced numbers by ELO. This kind of music wasn't sexy or life-affirming or angry or funny or real, but knocked off by thirty-something men with big hair and easy access to seventy-two-track recording studios. If I had to make a compilation tape of the first few months of 1979 for someone I didn't especially care for, it would start with stuff like this:

'Sultans Of Swing' – Dire Straits
'Clog Dance' – Violinski
'Lay Your Love On Me' – Racey
'Hold The Line' – Toto

None of this was inherently evil. Some quite nice melodies in there. It was just all very boring, over-produced, slick and lacking in the repressed anger we all felt – an anger that manifested itself in the heavy use of instant coffee.

19. UFO

The theory that Lincolnshire shares some characteristics with the Midwest of the USA was borne out during a period of change and low-level paranoia. Over a six-month period in 1978, three different UFO sightings made the front page of the local newspaper, the *Market Rasen Mail*, a sober publication not noted for its sensational take on events. First a schoolboy from Wragby saw lights in the sky that he took to be a UFO, then, a couple of months later, a local bus driver saw strange flashing lights in the sky (which he thought might be a UFO). Then in March of '79 came the biggest story of all. Two schoolboys from Market Rasen ('two seemingly intelligent and thoughtful lads' said the paper) were confronted by a floating light 'with a curved bottom, like a UFO', whilst the whole area for two fields around was bathed in an eerie white light.

3 TRAFFIC SIGNS

Examples of **SIGNS WHICH MUST BE OBSERVED**
A red ring or a red disc is normally a feature of these signs.

SIGNS FOR APPROACHES TO MAJOR ROADS

UFO
AT
MAJOR
ROAD
AHEAD

SLOW
ALIEN
CRAFT
AHEAD

UFO ahead. The craft will probably have bright lights and will float above you for several seconds before heading off at speed towards the woods. You have probably been drinking cider.

STOP and watch UFO, but only remember your camera after UFO has disappeared.

SPEED
LIMIT
20
M.P.H.

I'd like to be able to state that everyone at school was curious and sensitive towards the boys' experience. But I'd be lying. References to little green men and flying saucers were the order of the day. For years after the incident they were known as the kids (whose names nobody could remember) who'd seen a flying saucer.

But they weren't alone. Over the years many sightings have taken place in different parts of the county, usually by people on lonely back roads where there aren't any witnesses. It is still a mystery why aliens always seem to appear to people in obscure rural backwaters. Maybe rural people check the sky a lot more than urban dwellers? It's a form of cheap entertainment and also gives signs of changes in weather patterns, useful if you're a farmer or captain of a cricket team. Perhaps these UFO sightings were a way for rural people to make sense of the mistrust they felt for the modern world at this time.

Then again, maybe we *were* visited by aliens because they just liked the space and quiet in Lincolnshire. Or perhaps they liked the preponderance of crops in the huge fields so that they could leave their weird coded messages in the cereals stocks, something that started in the late 70s. Or was it just the proximity of various airforce bases nearby?

Or was it that Lincolnshire people were often just totally wasted?

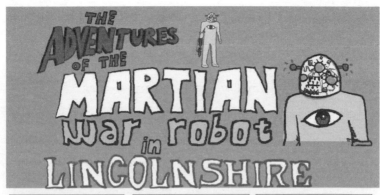

20. The Three Punk Nigels

In Lincolnshire we were behind the times with everything. Hairstyles, fashions, musical movements. These things arrived by train and had to be vetted by the relevant station masters before moving on to the outlying villages. Punk music had finally arrived in Lincolnshire in 1978 but only in small drips, and hadn't caused any kind of social upheaval, apart from giving some local hardcases an excuse to beat up anyone who wasn't wearing Oxford bags.

Punk was perfect for Lincolnshire. A guitar thrashed at high volume through an amp and fuzzbox is a very rural sound. It brings to mind farm machinery. It was of the sounds we grew up with: tractors trundling across fields the size of Scunthorpe; combine harvesters thrashing the hell out of just-cut crops.

The first proper punks were three local middle-class kids – all called Nigel – who began wearing tight, brightly coloured jeans, old blazers and punky T-shirts to discos and parties. Their cropped, messy hair contrasted with the basin mops sported by the rest of us. The three Punk Nigels were two or three years older than us yet somehow they had gained access to different cultural channels. The three Punk Nigels all came from the same village. They lived only a few minutes' walk from each other.

Each of the Punk Nigels had a separate and fully defined punk/New Wave philosophy. (This must be how major religious factions start. Three guys with quite a lot in common hang out together but they interpret their experiences differently and each comes up with a slightly different strategy to cope with their experiences.) Nigel S, the first Punk Nigel, was a hedonist, into drinking and going out with pretty girls a couple of years younger than him. His favourite drink was Malibu and milk and his favourite girl was a tall, lithe

brunette called Elise. His most 'punk' skill was a special breathing technique that enabled him to get through the police breathalyser test even when he was plastered.

The second Punk Nigel, Nigel V, was inscrutable. Nigel V was so quiet you'd hardly notice him, but then he'd come out with something extraordinarily profound and simple such as 'Heavy metal is shit' or 'Have you heard the new Buzzcocks song? It's ace!' and everybody would nod their heads and say to themselves 'Nigel V is a total punk sage'. He was a sort of cross between Tommy Ramone and Yoda.

While the first two Punk Nigels had a kind of medieval Japanese Zen punk monk dichotomy of drinking and serenity, as is the tradition of folk tales it was the third Punk Nigel, Nigel Richardson, who had the most going for him. He, too, had a younger girlfriend, but she was punkier and funkier than Nigel S's girl. Nigel Richardson also played guitar and had a band. Before he became one of the Punk Nigels, Punk Nigel 3 had been a quiet kid. I remember he was the only boy who was even worse than me at cricket. We'd sit on the sidelines as perennial substitutes, doodling in the scorebook. It was punk that had made him. Punk had done something to him, given him a new persona. He seemed to throw off his former self and, on his trusty Honda 70 moped (he was nicknamed 'Scooter'), ride off in the general direction of a more interesting life.

I wanted some of that. It couldn't be that difficult, surely? I decided that I would finally shed my image of clean-cut rural caterpillar and re-emerge as a rebellious punk butterfly. I'd read in the *NME* about The Clash wearing leather jackets and brothel creepers and so I approached my dad one day to discuss my new image ideas. In retrospect, this doesn't seem like a very 'punk' thing to do, but I considered it courteous to run it by him first before I got the train to Lincoln to buy my new

outfit. Dad was in the garage putting petrol in the lawnmower. I don't think I did any clever 'making smalltalk' thing about the latest rugby results; I just came out with it and said I wanted to buy a leather jacket and a pair of brothel creepers. I didn't actually

know what brothel creepers were. I thought it best to steer the conversation away from brothels.

Dad looked at me in the way that Aztec tribes people must have looked when they saw *La Niña*, *La Pinta* and *Santa Maria* sailing towards their shore. Sort of 'Eh?' mixed with 'This must be a dream.' And 'Shite!' He kept that confused expression for about half a minute, while I furrowed my brow and stared off into the middle distance, pretending to be nonchalant about the whole thing.

'No, you're not. No way are you getting a leather jacket. And what are brothel creepers?'

'Dad. Dad, Daddity, Dad,' I sighed. I put an arm around his shoulder. 'The world you knew is changing, old fella. It's our turn now. We are the punks. This new punk world is going to be good, and because you're a  decent bloke, you have nothing to fear. Granted, some fascists, like, erm, maths teachers, will be put against a wall and shot. But on the whole we punks just want the world to be full of creative expression. The world will be good and we'll all be wearing leather jackets and brothel creepers.'

Of course, I didn't really say any of that. I didn't even think it. What I said was: 'Aaaaaawww, Dad, s'not fair. You never let me do anything!' then I stalked off to my bedroom.

This setback had a creative side-effect as I set about turning a pair of old school trousers into bondage trousers, using Mum's sewing machine and various zips and an old dressing gown cord. I worked for several hours fine-tuning them but when I tried them on I had to admit that I looked completely stupid, plus I couldn't walk because the legs were too tightly sewn together. I put them in my chest of drawers and never wore them again.

I'd read it in *NME* about the bourgeoisie being to blame for all of society's ills. Who were these bloody bourgeoisie ruining it for everyone else?

Then it dawned on me that it was people like us, the complacent middle class, who were somehow at the root of the problems facing society. I started to believe I should probably reinvent myself as a working-class punk rocker, albeit one who wasn't allowed to have a leather jacket or brothel creepers.

Around this time I decided to rebrand my previous year's *Sunday Times* Rugby Union diary. The cover was scribbled over and on top of it was scratched PUNK DIARY. The first half of it is filled in in a very terse, matter-of-fact unselfconscious way, which means it's a goldmine of information. From September onwards I filled in most of the blank spaces with a 'punk' voice, as if I was retrospectively covering my tracks, trying to eradicate the me that had existed before. By now, to complement my punk persona, I had tired of talking like a 1950s kid and began to pick up an East Midlands nasal whine. As my voice dropped so did my aitches. My parents accused me of putting it on and wished I could talk like the young Prince Charles.

I suppose in a way it was all Suzy Fry's fault – I was still trying to do anything not to be the 'rich puff who lives in a big house'.

21. The Sound Gets Diffused into the Wires of the House

I had to accept that I was never going to look like a real punk so I had to change tack and put all my efforts into trying to sound like one. In other words, I had to get that electric guitar.

But which one? I did lots of research. I scoured the back pages of *Melody Maker* for weeks and looked at photos in *NME* of what guitars different musicians were playing. Hugh Cornwell of The Stranglers and Joe Strummer of The Clash played a Fender Telecaster. Steve Jones of the Sex Pistols played a Gibson Les Paul. Ritchie Blackmore of Rainbow/Deep Purple played a Fender Stratocaster. Paul Weller played a Rickenbacker. The bloke out of Kiss, Paul Stanley, played some monstrosity that he'd helped to design himself.

Lincoln was fifteen miles from Market Rasen, only twenty minutes away on the train, and it was in this unlikely town that I attempted to find my guitar. The city is done up and smart now, but back in the late 70s it seemed run-down, drab and grey, always raining, with a couple of pissed-off-looking swans on the river. It seemed as though progress had passed Lincoln by.

Woolworths in 1979 seemingly had everything a fourteen-year-old boy could want. Records, magazines, comics, books, sweets, blank cassettes, Winfield football boots, more sweets. It was a shop whose time had come, a jack-of-all-trades Colossus.

And they did indeed have an electric guitar, in a sort of Strato-caster shape and with a tremelo arm. I can't remember whether it was a Squier, a Futurama or an Audition. I do remember that it was thin and plasticky and I didn't fall in love with it. None of my heroes played a guitar like that. I would be The Bloke With The Woolworths Guitar.

I trudged down the high street to the other end of town in the hope that Rose's, a 'proper' music shop, might have something. Inside the shop were several classical guitars hanging on the wall, as well as a couple of mandolins. Just as I was about to leave in abject disgust, towards the back of the shop I saw a black Les Paul copy, with the name Eros written on the neck with white piping. It was beautiful, mysterious, and it was calling me. Two pick-ups. Oh, sweet scratchplate! I edged towards it and started to sniff it. Smell is all-important with big purchases. It was like the smell of a dining room in an eighteenth-century smallish French chateau. I was too excited, shy and nervous to ask to take it down so I caressed it for a little while longer then left the shop. At £65, it was well beyond my price range.

The weeks and months leading up to my full purchase of the Eros Les Paul electric guitar were perhaps the most stressful yet most exhilarating of my life. When I returned that day from Lincoln I realised I had to save up. I had about £40 of savings so needed another £25. Even now I marvel at the audacity of the operation I put in place to find the extra funds needed. Every day I walked around the house and picked up any bits of loose change lying around. My parents were both in the habit of leaving money lying around but I liked to think of it as the Electric Guitar spirits helping me out. It was rightfully mine.

When I had the money and announced to my parents my intention to buy an electric guitar, they panicked. Perhaps fearing that this was the first step in a life path of drugs, seedy hotel rooms, bad hair and no hope, they refused. They seemed determined to thwart any effort I made at teen rebellion, worried that any deviation from the norm might result in heroin addiction, a spell in prison or, worse, an attempt to get into art college. I persisted but they were adamant. For my birthday they bought me an illustrated *Encyclopedia of Jazz* then, in desperation, took me to a Dutch Swing College reunion gig at Lincoln's Theatre Royal, hoping that I'd be brainwashed by the geriatric sounds of Low Countries Dixie. But it was no use. They could not crush my spirit. To them this was just some symptom of the comprehensive school system, and an electric guitar represented dumbing down and cheap noise. Dad wanted me to be a top student and jock, not a layabout. He seemed to view bohemians as wasters.

I was incensed by their stubbornness. All I could see was the guitar and I didn't care about anything else. I upped the stakes by going on a talking strike, refusing to converse with them until they saw sense. After a couple of days of silence my parents started to crack.

(Scene – breakfast table. Me silent, reading back of cereal packet)
Dad: Hello
Me: –
Dad: Are you not talking?
Me: –
Dad: Is it about the guitar?
Me: –
Dad: I've told you what I think.
Me: –
Dad: You're being very silly about this.
Me (Reading the ingredients list over and over very slowly): –
Dad: OK, OK, let's talk about it, alright?

Finally my parents re-entered negotiations. But my dad still had some pretty tough conditions. On no account whatsoever must it be loud. I convinced him that I could just plug it into the wall socket and play without any amplifiers.

Dad: Great. So it won't be loud then.
Me: No. The sound gets diffused into the wires of the house and, um, feeds back into the National Grid.
Dad: So it's the mains socket, then. You definitely won't be buying an amplifier.
Me: (Smiling, thumbs up, lying through teeth) Won't need one, Dad. Got the mains plug.
Dad: Fine.

I brought the guitar home in a big guitar-shaped cardboard box. It was heavy, a serious piece of gear. There was a lead as well but, as I'd guessed, it didn't have a three-point plug at the other end. Improvising wildly, I got the local electrical shop owner to fashion a lead with a guitar jack at one end and a DIN lead in the other, then plugged it into Dad's new Hitachi hi-fi system, much to his terror. It still wouldn't work. I tried it with a tape in and on record and this time a beautiful distort sound came out, a bit like the heavy, dirty noise of Stiff Little Fingers

My first guitar

or a reverby cross between Jonathan Richman and Led Zeppelin. For a few weeks Dad's hi-fi became my recording studio, but soon he started to get worried that I would blow up his expensive equipment, and I decided that a small amplifier might, after all, be better.

A few weeks later I ended up taking my Yorkshire grandad to a big music warehouse in Bingley. As he walked slowly from the car with his stick, I raced ahead then kept stopping to wait for him to catch up. Inside I very quickly saw a lovely little practice amp with a tremelo for £20, just what I needed. A few yards away a bloke in his early twenties with long hair was doing a Ritchie Blackmore impersonation, cascading fast scales around the 'Smoke On The Water' riff.

'Why don't you try it out then?' asked my grandad.

Sigh. I plugged the guitar into the little amp and switched it on then strummed a chord over and over again for about five minutes. Strumm strum strummity strum. Then when I'd got really confident I added another chord to the mix, to see where it would take me. Strumm strum strummity strum.

'Why don't you play something?' Grandad asked.

I looked up, halfway through my self-penned folk ditty entitled 'Strummity Strum'.

'I am playing something.'

'Are you? I meant a tune. A song.'

I bought the amp. And later, back at home, there was much rejoicing.

Dad: What's that? Is it an amplifier?
Me: Ha ha. No, Dad. It's an early prototype of what's called a 'personal computer'.
Dad: Why is it making so much noise?
Me: That's the computer's memory.
Dad: Why is your guitar plugged into it?

One of the big problems with buying an electric guitar is that you have to learn to play it. It's very tempting to simply put it on your wall and caress it every morning, lie on your bed and stare lovingly at it. I was lucky in that my younger brother was a guitarist. Tobe had done classical lessons for a while at school and was meticulously working his way through The Beatles Complete Songbook. I didn't have time for such old-style learning techniques. I had no interest in learning for learning's sake and just could not remember the names of chords. I learned by putting my fingers (all three and a half of them) on the strings until I made a noise I liked. A good system for learning, but once I'd discovered a chord I didn't actually know what it was called. I could only describe what they sounded like in sub-wine-buff language: 'It's kind of optimistic but aware of the fragility of life. A very English chord, imbued with melancholy. On a day-to-day basis this chord is happy and optimistic but underneath, its heart carries layers of scar tissue to protect itself from further sorrow. Kind of like a Leeds United supporter.'

That chord is A minor.

Another one would be described as: 'It's bombastic and loud, dynamic and aggressive. See it at a party and it mouths off about politics, surrounded by onlookers. It exudes authority but it has to be played loud otherwise it doesn't sound very attractive. There's also something a little predictable about it. You sort of know where it's going to go next.' This would be E major. In this way I developed a kind of intuitive approach towards the guitar, making up for the fact that I couldn't really play barre chords (chords needing the use of fingers long enough to press down two or more strings at the same time, something that wasn't easy owing to the chipped-off little finger of my left hand).

I also have farmer's fingers. Not real farmer's fingers – if I had to work on a farm the farmer would laugh and tell me I've got weedy guitarist's fingers. But as a guitarist my fingers are just big enough to seem clumsy and too thick. Even if I had wanted to branch out and become good, my inability to play barre chords meant I was forever stuck in a desperate punk thrash/folky strum limbo of a sad busker.

Then I bought The Clash songbook and it all fell into place. The first song I learned was 'I'm So Bored With The USA'. Apart from '(White Man) In Hammersmith Palais' and 'Police And Thieves', I didn't really know any of The Clash's songs, but 'I'm So Bored' only had two chords so was really easy to play. I had no idea why The Clash wanted to shoot the skag and what the skag had done to offend them. The Clash were cruel, I supposed.

I decided that if I was going to learn to play Clash songs, I had to actually have some idea how the songs went. Which meant I had to listen to them. Which meant I had to *buy* them.

22. I Was a Teenage Clash Completist

'When I have money, I get rid of it quickly, lest it find a way into my heart.' – John Wesley*

Sanctuary had to be the coolest record shop in Lincolnshire. It was tiny, on a small street just off the upper part of the High Street in Lincoln. It smelled of incense or some sort of illegal drugs that I didn't know anything about. I had been in there a couple of times before, just browsing in a half-ecstatic, half-terrified sort of way, like a deep-sea diver going down for the first time. It had been a while since I'd had a religious experience but this came pretty close to one.

I had gone to Lincoln with Mum with the intention of going to Sanctuary and buying as much Clash product as I could afford/morally get away with it. Mum went to Moore and Collinghams, a big department store nearby, and gave me an hour.

As I entered the music shop, the smell hit me, then the fear. Everyone in the shop was cooler than me by some distance. I was obviously a phoney. Someone would probably point me out and shout, 'I saw him playing rugby the other day.' And

Sanctuary

THE ONLY
ALTERNATIVE
WHEN IT COMES
TO RECORDS.

8 PARK ST. LINCOLN.

---

* Methodist preacher, born Epworth, near Lincoln.

everyone would laugh. Just in case, I had put on my little black Harrington jacket with tartan lining (the latest expression of my individuality which everyone else wore too) and was trying to look as nonchalantly New Wave cool as possible. There is a ridiculous hierarchy of cool in teenage society but it is also contextual – if I was a punk in a roomful of rugby players at this point, I'd have been laughed at, de-bagged, had beer poured over my head while a rugby song went at full swing then forced to turn out at prop for the 4th XV away at Rotherham.

It wasn't just punks in the place; there were heavy rockers and hippies too. With my heart beating fast I quickly took the sleeves for The Clash's *The Clash* and *Give 'Em Enough Rope* (the over-produced second album), along with the sleeves for three singles – 'White Riot', 'Complete Control' and '(White Man) In Hammersmith Palais'. There were a couple of others but I felt I'd reached my limit. I didn't want to overdose on The Clash straightaway.

I was at the counter. I was nearly there. But the fear hit me again. I was convinced that my voice would come out really high-pitched and I'd be told I was too young to buy Clash stuff and did I want to see some Rolf Harris? I felt a bit like a spy trying to make it across a heavily guarded border checkpoint. Would I be found out?

I tried to come across as relaxed yet firm, a technique I would later employ when trying to get served in pubs. I also had a fallback plan: if the bloke behind the counter (a cool bloke with a cool punk T-shirt) said to me, 'Ha ha – are these your first punk records, then mate?' I'd reply with, 'Ha ha – naaah, these are for my little brother.' But when it came to it, he just told me the price. 'Where's Captain Kirk?' by Spizzenergi was playing. I gave him the money, he bagged up the records, gave me the change, then almost smiled as if to suggest that I was part of the Sanctuary now, the smart New Wave gentlemen's club of choice. I walked out of the shop. I wanted to punch the air with a 'Yes!'

PIP's view on taped music

(but people might be watching). Like at a checkpoint, I had to keep walking. But I had done it. I was a punk at last.

I began listening to the albums on strict rotation and although the first album was far superior, there was something compelling about *Give 'Em Enough Rope*, from its knocked-up-in-an-afternoon cover to the strange, non-punk soundscapes of the music. The song I kept going back to was 'Safe European Home', the first on side one. The chorus had Mick Jones shouting in his high-pitched market trader's bark, just like someone trying to get punters to hook a plastic yellow duck at a fairground – The verse involved Joe Strummer yelping 'was aman s lamba lopalazza barma' or something.

But I wanted more. I wanted *more* records, more product. I had to *own* songs. Taping wasn't the same. When Pip Podland had asked one morning in school who owned *Never Mind the Bollocks*, I had said in a tremulous voice: 'Yeah, Pip... I got it...' Pip looked at me approvingly with thumbs up. '... on tape.' Pip frowned and shook his head vigorously.

'No, no, no! Taping doesn't count.' He'd then put his hands into the pockets of his denim jacket and given me the full broadside, lecturing in a loud enough voice for other smirking boys to hear. Only by handing over money to a shop did you fully enter into the music.

As 1979 wore on I began to keep a list of what records I had and when I bought them. In this way I knew who I was and what I was becoming. The stats didn't lie. I was keen to create a punkish collection, so 1979 was The Damned's first album, *Damned Damned Damned;* 'Silly Thing' and 'Something Else' by the Sex Pistols (though I sold these two later at a hefty mark-up to Tobe – 'They've got picture sleeves… they're collectors items'); 'Milk And Alcohol' by Dr Feelgood; 'Just What I Needed' by Cars and 'Spiral Scratch' by the Buzzcocks. I also sold Tobe the risible *Jazz* by Queen ('It's got a poster of naked girls cycling!'), and tried to flog him the *Grease* soundtrack album (he told me to get lost). But the bottom line was that every Saturday morning I had to get down to Langfords Records and hand over all my pocket money to Mrs Langford as soon as I had the opportunity. I became addicted to her little handwritten notebook with all the singles she had in stock.

Occasionally I'd see a really uncool countryish song written down that I sort of liked and I thought maybe no-one would know if I bought it and hid it away: sad, sentimental stuff. But there were invisible guardians at my shoulder, warning me off – an invisible Pip Podland who threatened to beat me up for such thoughts, and an invisible Scooter 'Punk Nigel' Richardson who, priestlike, would try to show me the true, three-chord path.

Who Left That Radio On?: 1979

Lene Lovich 'Lucky Number'

Dr. Hook 'When You're In Love With A Beautiful Woman'

Sister Sledge 'He's The Greatest Dancer'

Cars 'Just What I Needed'

Blondie 'Heart Of Glass'

Dr. Feelgood 'Milk And Alcohol'

Gary Numan 'Cars'

The Specials 'Gangsters'

Joe Jackson 'Is She Really Going Out With Him?'

Rainbow 'Since You've Been Gone'

Sally Oldfield 'Mirrors'

23. Left-Wing Sixth-Form Girls Move Their Hips to Earth, Wind & Fire: Local Politics

Country people are on the whole dead friendly, but bring politics into things and there's an utterly depressing right-wing knee-jerk response to many of the big issues. Is there something in the rural English psyche that makes people reactionary? Earlier in the 70s, politics had been more fun. During the two 1974 elections we would walk around in a gang of kids all wearing Jeremy Thorpe/Ted Heath/Harold Wilson badges singing 'Join in the gang' in high-pitched East Midlands accents. We could all do impersonations of Ted Heath and Harold Wilson. But by '79 things had got more serious and partisan, perhaps because Labour people sensed that the Tories would no longer play by the same rules, rules that had stood for decades. In the *Market Rasen Mail*, in the months leading up to the election, there had been propaganda from both sides. Marcus Kimble, the sitting Tory MP, was forever giving speeches to special interest groups, which the paper felt duty bound to report.

'**Growing Marxist Influence**' screamed the headline reporting Kimble's speech to Keelby Conservatives: 'Labour want to see our society and economy organised along the lines

of a collectivist East European state.' A few months later it was
'**Socialism Holding Back Agriculture**'. Kimble was reported
to have said to a group of farmers, a week before the election,
to not trust 'the dead hand of socialism'.

But although it might *seem* that Kimble was getting pref-
erential treatment in terms of newspaper reports, from a fourteen-year-old's viewpoint the Labour party bizarrely always
got a better press. Every week there seemed to be some kind
of fundraiser, or meeting, or discussion, usually in a local pub.
The report would consist of a big picture showing glamorous
young people in their leather jackets with fresh faces and big
smiles – including both of my favourite attractive young feminist teachers, Mrs Greenwood and Mrs Fountain (née Cornhill) – plus some ugly male teachers and Bandy's dad (who
was the local Labour Party chairman). Wedged in the middle
of a bevy of left-wing lovelies would be Willy Bach, the candidate. This propaganda dance continued right up to the vote,
after which politics seemed to disappear from everyone's lives
for a while.

In May 1979 there was a General Election. As both of
Bandy's parents were Labour Party members, I'd go out with
him and his family delivering leaflets around Market Rasen. If
anybody asked me anything specific I'd get flustered and mutter
something about feminism that I'd heard from Miss Cornhill.
Scrap nuclear weapons. Er. Be nice to old people. Erm. Don't
be racist. Rather than having a clear grasp of Labour Party
policy, I was more motivated by the desire for the UK not to
vote for a right-wing lunatic. But left-wing politics didn't seem
that different from the mild C of E philosophy I'd been
brought up with.

Our main battlegrounds were the two big estates at the
south of the town, Gordon Field and Churchill Avenue. The
latter, being council houses, was thought to be Labour heart-
lands. We went up and down the drives of most of these houses.

But being vaguely left-wing did not make you popular around Market Rasen. We had people making veiled threats to us as we put up flyers and posters. But all this stuff was worth it, because... well, Labour didn't want to lose their deposit, I suppose. At least Labour had all the teachers at our school voting for them.

And there would be one more Labour party function. In the middle of the summer Bandy's parents held a big party at their house for all the downtrodden and defeated local Labour party supporters to say thanks for all their effort. Excitingly, Bandy was allowed to invite me. The place was rocking. The brother of the bloke who cut off my finger in the door back in '67 was doing the disco and, once the music got going, it seemed that the only people who voted Labour were beautiful, left-wing sixth-form girls, most of them friends of Bandy's older sister.

I had taken my new electric guitar along, thinking it would come in handy when trying to impress the sixth-form girls. Obviously they were as far out of our league as the most celebrated film stars, but at least they were within fifteen yards of us and they were all drunk. But the sixth-form girls were far too busy moving their hips to Earth, Wind & Fire to notice that I was strumming a new guitar from an upstairs window while trying to look interesting and rebellious. I think I walked around with it for a while, but to no avail.

This is what politics is all about, I thought to myself. Sexy, older women, good music and masses of free booze. Everyone got really drunk – for me and Bandy, that only took a couple of small cans of McEwan's Export – then got maudlin and some, as was the way of things in those days, tried to flirt with each other's partners. Bandy and I had no partners so we just observed, though I did eventually dance with Mrs Greenwood while a cider-addled and deluded Bandy convinced himself that one of the nubile left-wing sixth-form girls – Wendy Marchant – fancied him. What was he thinking? She fancied me and my guitar; that much was obvious.

By the end of the summer Bandy's parents had split up. Bandy's dad would soon move up to Scotland (and end up joining the SDP). The party was very much the end of an era for us all. But I had hope of a better future. I felt in my gut that Labour would wipe the floor with the Tories at the '83 election and then the socialist utopia of free drink and attractive sixth-form girls would be upon us.

THE SECRET SUPERGROUP OF THE FORBIDDEN MUSIC ROOM

AT WINDBAND PRACTICE I'D SIT IN A ROOM WITH THIRTY OTHER KIDS AND WE'D MURDER EASY LISTENING CLASSICS. I WAS THIRD TROMBONIST, TASKED WITH PROVIDING SINGLE NOTE BACKING FOR THE CLASSY SHOW-OFFS ON FIRST AND SECOND TROMBONE...

DURING LULLS IN THE ACTION I LOVED TO LISTEN TO THE STRANGE SOUNDS COMING FROM THE REHEARSAL STUDIO.

THIS WAS THE FORBIDDEN MUSIC ROOM — OFF LIMITS TO ANYONE UNDER 16

OLDER KIDS IN THE 5TH FORM, LONG HAIR, BIG TIES. THEY PLAYED ONE RIFF THAT STUCK IN MY MIND DER DER DER DER (DER DER DER DER DEERR DER)

THE BAND WOULD PRACTISE IT OVER AND OVER. I PRESUMED IT WAS A SELF-PENNED NUMBER AND THEY WERE PREPARING THEMSELVES FOR GLORY.

THEN IT WAS TIME FOR US TO DO OUR VERSIONS OF UNA PALOMA BLANCA AND HAWAII FIVE O AND THE RIFF WAS DROWNED OUT.

AFTERWARDS WE'D GO INTO THE ROOM TO LOOK FOR CLUES. THE GUITARS HAD GONE BUT THE AMPS WERE STILL THERE.

THERE WAS ALSO A MASSIVE DRUM MACHINE WITH ONLY TWO OR THREE RHYTHMS.

IN LATER YEARS I SOMETIMES WONDERED WHAT HAPPENED TO THE SECRET SUPERGROUP. DID THEY MAKE IT BIG?

AND THEN, AT A PARTY, I HEARD THAT RIFF AGAIN...

HEY! THAT'S BY THE SECRET SUPERGROUP FROM MY OLD SCHOOL - BOWERTHWAITE, BUMCRACKLE AND PINGLE!

ER, NO...

..IT'S 'SUNSHINE OF YOUR LOVE' BY CREAM.

24. Girls Girls Girls (Girls) 3: My Glenda Jackson Lust Phase

I fell in love with Glenda Jackson in the late summer of 1979. It was most likely due to a showing on BBC2 of the Ken Russell film *Women in Love*. More specifically, it was the moment where Glenda, playing Gudrun, takes her dress off while sitting on a bed. What on earth was it about the topless Glenda Jackson that appealed to the fourteen-year-old me? No, actually it wasn't *just* that. It was also that she was lippy, gobby. Opinionated.

I learnt to keep my film-star crushes to myself. If I mentioned fancying Glenda Jackson to one of my mates, I'd be laughed at and pilloried for my lack of taste. You were allowed to fancy the women off *Charlie's Angels*. Or popstars like Debbie Harry and TV presenters like Sally James, girls whose beauty was used to flog product. But what is not to like about Glenda Jackson? Even nowadays, as a battleaxe Labour MP, she's got knowing, I'm-up-for-it eyes.

You were also 'allowed' to fancy the girls out of *Magpie*. Whenever people talked about *Magpie* when I was younger I'd go quiet. I didn't want to blurt out, 'My dad doesn't like us watching commercial TV,' but I had never seen *Magpie* much. Susan Stranks was very pretty and Jenny Hanley was also quite nice, but because I never spent that much time getting to know them, I never really fell for them. *Blue Peter*, on the other hand, which *Magpie* tried so hard to emulate, was always on in our house. Valerie Singleton was like your mum, so you weren't allowed to fancy her unless you came from Norfolk. Lesley Judd, on the other hand, had been one of the Young Generation dancers, the ones that used to prance about on *Saturday Night Special*. She was like a slightly sporty and racy teacher, and wore nearly revealing denim clothes.

Then, one night when Mum and Dad were out, I watched Jean-Luc Godard's *Pierrot Le Fou* and had a new film-star crush. Anna Karina. She was not just lippy but French lippy, which made everything she said sound amazingly sexy. She could have been talking about how much petrol she'd need in her car to get her from Paris to Montpelier but she would still sound like a honey-voiced goddess of dark-eyed beauty.

The trouble was, all this falling for actresses took me away from what was happening in *real life*. It's hard work getting a real-life girlfriend. It's like the moment when the dodgems stop and you have your eye on one but someone else gets there first, and then it's usually too late to find anything else.

I decided I would ask out Gina Healey, the leader of a gang of girls we sometimes hung around with. Gina Healey was the star of the school hockey team and had thighs like a Tongan rugby player. She looked like a cherubic but slightly dirty schoolboy with a mess of platinum-blonde hair. I tell myself now that I was on the verge of asking her out, sure thing, just a couple of days away from it – to do what, exactly, I'm not sure, maybe just a bit of lunchtime snogging, which would have suited me fine – but she was a mate and it seemed so drastic that I backed off. She was then, of course, snapped up by some brazen good-looking lad with neat hair, and my chance was gone.

25. Heart Attack On Tape

The Heart Attack project had become much more exciting now that we had a real instrument. The guitar, when it was plugged in and the volume on my weedy little amp cranked up to ten (it was always up to ten), didn't sound that different from the guitar sounds on the records we liked. Well, that I liked. Bandy was still persevering with Wings, ELO, 10cc and Creedence Clearwater Revival.

But all of a sudden we had gone from being a bit of a personal joke and something to do on a Saturday night to a real band. I started to believe that I was a proper musician. I could talk technical when it came to strings and amps and stuff; I just hoped no-one asked me about chords and music. Bandy too was getting excited. It meant that his shrill punk poetry was going to have proper musical backing. And we didn't have to practise on the Bontempi air organ in his dining room any more. Which was just as well, because he, his mum and sister had moved to a smaller house in an estate in Middle Rasen. From now on, all recordings would be done at my place.

I was spending all my spare time looking for music: new music, old music, good music, shit music, as long as it was punk/New Wave. I became a voracious collector of punk singles. My copy of Thin Lizzy's *Live and Dangerous* was banished to my wardrobe just in case anybody cool came round. I was trying to synthesise all the stuff in my collection – The Clash, Devo, The Ramones, The Monkees, Rolf Harris – into a vision for a new musical sound. Unfortunately my fingers couldn't play what my brain was writing.

A new boy called Egg had arrived at our school. He was mature beyond his years and had to shave twice a day. For some reason he reminded us of Brian Epstein and I think we decided he had to be our manager as soon as we saw him – maybe we were just keen to impress him because he was quite posh. Eventually we got chatting to him and he asked to hear a tape of some of our songs.

A tape. We had tape recorders. We taped everything, in fact – *Top of the Pops* (obviously – didn't everybody?) with the microphone on the kitchen table, glaring at any family member who looked like they were about to make a noise. Occasionally my dad would come in halfway through a really important recording and say 'What's all this rubbish?' or 'Have you seen my Benny Goodman EP?' We also taped the Top 40 countdown on a Sunday evening. I taped some of my favourite TV programmes, such as *Monty Python, Tomorrow's World, Rugby Special* or *The Goodies.* Or we'd wind Snake up then tape him screaming. We'd even taped the 1978 World Cup Final on a two-hour Scotch tape that included our swearing when a last-minute Dutch attempt hit the post. So taping our band should be relatively straightforward.

I usually used BASF tapes. Since as long as I can remember we had disliked many things about Germany – football teams, planes, Eurovision Song Contest entries, the calendars my mum got every year from her penfriend in Cologne. But their cassette tapes were a different matter. BASF seemed reliable and high tech. It was music equipment made by super-boffins. The tape was a slightly better quality than the competition because they were made of chromium dioxide (CrO_2). This meant that chromium dioxide particles stuck to each note of the music and 'enhanced' it, making it sound much more fluid. Whatever that means.

Before going in the 'studio' (our sitting room), we had to decide on the recording equipment we would use. For most music taping I'd used my dad's Hitachi portable tape recorder or my brother's even smaller Crown model from Woolworths (which had a detachable recording microphone for miming in front of the mirror). My dad also had his hi-fi, so I got a stereo microphone fitted with a DIN plug at the local electrical shop so we could use them together. What we tended to get was hard-panned instrument separation like in the stereo versions of The Beatles LPs, where the vocals came out of one speaker and the guitar out of another.

We decided on about five or six songs to record for Egg. Our songwriting technique was simple. Again, like The Beatles (*Let it Be* period), we'd use the 'studio' to write, then almost instantaneously record our songs. Sometimes I'd come up with a chord sequence and Bandy would write a chorus, then he'd go away and write some verses. Other times he'd write out a whole song and I'd add music to it. We didn't believe in too much practice as that was anti-punk and elitist. We wanted to capture the rawness of a barely learned new song. Hmm.

⌐New technology

Heart Attack Egg Tapes Vol. 1
Slit My Gullet (Faeces/Slitgullet) 1m 30
The rumbling opening chord was undoubtedly influenced by (i.e. ripped off) The Clash's 'I'm So Bored With The USA'. One of the problems for me as the guitarist was changing chords. There was no guarantee that I'd be able to find the correct finger positions when playing at speed. What I really needed to do was press pause, move my hands to the new position, then start the tape recorder again.

And again, the recording was pure stereo, with the guitar coming out of just the right-hand speaker. From the left-hand speaker came a moment of classic rock history as Bandy's pre-pubescent squeal came in:

> *Well, I was walking down the street*
> *And I met an old man*
> *I said 'Give us yer wallet'*
> *He said No*
> [Lincolnshire nasally whine – '*No no no no no no no*' – by guitarist]
> *So I slit his gullet*

Although on the face of it, the song sounds like it's about blood, gore and violence, Bandy's lyrics are really all about being stuck in a crap village with nothing to do, and hating the bourgeois (we'd had to look the word up) safeness of everything.

She's Got VD (Faeces/Slitgullet) 1m 40
This was a song inspired by our habit a year or so earlier of walking in the woods, picking up used condoms and collecting them in an old biscuit tin. Each time we'd find one we'd theorise as to who had been the users. Sex in the local imagination was always connected to cars. Cars took you from the pubs three miles away to the woods and back again. We took the piss out of, but also celebrated, sexually voracious girls.

Wicket Den (Faeces) 1m 45

It was the first of the Heart Attack songs about cricket on this tape, about a local kid who laughed at Bandy's skinniness and compared his body to a cricket stump (at this stage most of our songs were about local people). The song has a combination of buzzy bass guitar played on the low strings followed by a folky strum chorus in a totally different time signature. I originally wrote this on Bandy's crappy Bontempi in his parents' dining room.

Invasion (Faeces/Slitgullet) 2m 10

The longest song on the tape, it's seemingly improvised thrash that stops halfway through, then starts again with a slightly different riff, and ends on a terrible three-note guitar solo played by someone with farmer's fingers. The song is all about boneheaded violence at football matches, and Bandy does the commentator voice at the start in his Bill McClaren voice. However, as McClaren was a famous rugby commentator, I wondered why he would be commentating on football. I wanted to do the song again because it had somehow lost its authenticity but then I came to my senses.

Cooky Caught A Catch (Faeces/Slitgullet) 1m 30

Sung to the tune of 'Where's Your Mama Gone?' Another cricket song, inspired by an incident in a school cricket match in which a young lad unexpectedly held a catch and spent the whole minibus journey home revelling in his feat. There might have been a peculiar beauty to the sentiment of this song if it had been done more deadpan, rather than as a savage piss-take:

> Cooky caught a catch
> In a cricket match... (etc.)

I can still see the faces of our friends when we first played them our tape. I think they were impressed but they had to laugh. We played our first proper gig around this time, on my parents' roof. Just like The Beatles! (Well, when I say 'roof' what I mean is the flat bit over a window gable.) Seven people turned up and sat on our front lawn. Halfway through the gig Bandy, in a worryingly Rubble Man type episode, poured water on me while I was playing the guitar.

'You could have electrocuted me, you twat!'

We also got into merchandising, and had a load of T-shirts made up. Well, two, done by a friend of Bandy's dad. They said 'Heart Attack' in a kind of multicoloured hippyish script. I gave mine away to my penpal Alain, much to Bandy's annoyance.

In performance, Bandy was able to push himself to the point where he looked disturbed and absurd and had people laughing at him. I could never lose control in this way. Although I wanted to rebel and this was my chance to push against things, I was still the son of a respectable local solicitor. (A photo of me taken around 1981 confirms this. I'm in a school rugby jersey and a pair of grandad trousers with my guitar and I look like a public schoolboy in a Genesis tribute band. Bandy manages to look crazy and cool at the same time.)

Now we were suddenly 'the punks'. A real punk in the year above us, Jimmy Burke, said we were 'plastics' (i.e. fakes). He was obviously threatened because he didn't have a proper gigging punk band. Fame went to our heads. We produced a fanzine called *Rasen's Boreing* (I was always in need of sub-editors), in which we interviewed ourselves. We also decided to bring in some more of the local punk talent. Well, they weren't really punks, but then neither were Bandy and I. All names have been changed, except for Kev (who wished to remain non-anonymous) and my cousin Rob (who won't read this, because it hasn't got an early-70s cricketer on the cover).

Pubic Pete was Rob's short-lived punk pseudonym. 'Pete'

never joined Heart Attack; he was more an early fellow traveller. In fact, he formed his own band – Gang of Rob. We liked to think that the Gang of Rob/Heart Attack rivalry became Market Rasen's version of The Beatles vs The Rolling Stones. Our fear was that Gang of Rob would start eating into Heart Attack's traditional fanbase. (All seven of them.) It got to the point that, much as I loved Rob, we began to resent his band's success. Alright, we hated the bastards. His imaginary album titles were amusing, though. *Stations of the Rob. Magical*

Mystery Rob. Let It Rob. Rob pissed us off even more by starting up a correspondence with Stiff Little Fingers vocalist Jake
Burns, asking if Gang of Rob could support them on the
Lincolnshire leg of the next SLF tour. We mocked this but jeal-
ously worried that he might pull it off.

Our mates Kev and Chris became Kev Cretin and Cozy
Merde. Kev was going to play lead guitar, except he didn't have
a guitar and couldn't play one. Cozy – so named after the ex-
Black Sabbath drummer, Cozy Powell – was going to be the
drummer. A new, very thespianish and intellectual pupil called
Ed Wood was renamed Steve Spillage and would play bass. Ed
was a bigshot in the school drama club and a good friend of
Egg our sort-of manager. With five members, we would now be
a proper punk outfit.

It soon became apparent, however, that we had been a little
hasty in our enthusiasm to get new members. It was mine and
Bandy's thing. None of them could play, of course, but they
couldn't not play in a *good* punk can't-play way, but in a rubbish
can't-play-a-note *bad* way. Within about thirty seconds of our
'audition' with Cozy, we realised he was a terrible drummer.
Whatever we played, he just drummed the melody line, not the
underlying beat. Perhaps Cozy Merde was more into jazz. But
we still hung in there with him. There was something glamorous about Chris. He was a champion sprinter, the fastest kid
in the school. He was tall, about six foot one, sandy-haired and
good-looking in a 1950s 'good guy' sort of way. We agreed to
let Chris be the bassist. Kev would have to be a stage dancer or
something. Steve Spillage would be drummer. Or first reserve.
Chris seemed happy enough that he had to buy a bass guitar.
Everything was falling into place.

Then a couple of days later Chris got in touch and told us
his mum said he wasn't allowed to buy a bass. I knew what that
felt like, but I guess Chris wasn't as determined as I was to be
a punk legend. It was time to split up the band. We had to

destroy it to save it. At this point I suggested to Bandy that we change the name – it had been pointed out to me by cooler, older kids that Heart Attack was a bit of a comedy band name, but Bandy accused me of just trying to boot-lick Scooter. He was a little bit right, but the accusation stung me into acquiescence. We told everyone that Heart Attack had split up, then we reformed almost immediately. We were a two-piece again.

26. Girls Girls Girls (Girls) 4: Walking On Top Field

Thanks to the tape, we suddenly became more popular with the girls. How it was that songs like 'She's Got VD' or 'Flick-knives' gave us social cachet I'm not sure. I guess it just made us more interesting. Not long after our tape did the rounds, the Heart Attack Fan Club was formed by members of an existing gang called the School Girls' Union.

Now I was *really* ready for girls and I had, on paper, the great fortune of being in a band, which meant that I was, in theory, cool. It was 1980. I was fifteen, hormones raging. Girls were suddenly everywhere. And they were wearing bras! You could see the straps through their white blouses.

Our new fan club contained five girls in our year – Gina Healey, Jill Hopcraft, Debbie Horse, Anne Crumbe and Maggie Jefferson (though I might have sneakily added Maggie to the list without telling her). Maggie and I seemed destined to go out. Her birthday was the day before mine so she was an older woman by about nine hours. I wouldn't say I was in love with her; I just had a feeling she fancied me and decided that I had had enough of going for unattainable women like Anna Karina, Glenda Jackson and Julie Christie.

Around this time, every male in the school had gone utterly lovesick crazy over a new girl, Brenda Beamish, a tanned, blonde lovely with an Irish name and a soft Welsh accent. Even the teachers seemed mesmerised by her. Bandy fell for her, tongue lolling. Cozy too was in a trance. This gave me a relaxed, clear run at Maggie without competition. No-one noticed. The whole male population of the school was following Brenda around in a big crowd like a scene from a zombie film. How did I ask Maggie out? Did I phone her? Did I get someone else to ask her on my behalf? Maybe she asked me. Knowing Maggie, that was entirely possible. She probably phoned me and said, 'Look, do you fancy me or what?'

Maggie was small and clever with thick glasses, a quick wit and a big mouth. She was one of those girls who you knew would turn into a real beauty (like in Hollywood films where the star is a speccy swot but she takes off her glasses and lets her hair down and she's utterly irresistible). To start with everyone called her Gobby. Such feminist times – an opinionated girl given a crap nickname. I'd like to think it was affectionate but it probably wasn't.

The entry in my diary for Wed 30th Jan 1980 reads: 'That's today. What a day. Walking on the field.'

'Walking on the field' said it all. Maggie and I met, already in silent agreement of the terms of the contract we were expected to adhere to. We might have exchanged some words but it's unlikely. Silently we walked together, like two condemned criminals walking side by side through the main playground, out onto the field. When we were far enough away from the school buildings I put my arm around her, as if she was a child who had just fallen off her bike and I was taking her back to the house to clean up the cuts. In this way we walked around the field, she petite in her grey duffel coat and green skirt, me in my donkey jacket, drainpipe cords and DMs. We did the circuit of the rugby pitches, up around the all-weather hockey pitches and around the top of the football fields, then back around the tennis courts, looping round to the back of the sports hall. All done in stony silence, of course.

I hadn't been round the back of the sports hall since my first days of ciggy experimentation with Bacon Hawkins. It was like the cantina scene in the original *Star Wars* film. There were kids there I didn't recognise; faces that I was seeing for the first time. Were they actually at this school? They had the uniform on, or a version of it. Kids sat smoking, staring, looking surly, snogging, teasing, shouting, hanging out in little pockets. Maggie and I walked along the path, now hand in hand, until we found a spare bench. We sat down without a word and then we were kissing. It wasn't anything like real kissing – it never is, is it? Maggie and I opened our mouths as wide as possible, like the snakes that can dislocate their jaws to swallow whole antelopes. It was as if we were competing to see whose mouth could open the widest. When we'd reached optimum mouth wideness, we locked in on each other and our tongues met. It was only on impact that it dawned on me this was my first real French kiss. The English kissed with their mouths closed, the French with theirs open. Everyone knew that. I wasn't sure how best to breathe. Our kiss was completely airtight but my nose was a bit blocked, so there was the odd snot-filled snort. Our tongues flicked and wrestled for what seemed like the whole afternoon but was probably about two or three minutes. I couldn't taste anything. Maggie wasn't toothpastey like Debbie (The Girl Who Had Moved To Scunthorpe) or... blimey, I hadn't actually kissed any other girls, not even with an old-fashioned English kiss. My mind started to wander, and

I suddenly felt trapped, stuck in a relationship that was going nowhere. I need space, you can't tie me down, I'm too young to get married, have kids, did I really love Maggie or was I using her to better my French kissing technique? I wanted to do the right thing, though. We were boyfriend and girlfriend now. I had made a commitment and I would stick to it.

But not at afternoon break. I told Maggie I had to hang out with my mates and play football. Actually, I didn't tell her that; I just presumed she would know, telepathically. The next week we met up intermittently for arm-in-arm walks, but we didn't try too much French kissing. My diary for that week appears to have been written by a manic depressive who's in solitary confinement rather than a fifteen-year-old boy with a girlfriend. *I hate school. It's horrible. I don't want to go there.*

By Friday 8th Feb it must have been all over, because there is a reference to the School Girls' Union not being happy with me. I expect this was the first experience I had of trying to end a relationship, which I did rather ungallantly by utterly ignoring the poor girl until she got the message.

So that was that for a while, though I began to realise that I liked athletic girls. Some time after that, I rolled around on the floor at a party for twenty minutes or so with a keen fan club member, the tall blonde Jill Hopcraft (who was built like a 400m runner), showing off my new French kissing technique, whilst manfully pretending to be asleep. When quizzed about it by Bandy afterwards, I claimed 'It must have been my subconscious'. Jill looked at me a bit funnily for a few days afterwards, but she, too, soon got the message. Keen to show Bandy that I hadn't turned into a total girl-loving jessie, the next time we went to a party I took along an old bottle of laxatives I'd found in a cupboard at home and we made some baked beans for everyone.

'That was so kind!' said Guinevere O'Reilly, whose birthday party it was.

'Ha, any time.'

'But why are you leaving so early?'

As we pedalled furiously back to Market Rasen, I reckoned I felt more comfortable as a somnambulist seducer than I did as a bowel-moving prankster.

Then, at the start of the summer, I decided that I fancied quiet Gwen Cobner, mainly because I'd seen her doing the 200m race in an athletics match and thought she had nice legs. This time I got Cozy to ask her out for me. But I couldn't get as far with Gwen as I had with Maggie. Even an English kiss seemed out of the question. We just walked around and made small talk and I felt terribly self-conscious. After a couple of days I was single again. Just in time for the holidays. Phew.

GIRLS GIRLS GIRLS (GIRLS)

FINDING MY FEET

In the late 1970s I fancied different girls. And that didn't include my long relationship with the film star Barbara Bach nor my ongoing commitment to Babs Lord out of Pan's People.

GINA HEALEY
The legs of an East European 60m Sprint champion

CLARISSA BOLT
We swapped Valentines cards and then it ended

CARMEN WILLIAMS
I wrote her name on my pencil case

JILL HOPCRAFT
Built like a 400m runner

MADELEINE LISIÈRE
French girl who kissed me (to say hello)

LILY FLINT
Told me her bra size (whatever that is) on French trip

DEBBIE HORSE
Quiet girl with big tits

MISS CORNHILL
Feminist English teacher with a love of denim and DH Lawrence

ANNABELLE BRIDGET-JONES
Posh and pretty – a good combination

MAGGIE JEFFERSON
Small girl with a big gob and big glasses

WENDY MARCHANT
Totally unattainable 6th former with dancer's eyes

27. Mutually Assured Destruction During Double Maths

There had been various heights of the Cold War, but now it seemed we were *really* at the height. The Soviet Union apparently had enough long-range strike missiles aimed at the UK to turn it into a fine powder, and although the SALT II had been agreed, we were all still – when we thought about it – shit scared.

The USSR-Afghan war began and the West was already taking sides. Then there was trouble brewing in Poland. The Iran-Iraq war was just kicking off. On bad days we expected nuclear conflict to happen at any time.

Hopefully this would happen during double maths with Mr Webb-Williams. We quickly learned how to notch off the minutes in the squares of our exercise books all the way up to seventy every double maths lesson, powerless in the face of a teacher who could slow down time. Webb-Williams nicknamed me 'Dumbo' and would delight in asking me questions he knew I didn't know the answer to. Over and over I would imagine the exquisite pleasure – just as the sadist was asking me about the differentiation of the trigonometric square root of something or other –

This booklet tells you how to make your home and your family as safe as possible under nuclear attack

of the end of the world. Being vaporised would also bring an end to my maths 'O' level revision plan. What would it feel like? Would death be instantaneous? Would the flesh be burned from the bones or would we all just melt instantly? It would be good if paper burned first, so at least you could see your maths books die.

At night I would lie in bed and think about nuclear war. It was bound to happen sometime soon, that was my philosophy. It was only a matter of time, we surmised, before the Ruskies attacked. I was constantly worried, but not in an obvious way. It was more of an underlying keeping-me-awake-at-night thing that I didn't quite understand. Looking back, I was right to be worried. At one time Market Rasen had been surrounded by nuclear bases. One, RAF Faldingworth, only three miles away, had been a secret nuclear bomb storage site. Far from being happily detached from war, out in the sticks, for us it would all have been over in the blink of an eye.

There was a hilarious (yet scary) new government pamphlet being circulated entitled 'Protect And Survive' that explained in detail what we were all supposed to do in the event of nuclear attack. My particular favourites were 'Hide under a bridge if you're out of doors' and 'If someone dies put them in a separate room, wrapped in a polythene bag with a name tag'.

We also went to watch two films at the Liberal Club about what to do in the event of a nuclear attack. The first was *Duck and Cover*, the 1950s public information film from the USA that starred a cartoon turtle and showed how you could survive a nuclear attack by hiding under a desk or putting a newspaper over your head. The other was the public information film *Protect and Survive*, with its chilling air-raid siren noises and a voice-over by the man who did the Barratt Homes advert on TV.

With Market Rasen being so close to several important military installations – Binbrook, Faldingworth, Hemswell, Ludford Magna and Scampton – the silence of a summer's day would

often be pierced by the deep rumble of a Vulcan bomber flying low overhead, or the high-pitched sonic boom of F-111s. It was a shame we couldn't use the (Russian) MIG 15s. These were my favourite planes as well as sounding like a nickname you'd give one of your mates. I also liked the Mirage jets as used by Tanguy and Laverdure in the late 60s French TV series *The Aeronauts*.

Around this time a rumour went round the school that one of the teachers – nicknamed Titty – had acquired a nuclear shelter at nearby Hambledon Hill. Bandy wrote some lyrics and we recorded a song called 'Titty's Got A Nuclear Shelter'.

> *Cos Titty's got a nuclear shelter*
> *And she'll go there if there's a nuclear war*

A few months later the nuclear issue re-emerged in a conflict between local residents, stout-hearted warriors who refused to be beaten by the communist hordes, and lily-livered cowardly

peace lovers from communes deep in the countryside. The fight
was over a question: What was Market Rasen supposed to do if
there was a nuclear war? With military bases so close, the simple
answer would be 'Prepare to be instantly vaporised'. The
County Emergency Planning Officer had other ideas, and held
a meeting in the Festival Hall with the intention of preaching
the importance of trying to survive a nuclear attack. He seemed
to think that the county was pretty indestructible, and tougher
than the USSR realised:

'It will take *at least* forty two-megaton weapons to
completely devastate Lincolnshire.'

What? Don't *tell* them. Now they'd know how many
weapons to fire at us…

A town councillor of the moustache-and-leather-jacket
brigade stood up and said that if a bomb was dropped by para-
chute and detonated above RAF Binbrook then we were all
goners. Then a load of CND protesters got up. According to
sources, they were 'not from Market Rasen', a euphemism for
'conchie bastards – let's string 'em up'. (This dig had even more
potency, locally, as during the Second World War a lot of
'conchies' came (or were sent) to live in the village of Holton
cum Beckering, about four or five miles from Market Rasen,
where a family of fellow conscientious objectors opened up their
farm to try and help them eke out a living from farming. They
became the local bohemians – writers, artists and actors who,
while commanding a certain grudging respect, also attracted a
lot of derision from people in the town.)

The only concrete action, seemingly, to come out of this
conflict was the setting up of the Market Rasen branch of the
CND in a local pub.

28. Love and Tears at the Festival Hall: Local Disco Fever

Back in the 1960s, songwriter Rod Temperton (who wrote 'Thriller' for Michael Jackson) went to De Aston school in Market Rasen. When he penned 'Boogie Nights' for his band Heatwave (in 1976), I like to think that he might have been reminiscing about going to teenage discos around Market Rasen:

Boogie Nights
Ain't No Doubt We Are Here To Party*
Boogie Nights
Come On Out Got To Get It Started
Dance With The Boogie Get Down**
'Cause Boogie Nights Are Always
The Best In Town***
Got To Keep On Dancing Keep On Dancing****

('Boogie Nights' written by Rod Temperton. Published by Rodsongs/Chrysalis Music Ltd (c) 1976. Used by permission. All rights reserved)

---

* Possibly, though many of us are under 18 so that might be a problem.
** Look out, someone has thrown a half drunk pint of snakebite onto the dancefloor.
*** Let's face it, the only thing in town.
**** Got to keep on dancing, yes – those blokes near the door are out to get you because you looked at their girlfriends and the dancefloor is the safest place.

Rod obviously didn't specify that this was *about* Market Rasen – he wanted to sell more than seven copies – but as a motif for the interests and desires of teenagers in a town like this, it tells a true story. And he certainly never imagined Boogie Nights in the Festival Hall.

The Festival Hall was an early 70s redbrick building, as functional and ugly as all structures of that time were supposed to be. Architects in big cities at the time perhaps had grand visions of interpreting modernist philosophies in concrete and glass, but in small provincial towns like Market Rasen, early 70s 'modern' was a big brick shed with a stage and a bar, cloak-rooms and a toilet. The hall was at the back of a large car park, by far the biggest in the town.

The 'Fezzy' or 'Fez', as it was affectionately termed, was where, each year, we crowned our town's greatest beauty and worshipped her as a mini deity for a whole twelve months – well, gave her free vouchers to some of the shops in town and a ferry round trip to Ostend.

The annual Miss Chamber of Trade competition – a lyrically Lincolnshiresque way of branding a beauty contest – was one of the highlights of the year for boys of all ages. It was a chance to get an eyeful of hotpants and false eyelashes and female leg, and a chance for whichever balding middle-aged no-hoper was the local mayor or head of the Chamber of Trade to

get close enough for a kiss from one of the beauties, who was to be displayed next week in the local papers. The whole town went a bit crazy every year during this competition. People poured in from the outlying villages to see it. I always presumed that every town in Britain had a Miss Chamber of Trade contest but apparently not. This glamorous beauty pageant is unique to Market Rasen.

When I was little I sometimes wondered why the girls in the Miss Chamber of Trade competition weren't quite as pretty as the women on Miss World or Miss Great Britain, but that didn't stop me being fascinated by it. Of the contestants, there was always a sensible one with a long dress or skirt; a sexy librarian one with thick glasses; a raunchy looking brunette; a tall one with long blonde hair; and one with short hair, massive false eyelashes and amazingly athletic legs. The winner would usually be the one with the really amazing legs. The judges of the Miss Chamber of Trade competition liked good legs. Perhaps it was because of the town's love of racehorses. The raunchy brunettes never won, I suppose because they posed a danger to the natural workings and morals of the town. You couldn't have raunchy brunettes opening supermarkets, or riding in an open-topped car through the town; they would cause a riot. This year's Miss Chamber of Trade was actually someone who had been at our school a couple of years before. The great beauties of the age were now only just out of reach. I had once fallen in love with one of them – Stephanie Dray, the 1970 Miss Chamber of Trade, a tall, tasty woman with a strong nose and long legs. It was hard for Stephanie and I to meet up in our small town without tongues wagging. She was twenty, I was five.

In the early 1980s there was a disco every fortnight or so at the Fezzy, and it was the biggest teenage social occasion in the area. And so it's Saturday night, 1980, and Bandy, Cozy, Kev, Sidebottom and I are in a small pack coming off the main road, passing the chippy where Kev had a plum job as chief potato peeler (Kev's job gave the rest of us an excuse to hang out in the chippy on a Saturday night, playing Space Invaders and Asteroids and trying unsuccessfully to chat up girls like Carmen Williams. Kev was always getting jobs – he was always saving for something). We get to the Festival Hall car park, talking loudly and taking the piss out of each other. As we approach the entrance the caged disco noise hits us and with it the rush of anticipation. There are others waiting, girls in twos and threes, quite a few couples. There's a jostling excitement as we get through the door. Each time it is still a thrill that we have been allowed in and we enter the main hall, wide eyed. We look around nervously, laughing at each other and eagerly but nervously doing a quick scan of the hall for people we know or people who don't like us and of course girls we fancy.

As we entered there had been the growl of small motorbike engines. A gang of denim-clad hard-rock acolytes from the rural farms and hamlets to the north and east of Market Rasen had arrived. They would take up a position near the big windows and at each side of the stage, as if pressuring the DJ in a pincer movement to play loud heavy rock. We instinctively moved in the opposite direction and walked nervously to the bar area to discuss who's looking the oldest that day, to get the beers in. Bandy won't get the job as his voice still starts to squeak at moments of high tension.

Barman: Are you eighteen?

Bandy (squeaking): Yeah, course. In fact I'm forty.

It would often be me or Cozy who'd get the job. My technique for looking older was to frown. I figured that grown-ups were less happy than kids, so by looking serious it would appear as if I had the weight of the world on my shoulders and must be over eighteen. I'd ask for the drinks in one of two ways – either in a nonchalant, disinterested way, in an I'm-not-really-bothered-I drink-pints-of-Strongbow-every-day-so-it's-no-big-deal sort of way – or in a defiant, urgent, focused way – we are busy gentlemen, men, *busy men* with a mission, we need those drinks *now*. Cozy was tall, looked older and serious, and had a proper haircut. Sidebottom was even taller, but he was one of those people who wouldn't make it to the bar for ages because he'd get waylaid by too many people to say hello to. Sidebottom knew most of the lads two years older than us who were friends of his brother, as did Kev whose older cousin Douglas was usually in the thick of things. The rest of us stood on the edge, unimportant, invisible and vulnerable. Eventually, armed with our bitters, ciders or lagers, we'd stand near the back of the hall, at the edge of the bar area, and start to do what we loved. Slag off shit music.

'Supertramp! This is shit.'

'Shit. Really shit.'

'Yeah, shit.'

Sip pints. Look around. Try to catch eye of girls.

'ELO. Fucking rubbish.'

'Shite.'

'Hold on, Bandy, I thought you liked ELO.'

'Er, yeah.'

Sip pints. Talk about football. Try to catch eye of girls. Martha Tidy walks past and we all go quiet. Martha Tidy, nearly nineteen, always wore the same shiny turquoise spray-on trousers at each disco. And with good reason. An open-mouthed silence followed in her wake. Why didn't she save us all a lot of bother (and guesswork) and just paint her naked legs turquoise?

'I'd do it for her,' said Kev.

'Dancing In The Moonlight' by Thin Lizzy comes on. My God, what is wrong with this DJ? He is taking the mickey.

'Fucking rubbish.'

'Jesus Christ, it's shit this week.'

'Look, some of the rockers are dancing.'

'Ha ha. They think they should cos Lizzy are a rock band.'

'Listen to those twin guitars. Loyalty.'

Sip pints. Sigh.

The disco music comes on. 'Le Freak' by Chic.

'Bloody disco now.'

'Yeah. Bloody hell.'

'Hold on, Tim, you like this.'

'Er, yeah, it's alright, I suppose.'

Then something by The Gibson Brothers. We all look on as the girls start to fill the dance floor. We can't dance to it because we are too inhibited (i.e. sober) but we'd like to. I'd certainly like to. There are loads of girls wiggling and bouncing around to this. We all go quiet as some of the older, cooler town lads allied to the rockabilly revival, plus the older blokes with cars brigade, move onto the dance floor and take up strategic positions near the best-looking girls. Older blokes can somehow do disco dancing with a nonchalant style, like their heart isn't really in it and they'd rather be off reading the paper or washing their car, whereas we always go hell for leather whatever we're doing and end up looking daft. Our hearts sink a little as Babyshams and rum and cokes are offered by these older blokes, and the first layer of available girls is stripped away.

If I had been sitting in a laboratory, wired up by scientists doing research into attraction, I would probably not have got that excited by many of the girls as seen in the town. But at a disco, things are different. In fact it might not have been the disco so much as the Festival Hall itself, which turned country girls into fashionably dressed, gyrating gorgeous dance starlets with cherry gloss lipstick and big mascara eyes. When women entered the doors of the 'Fezzy' they became something different – powerful rural love goddesses whose favours would only be won by the most charming and courageous hero.

From the safety of our position near the back we can mock those dancing to shit music and be near enough to the bar to get

another round in. Having said that, we had very little money, so after the initial success a lot of the time we might be hanging around in the cloakroom begging drinks or sips of drinks off other people, or just stealing people's beer to try and get drunk. Or sneaking in small bottles of rum and black in our pockets.

What we're waiting for is the silence at the end of a crap song – probably The Nolan Sisters or Liquid Gold – and the charge that will go through the hall. When it comes, the atmosphere changes completely as the opening bars to 'Into The Valley' by The Skids comes on, a breathless urgent bass riff, and everyone's brain scrambles – Der der der dah dah duh duh doh doh doh doh doh doh doh doh... We all slam our drinks down on the table, and, arms flailing, legs kicking, already dancing like jerky ants as we run, we try to get to the dance floor as quickly as possible. We have the whole floor to ourselves as we laugh like maniacs, jumping up and pushing off each other's shoulders. We are going absolutely mental, banging into each other – some say punk started at St Martins Art College in 1975 with the first Sex Pistols gig but, no, tonight it's here, at the

Festival Hall in Market Rasen in 1980. This is what punk is all about, right now.

We are joined on the dance floor by the three Punk Nigels, plus part-time punk Carwyn Lovehandles – this is the town's New Wave contingent in its entirety, unless some of Nigel's mates from Wragby or Lincoln are here – and there are some rockers whose feet are moving because the guitar is cranked up pretty loud. We are in a bubble of pogo thrash and hybrid jerky dancing, with Bandy doing his mad personal chicken dance out of time with the rhythm; Kev bouncing higher and higher; Sidebottom lashing out like he's taking free kicks in quick succession; Cozy like he's simultaneously having a fit and running around looking for his lost house key and me; I've no idea how I dance. I can't feel my body; I am weightless.

I'm not sure how much time has passed. 'Into The Valley' lasts about three minutes but that might have been three seconds or thirty years. We all become fully conscious again as the song starts to fade out but, if the DJ is feeling extra kind, he will put on 'Eton Rifles' by The Jam. This again starts with a thudding bass line but it's more jagged punk pop so you do a more bouncy, jaunty kind of dance. The most difficult bit about dancing to 'Eton Rifles' is the chorus, because if you're not thinking straight you might inadvertently do a Pan's People-style literal mime interpretation and do a smile and wave followed by a sun effect with your hands then pretend to shoot a gun. What you are *supposed* to do is concentrate and do a strange little head-flicky dance. Then the DJ will be sneaky and put on 'Message In A Bottle' and we will dance but we know he's setting us up for a big rejection, because he can't do a disco with only six or seven people on the dance floor... and then sure enough it will be The Nolan Sisters again or The Dooleys or Gloria Gaynor, or it might be the rockers' turn – Status Quo, Jeff Beck, Black Sabbath – and our stint will be over.

Time would fly by after that, as the alcohol kicked in. Once in a while we'd be too drunk to stand up at the end. I can remember being dragged out of the toilets while in a fit of blind drunk sickness (brought on by an almost-lethal mixture of rum and black, snakebite and pork scratchings) and Roly Chesterfield bundling me into his car and driving me home.

If we were still in one piece by ten to midnight, we were in the running for the slow dances. This was the opportunity to get a last-minute snog from someone while dancing to some rubbish ballad. Once in a blue moon I'd pluck up the courage to ask a girl I barely knew for a dance and maybe get lucky with a tongue wrestle up against the wall at the end, before the lights would go on and you could suddenly see everyone properly.

And what people! Presiding over the edge of the dance floor like a seasoned MC is Pip Podland, small-town tough, a pink-faced, smiling hard-man with a mop of unruly brown hair. Pip resolutely refused to take anything seriously. No-one ever saw Pip physically threaten anyone. It was just the sheer force of his personality. It was all bravado with Pip. Pip often held court, telling us all about stuff he'd nicked, goals he had scored, people he *could* beat up. Strangely, Pip never boasted about girls. I don't ever remember him having a girlfriend. He was of the old school, in which an interest in girls suggested a slight effeminacy, as if his friends might think he was gay if he said he fancied someone.

And you had Garp, the five foot nothing rocker with a little blond 'tache who would always try to catch your eye then make something of it. He was like Medusa – you could not look at him, particularly when he was spoiling for a fight. One night I was in a huddle chatting with a few lads. After a while I noticed a figure in the middle of the group staring at me. It was Garp, gazing up into my eyes.

Garp (imagine the most nasally East Midlands accent imaginable, like a reedy Brian Clough): What... are... you... starin'... at... mate?

Me: Eh, I, er, I…

Garp: (Looking deep into my soul) Wanna… make… something… of.. it… do… yer?

Disaster. I had been Garpised. If I didn't disengage that second, Garp would paralyse my whole nervous system with his eyes before a couple of his accomplices would manhandle me out the back of the Fezzy and he would beat me up – below-the-belt punches, too, because Garp was, well, so small. I used all my willpower to avert my eyes from Garp's trancelike stare and carried on the conversation, with Garp still standing there, staring up at me. After a while he got bored and found someone else to stare at and, possibly, beat up.

Although most of the characters at the Fez existed in relative harmony, violence did occasionally erupt, usually connected to impressing and fighting over girls. Or if someone suggested that nearby town and arch-rival Caistor had a better chance of winning the Lincolnshire Tidy Towns Contest.

One of the major episodes in the Festival Hall's mythology was when the mods turned up towards the end of a disco and threatened to beat up every local bloke with hammers that they carried around in their parka pockets. It was a bank holiday and, after the disco started, a rumour started going around that the mods were on their way there. We all started to get a bit edgy, especially those very close to the bottom of the food chain. We hung around for a while but our hearts weren't in it. Then someone shouted 'The mods are here, the mods are here!' and that was it. In the confusion on our way out, Kev got hit by a mod, who was possibly enraged by Kev's slightly beatific George Harrison-like demeanour when it came to violence – he would point out in his ever-so-reasonable way, 'I am a pacifist, actually' – then we just legged it, up the back lanes and paths, hiding in cornfields and taking a very long way home. Up on our local hill, Mount Pleasant (it was more a slight slope), we could see a group of mods on their scooters stop in the road. They could smell our fear. We were convinced they were looking for us so crouched down lower in the field we were in. Running was our fighting technique.

As long as we weren't chundering our guts up, the end of a typical Festival Hall experience would be round at a mate's house for instant coffee (as ever), analysing the evening's events like middle-aged sports pundits, and teasing and congratulating anyone who had got a snog during the slow dances (usually Cozy). We would agree that 'Into The Valley' was a work of genius, The Skids would become as big as Genesis, that 'Message In A Bottle' was shit and that we probably would never go to another disco in the town again. Well, not for a week, at least.

29. Shining at the Buxton Pavilion

Brass band music had been important in my life but in 1980 I was about to give it up. I'd been playing in bands since I was nine but it was now getting too much. I got my music fix from thrashing around in Heart Attack, plus I played loads of sport too and I just didn't have time for it any more.

My career had begun in the school band, with a euphonium, which was a big lump of brass full of holes that had been at the school since WW1. In fact, it might have been used in the First World War as some kind of low-tech cannon. It made a sort of *fwump* sound, like an old man snoring and farting at the same

time, due to the countless leaks. Pressing the keys didn't affect the quality or variation of this noise in any way. Still, I persevered and the next year graduated to trombone. That was when the town band head-hunted me – there was a spare baritone lying around and would I fancy it? They already had three trombone players, two of them older girls. Yeah, why not? That was my stock prerequisite when asked if I'd like to *join* things.

And so I entered the heavily competitive world of band concerts. Brightly coloured jackets, military-style discipline and lots of chain smoking and male banter. I felt like a tit. Conversely, playing was good

makes your lips rubbery

for my still slightly asthmatic chest and also made my lips go big so I looked like a vaguely alluring albino Jean-Paul Belmondo.

The soft warm sound of a brass band on a cold winter's afternoon is at once both uplifting and melancholy. The best tunes to play in a brass band are hymns, which work better without the words. But our band was well known for its 'groovy' repertoire such as 'Swinging Safari', the James Bond theme, 'Save All Your Kisses for Me', *Hawaii Five-0* theme, the *New World Symphony*. In 1976 we did a sponsored play in the Corn Exchange to raise money to buy new uniforms. The old jackets were in the firm tradition of brass bands. Royal blue with a gold trim, a timeless classic. The new uniforms were firmly rooted in the mid-to-late 1970s. Lime-green jackets with a fashionable cut.

Branded forever on my mind is the faux pas I committed at a Christmas concert at the end of that year in a village church. I turned up in my new blazer, beaming away, all proud. But grown men began hissing and cursing me, calling me an idiot. Hadn't I realised? We were going to be unveiling our new uniforms at a big competition at Buxton Pavilion in the new

Cornet

flugelhorn

French horn

trombone

baritone

tuba

year. I must have missed that bit (I had probably been staring at the glamorous trombonists while the lads were planning their wickedly tantalising strategy). Humiliated, I had to play like the girls with no jacket, just a white shirt. I sat in silence. No-one would talk to me. Even Hank, the man who had got me into the band, my mentor, refused to look me in the eye. For the next couple of weeks, on reading the local *Market Rasen Mail*, I was fully expecting that an eager journalist 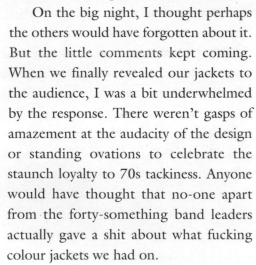 would have picked up on this controversial story and would have revealed his scoop to the world...

On the big night, I thought perhaps the others would have forgotten about it. But the little comments kept coming. When we finally revealed our jackets to the audience, I was a bit underwhelmed by the response. There weren't gasps of amazement at the audacity of the design or standing ovations to celebrate the staunch loyalty to 70s tackiness. Anyone would have thought that no-one apart from the forty-something band leaders actually gave a shit about what fucking colour jackets we had on.

I continued in the band for another year, still going down to Uncle Joe's afterwards for my dripping sandwiches. Yet the magic had gone for me. I had lost my status as the bright and talented young prodigy. There was now a younger kid than me in the third cornet section. I was just the lanky lad who plays the same note over and over again and who doesn't listen when you're explaining the special secret plan for unveiling the new band uniforms. But I didn't like giving up on stuff so I soldiered on.

The school windband was different. Run by Mr Hair, the music teacher, it was more fun because the music was more varied and contemporary, and the atmosphere wasn't competitive. And there were more girls in it. Nor did you have to dress in stupid lime-green jackets. Rather than playing third baritone, I was second trombone, a subtle difference in the brass/wind hierarchy. But playing an instrument at school meant that I was stuck in the Royal School of Music grade system. I disliked the stale, stilted, old-fashioned 'classical' music we were forced to play over and over again. I knew that in the long term I was unlikely to be able to practise properly because I didn't love the instrument enough, though if there had been a Royal School of Ska Music, run by Rico of The Specials, it might all have been different. So I started to look out for an excuse to leave. Mr Hair and Mr Minting the PE teacher had already clashed about who had priority when there were sports fixtures and concerts coming up and the fact that it was getting harder to combine music and my burgeoning school sports career made the decision easier for me. At the end, it still felt strange jacking in the trombone. If only for those great big lips.

30. Ian Curtis Died For Us

Like any normal fifteen-year-old I was now spending all my spare cash on records. I liked masses of stuff. But I didn't like *everything*. A combination of my slow, big-skies rural life and the buttoned-down nature of the middle-class thread running through my family meant that when it came to pop stars I could worship I was not turned on by the flamboyant, the extrovert, the showbizzy brash (Bowie, Bolan, Pistols) but the more nerdy, introverted trying-to-be-clever strain of singer. I tended to go for stuff with lyrics I understood while listening to the music, rather than having to read the lyric sheet afterwards as if dissecting poetry. The Sex Pistols' *Never Mind the Bollocks* did nothing for me, apart from 'Anarchy In The UK', whereas The Clash had stories and polemics that made sense.

By 1980, the post-postpunk musicscape was throwing up myriad leftfield bands that I could relate to. Around that time I had gone into Lincoln with a load of money (£6) and at Vallances electrical shop I had a choice between Joy Division's *Unknown Pleasures* and *Entertainment!* by Gang of Four. Rob, ever ahead of me on the music front, already had Joy Division's album, which I'd taped. Gang of Four's lyrics were straight out of a plate-glass university's Critiques of Culture course, with quotable platitudes I could repeat in the pub to try and impress any left-wing rock chicks that might be hanging around. Their vocals were shouty and high-pitched and aggressive and know-it-all smart, the music fast, relentless, impatient. Joy Division had opaque lyrics I didn't understand but I guessed they were about alienation, depression, a mood. The music had lots of spaces, moments where the band seemed to be jamming or resting, with vocals like those of a hungover north of England Sinatraesque pub crooner.

So I ended up buying *Entertainment!* for the amazing sum of £5.25, which in today's money is probably about £10,000. Like a wonderful, psychotropic, £5.25-perception-altering drug, *Entertainment!* opened new doors in my mind. I became aware that:

1. The military industrial complex dominated world politics.
2. History is not made by great men, but by the actions of the masses.
3. Don't fall in love because it's comparable to catching anthrax.
4. The bikini was named after bikini atoll, site of the first H-bomb trial.
5. Punk could be funky.

Gang of Four guitarist Andy Gill played punk in a funk style. Or he played funk in a punk style. This was the breakthrough influence I had been waiting for. I turned the bass down on my little practice amp, turned up the treble, switched the pickup selector control to treble and brought my hand across the fretboard, attempting to send out shards of metallic punkpop chord magic. To start with I didn't really play proper notes; it was mainly discordant. The first Heart Attack song we recorded using my new Andy Gill style was called 'The Castrated Conservative Councillors'. (I would later refine this style with riffs nicked from Echo and the Bunnymen – in fact, I deconstructed and resassembled the opening motif to 'Rescue' so many times that even I could no longer recognise the original.)

A few months earlier, in late '79, Scooter had asked me if I fancied going to Derby (or was it Sheffield? Scunthorpe?) to watch Joy Division. I could cadge a lift on his moped. It sounded exciting. But I'd never been to a gig before. At that time I had only just started going to discos, which were as we've seen magical and exciting and full of unattainable older girls out letting their hair down. I decided that I would prefer to go to the Fezzy Hall to the disco as I had an idea that I might bump into Maggie Jefferson, or possibly even Carmen Williams, and maybe get someone to buy me a pint of Stones bitter. As usual my brain had been so scrambled by thoughts of snogs and unbelievable girl perfume that I got my priorities all mixed up. Some warm pissy ale and the (not very likely) possibility of a cherry lipgloss snog versus a chance to see one of the best bands around? In the end, I convinced myself that it was early days for Joy Division and I'd get loads more opportunities to see them at a venue closer to home, when they had become as big as The Jam and I would be their number one fan in Lincolnshire. Forward thinking, you see.

My first gig was in March 1980, when I was fifteen. Stiff Little Fingers were playing at Cleethorpes Winter Gardens. The Winter Gardens was a kind of 1930s Taj Mahal, famous at the time for having hosted punk bands like the Sex Pistols and The Stranglers (the latter band, according to local legend, were beaten up by local dockers). Outside in the queue, I had never seen so many grumpy-looking kids. Most were sixteen-plus, but I reckoned they must all be exceptionally cool and hard and serious by the frowning faces and pursed lips that said: 'Don't mess with me, I'm tough. And don't try and get in a debate about pop music or European cinema with me, either, because I'm dead clever too. Well, maybe not clever, but I've got an anally retentive ability to remember names and dates.' I didn't mess with any of them.

Cozy and Kev were there too. I was in my Clash T-shirt, donkey jacket, drainpipes and DMs. Kev was in his Sex Pistols

T-shirt, donkey jacket, drainpipes and DMs, while Cozy was sporting a Jam T-shirt, donkey jacket, drainpipes and DMs. We were expressing our individuality. The general style of the waiting crowd was more flamboyantly punk than we could hope to attain. Some wore really smart leather jackets, some of them remarkably new-looking. We all furrowed our brows and stared straight ahead off into some imaginary middle distance.

Looking at these Sid Vicious clones made me realise, if I didn't already know it, that I had never been and would never be a proper punk. For a start, I had the wrong hair. I looked like a farmer's son with my wavy, straw-like locks. No matter what kind of expression I affected I couldn't escape the feeling that I was just too clean-cut. I had often been accused of dying my hair blond. This was due to the white streaks on the left-hand side of my head that were a throwback to my early childhood when all of my hair was that colour. What was left now looked like a very cheap highlight job that always fascinated hairdressers – I should say, always fascinated female hairdressers.

'Gosh, it's amazing!' said Sue at Cynthia's, while all the other girls stopped what they were doing to crowd round and have a look at me.

'Ooh, I wish I could get my hair like that,' said another.

Kev was different. Ever the rebel, he offered to help his mum serve the Sunday lunch and had surreptitiously hidden the pan of cabbage water in the garden shed, then later washed his hair in it. At school the next day he triumphantly told us what he'd done.

'What do you reckon?'

'Er, reckon to what?'

'My green hair. Is it punk or what?'

'What green hair?'

He held some hair up in his hands. 'It's not that green but when the light hits it in a certain way it's got a sort of green tinge.' True enough, there was a certain cabbagey green quality to Kev's barnet that morning. We all agreed that his punk credentials were enhanced.

In my 1980 punk diary, at the back in the address book section, is my first ever gig review.

> *'LIVE!'*
> *SLF Winter Gardens*
> *Another Pretty Face started, with their post-punk pop. The crowd weren't very responsive though* [they were too grumpy and cool for that], *and this came out in the band, who didn't communicate very well* [it sounds like I'm writing up the notes for a job interview – it's not exactly Lester Bangs].
>
> *SLF came on amid the rousing 'Dam Busters' theme. This is a bit pompous and commercial for a so-called street band such as SLF.*
>
> *The songs were powerful and well executed. And the front ½ of the audience pogoed and swayed eagerly* ['swayed eagerly'? Eh?].
>
> *At the end they played an encore of 'Ghostriders', which was crap.*

On Monday 19th May my diary entry reads as follows:

'I was listening to John Peel, when suddenly the news came. Ian Curtis is dead. End of an era!!' Yes, I really did use two exclamation marks. And I'm not sure what era I was thinking of. I had only been aware of Joy Division for just over a year, so to describe it as an era seems somewhat hyperbolic. I think I was trying to get across my feeling that this seemed genuinely important. At this point, apart from my *Unknown Pleasures* tape, I only had one Joy Division record, 'Transmission'.

I bought this in Grimsby on the morning of the 1980 FA Cup Final (West Ham vs Arsenal. Trevor Brooking scored the winner. It's one of the handful of memories from 1980 that are fresh in my memory, plus I have my erudite entry from the 1980 punk diary to confirm that day's events). But a quick check shows me that the Cup Final was the week after Ian Curtis died. So I *was* a plastic bandwagon jumper after all. The shame.

By 20th May I had taken a more philosophical stance to the tragedy.

'Nobody believed me at school when I said that Ian Curtis had died. Thought I might have dreamed it. Most of them didn't know who Ian Curtis is/was. Joy Division are bloody brilliant. What is going to happen to them?' With my alternative music soothsayer's hat on I predicted they would probably sink without trace now that their singer was gone. That day I wore an armband at school, but not a black one. I couldn't find anything black so I used one of those old fluorescent armbands that kids wore on their way to school in winter when they changed the daylight hours in the early 70s. As a consequence not many people noticed it, and those that did wondered why I was concerned about traffic safety all of a sudden.

31. 'We Used to Use Half a Brick'

Seen from the sky, by amateur pilots, skydivers, kids on Google Earth or an omniscient deity, Lincolnshire probably looks like a collection of massive fields of three colours. Yellow for oilseed rape; brown for wheat or barley; and green for football, rugby and cricket pitches.

It is little wonder then that those with sporting ability were among the most venerated characters in the community. In the natural pecking order, 'being hard' came tops, but being able to score thirty goals a season could put you up there, too. I might have moaned to myself about the ennui of living in Lincolnshire, but I loved sport, and sports-loving kids in Lincolnshire were pretty lucky. Our school was surrounded by fields, which gave space for two rugby pitches, three football pitches, a hockey pitch and a cricket field, with the town's rugby club and its three pitches in between. Winds whipping in on a Saturday afternoon in winter and early spring heightened the sensations of physical contact at high speed.

There were some kids who instinctively understood how sport worked, as if their body/mind was wired in a different way. They knew the length and breadth of the pitch without having to think about it, and had long ago internalised the myriad small movements, angles and rituals that make up sporting skills. They were kids with vision, able to play a kind of lifesize chess, whether it be football, rugby or cricket. Everything they did had grace and ease of movement: it was as if they had more time.

I was not one of those kids. In any sporting environment, my world was smaller, consisting solely of what I could see in front of me. The idea of a move unfolding, of a tactical plan being followed, was far too abstract and theoretical. At any one moment I could only cope with my immediate surroundings: a small patch of grass in a two-metre square around me (it makes me think of the hapless elephant seal thrashing around in its little pool at Cleethorpes Zoo). I sometimes felt trapped inside my own body and my own lack of hand-eye co-ordination. My childhood asthma had left me with a propensity to spend so much time gulping for air that my brain never seemed to have enough oxygen to think about what might happen next.

The idea I had of myself in the sporting arena did not, as a rule, correspond with reality. I thought I was ace. My sporting heroes were usually centre-forwards like Geoff Hurst, Joe Jordan, Mick Jones. I was thrilled when I was picked for the primary school's football team for the first time, aged just nine. Apart from fouling more skilful opponents, which was something all of us were able to do instinctively, I had one unique skill. I was able to dribble with the ball while standing still. So if someone passed to me I could evade onrushing tacklers by pushing the ball backwards and forwards underneath my foot.

But that was it. Mr Sharp, the teacher who ran the football team, perhaps having recovered from the blow to the head that made him pick me in the first place, decided to leave me out for the rest of the year. When I did feature again, in my penultimate year of school, it was as a rugged left-half, where I could just stand in the way of opposing forwards or dribble with the ball while not moving, until one of our team's more creative players could whip the ball off me and take it upfield.

But how I envied the natural sporting ability and athleticism of other kids, like my mate Bramley Edwards. I first met Bramley when he was playing for Faldingworth under-11s against Market Rasen under-11s in autumn 1975. I can safely say I wasn't really supposed to be marking Bramley that day. Nobody would admit to it at any rate. We were beaten 4-1 and I think Bramley scored a hat-trick. He finished off his third goal with a little diving header followed by a forward roll and I remember thinking to myself, What a complete cock, or something similar, while simultaneously thinking he was cool and marvelling at his skill. I could see what Bramley was doing. It was called pass and move. He would pass the ball then, rather than stand there with his hands on his hips and admire his own handiwork and shout 'Go on' as I would do, he ran into a better position to receive a return pass. This was alien football. It seemed somehow unpatriotic.

Then there was Bandy. He was now our school team's centre-forward and would take the ball from just inside our half and run with it really fast, while keeping control of it. How did he do that? Mr Sharp was always on at us to practise our keepy-uppies, and reckoned that we should be able to do at least 200. I know Bandy practised this skill on his own. Even though I was probably the team's best standing-still dribbler, I had only ever managed ten keepy-uppies.

If I did get time alone with a ball I preferred to play Imaginary Scenarios In Which I Score A Last-Minute Hat-Trick In

The World Cup Final. In this fantasy I was either the centre-forward who had received a blow to the head or had to fight off marauding German stormtroopers or I'd had to leave the pitch for a while to save a good-looking French actress from a pit of vipers. The general narrative was that towards the end of the game I would overcome insurmountable odds. Even I had to think I couldn't possibly save the game, the girl and the planet this time. Thankfully I always did, and occasionally I would look up in the faint hope that the current England manager might be flying overhead in his private plane and see something in my never-say-die attitude and my ability to dribble while standing still.

Sport became a problem when girls started watching, especially Carmen Williams. She had a certain magnetism which turned fifteen-year-old boys into quivering blancmanges. I never seemed to play well at football when Carmen turned up to watch. It was similar to having your dad watching, but subtly different. I would do things I wouldn't normally attempt, like trying to do silly tricks, and would have a running commentary in my head, thinking about myself in the third person, trying to imagine how Carmen would see me. This was, of course, disastrous. With Carmen around I was always aware of my appearance – was the muscle definition of my thighs good, did I look steel-jawed enough?

If there were girls watching, you were better off playing cricket. For a start you were so far away from the spectators that they didn't know who you were. And girls tended to get bored of cricket very quickly and they'd wander off and do something else. Also, because I was crap at cricket I could be a 'comedy' player and get a laugh, getting attractiveness points for not taking myself too seriously.

At primary school Mr Sharp was also the cricket coach. Coaching consisted of him whacking the cricket ball up into the air with his old bat and expecting us to catch it. As we watched the ball sail into the stratosphere, there was just too much time to think, to worry about it. Then it would take an age to come down.

'We used to practise with half a brick,' he'd say, seriously, as yet another kid fell yelping to the floor when the ball hit him after a failed catch. 'When you've played catch with half a brick, a cricket ball feels like cotton wool.'

My small-world approach to sports could be applied equally well to cricket. I liked team sports, the collective effort, but cricket seemed to be a bewildering series of individual events and duels in which you could easily be found out and isolated. When in bat I would have one goal – to stop the ball from hitting the stumps. The thought of playing a shot to score runs never really entered my head. If I did get off the mark that was just a bonus. I really came into my own when fielding. It doesn't matter what is going on around you. If the ball comes towards you at high speed you try and catch it or stop it. There are no tactics or strategy involved. In this regard I became an above-average fielder – I only came alive when the ball was near. And I soon learned that the closer in you were the better, so you didn't have time to think about a hard ball being clouted in your direction. Instinct took over.

Around this time my dad and uncle set up an under-13 cricket team in the town. This was a revolutionary concept with teams of eight rather than eleven. Two went in at once and it didn't matter how many times you got out, it was all done on averages: your final team total divided by the amount of times you were out. This worked against me because the stats-obsessed part of my brain took over and I was playing the sport at the same time as processing the statistics. So the ball would be coming down and I'd be facing and thinking, We have three runs and haven't been out yet. If I survive this ball we will still have no wickets. Ace. Oh, I've been bowled out. So now we have three runs and one wicket. Here comes the bowler again.

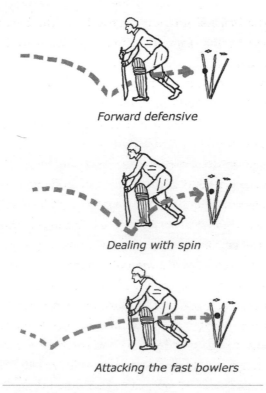

Forward defensive

Dealing with spin

Attacking the fast bowlers

My batting tactics in Under-13 cricket

If we score twenty more runs in our stint we will still have a respectable... Oh, I'm out lbw.

By this stage my partner at the other end would be frantically trying to run so that he could face the batting. And I could have stayed at the non-striker's end and had time to relax and work out the averages. The great thing about the under-13 cricket league was that people like me who were crap at cricket could stay out there for four overs. Of course that meant wrecking the team's chances of winning but it was good to have a proper go at it for a change.

We also used to play cricket on the field at the front of our house. There were usually between seven and ten of us. There were never any umpires. This was fine for most of the time, but any contentious decisions and there would be arguments. Quite often these arguments would involve cousin Rob and Roly Chesterfield. One memory I have is of us playing happily, the usual eight or nine overs, then the next minute Rob is chasing Roly Chesterfield down the drive, holding a cricket ball and threatening to throw it at him. Rob chased Roly, with all of us excitedly in tow, down the drive and into our yard, where he then let fly with a cricket ball. It missed Roly by a country mile, then Roly picked up the ball and threatened Rob in the same way. Rob legged it next door into Gran's house and told her that Roly was threatening him with a cricket ball. And when Gran emerged from her front door with a wooden spoon and fag in hand, we knew that was the end of the cricket match that day.

As a little kid I had always wanted to play rugby, like Dad, and got the chance when I went to secondary school. Although under Mr McTavish we were the worst team in the county, things improved the next year under Haydyn Thomas, so that we actually started to win games. This upswing had coincided with Bramley being persuaded to take up rugby. We also had two new boys in the team, Egg, the manager of our band, and a massive Adonis with a moustache called Michael Geddis. To this day I would not be surprised if I found out that Ged wasn't thirteen when he came to the school, but twenty-four and had a wife and kids and a proper job. I was reasonably sized for my age but Ged was at least four stone heavier than me. He was fast too, so our team now had two tactics:

1) Give it to Ged. Ged would get the ball in the centre then run really fast, knocking over opposing tacklers on his way to the try line.

2) Give it to Bramley. Bramley was just as fast as Ged but was small in comparison, so he was able to duck and weave.

Athletics was interesting because really you didn't have to think at all, just run as fast as you could. Perversely I chose a race that was more complicated than most, the 110m hurdles. But it meant I could break the race up into a series of smaller races, thinking only of the technique necessary to hurdle each barrier. I liked to imagine I was exploring in a field and suddenly a bull was chasing me. All I had to do was jump over the fence in as graceful a way as possible. Then I was in another field being chased by a different bull – or maybe it was the same bull that had found a way through the hedge.

In my head I was an electrically fast runner. I knew that I was physically capable of beating the world 100m record, which for most of the 1970s stood at 9.95 seconds, a time set by Jim Hines at the 1968 Mexico Olympics, and which would not be bettered until just after I finished my 'A' levels. Sadly it wouldn't be me who broke the record. But for some reason I could never convince my body that I could run fast. In the fourth year I won my one and only race, in a match against two other schools. It was the 110m hurdles and I won by an inch. A few weeks later I was representing the school in the East of England finals in Bedford. I didn't win that one, but got a decent enough time. And probably felt that was as far as I was going to go.

By the fifth year at school, it was not unheard of for me and some of my mates to play rugby on a Wednesday, football on a Saturday morning, rugby on a Saturday afternoon and youth football or Colts rugby on a Sunday morning, while keeping up a competitive pint-drinking regime.

What On Earth is On the Radio at the Moment?: 1980

Jam 'Going Underground'

Diana Ross 'Upside Down'

Sugarhill Gang 'Rapper's Delight'

Vapors 'Turning Japanese'

Roxy Music 'Over You'

Siouxsie And The Banshees 'Happy House'

Hot Chocolate 'No Doubt About It'

The Beat 'Mirror In The Bathroom'

Lipps Inc. 'Funky Town'

Ottawan 'D.I.S.C.O.'

Joy Division 'Love Will Tear Us Apart'

32. A Week of TV, 1980s Style (6-12 Sept 1980)

Saturday morning starts at the crazily early hour of 9.15 a.m. with an episode of *Battle of the Planets*, a kind of jerkily weird Japanese-style cartoon about spacemen with feathered capes who can fly. It's rubbish really, but the sort of thing Snake loves. He's working out the probability of it happening in a parallel universe using just his brain, his Rubik's Cube and an old radio he'd taken apart. I sit in the kitchen and read *NME* for the third time or stay in the sitting room and bait Snake:

'This is rubbish.'

'Why did he do that?'

'Who is Zoltar?'

'Why is Jason, of *G-Force*, taking part in a 9,000-mile road race?'

Snake smiles all the time but now his smile is turning to a grimace. In a minute he will surely scream, 'Muuuuu-uuuuuUUUUUUUUUM-MMM!!!!!' – but it'll be so high-pitched that only the local dogs will hear.

Telly ↑

Then it's serious telly at 9.35 with *The Flashing Blade*. This was first on when Tobe and I were little kids in the late 60s and early 70s and we loved it. It was set during the Franco-Spanish wars of the seventeeth century. All the Spaniards were evil sadists with moustaches. Most of the French were romantic poets with swords and George Best haircuts. It was, of course, made by a French TV station, in French and dubbed into English by what sounds like one really serious-voiced bloke on a tape recorder in his bedroom. I wished my voice sounded as cool as that.

The theme tune, recorded in a poppy late-60s style especially for the English-language version, was a work of genius. The final episode achieved a sort of notoriety when, due to some damage to the film, the dubbing went. The hero, Chevalier de Recci, was shown to have a really wet high-pitched French voice and the theme music was rubbish slow classical music.

After that it's *Bugs Bunny* and Tobe and I go outside to kick a rugby ball to each other. Snake stays in to watch. To become one with Bugs.

Grandstand starts early because the Gillette Cup Final is on. It's between Middlesex and Surrey – in reality North London v South London and therefore of no interest to me.

Football Focus... Leeds are playing Stoke City away. Two points in the bag there. Stoke are rubbish.

Down to the rugby club to play for the 4ths. Have a pint of shandy.

5 p.m. Back for final score. Leeds lost.

5.15 p.m. *The Dukes of Hazzard*. Worth watching for Daisy Duke, one of the most beautiful women in the world. When she is on, screen time slows down and I'm in a sort of hypnotic state. I imagine my English teacher sitting next to me talking vaguely about how I shouldn't objectify Daisy Duke. But, Miss, Daisy is wearing tight denim hotpants.

6.20 p.m. *Dr Who*. With Tom Baker. He's a bit thespy. Not as good as Patrick Troughton, though none of my friends agree. Most people think Jon Pertwee is the best Dr Who of all time. He played the Doctor as a kind of thuggish aristocrat antiques dealer and martial arts expert. Troughton was like a giggling Celtic poet.

Sunday

Not much on until *Mastermind* at 8.05 p.m. Gran will be watching this. I suspect she has the hots for Magnus Magnusson. One of the contestants does the life and works of Jung (not Neil Young). On BBC2 is the all-Ireland hurling final. What is hurling?

Monday

Watch *Hong Kong Phooey* with Snake and Tobe. Then potter about until *John Craven's Newsround*. Apparently by the year 2000 rabies will have made its way to the UK and we'll all be foaming at the mouth and going crazy.

Then *Blue Peter* with Sarah Greene, at the moment Britain's number one sex symbol. A new bloke has just started. I never warmed to Peter Purves but he was the last link to the old days and now he's gone the programme is not the same. The new guy, Peter Duncan, is a mere boy. I suppose the highlight of *Blue Peter* was when Bleep and Booster were on in the late 60s. The *Blue Peter* garden got vandalised a few months ago. We all laughed and Mum then gave us a stern lecture about ethics and character.

6.55 p.m. Watch the start of *Angels*, just for the theme music – sort of Buzzcocks meets Ritchie Blackmore.

8.05 p.m. Catch the end of *Star Trek* where they all laugh before the freeze frame.

9 p.m. Watch a bit of *Rhoda* with Mum while she's doing her yoga on the floor, right leg wrapped around her neck. It brings a bit of US glamour to our front room.

5.10 Blue Peter
with **Simon Groom, Sarah Greene**
and **Peter Duncan**
Today, *Blue Peter*'s new boy makes his first-ever appearance on the programme. Think you've seen him before? You probably have if you watched the *King Cinder* series where Peter Duncan played the daredevil speedway fanatic Kerry. Peter's keen to get into more action in *Blue Peter*, and today he has a go at navigating *Keying II*, a 20-metre Chinese sailing junk, up the River Thames. In the studio there's the first-ever television appearance of Britain's record-breaking litter of 17 poodle pups.

Tuesday

4.40 p.m. *Playaway.* I will watch this as long as none of my mates are around because Brian Cant is a comedy genius.

9 p.m. *Butterflies.* Because nothing else is on and Mum likes it.

9.30 p.m. *Not The Nine O'Clock News: The Bert of Not the Nine O'Clock News.* This is the funniest thing on television, though Gran wouldn't agree.

Wednesday

4.40 p.m. *Think of a Number* with Johnny Ball. Tobe and Snake love this programme but then they are boffiny swots. They even laugh at maths gags. You can see Snake smiling and fingering his Rubik's Cube and dreaming of becoming Johnny Ball.

9 p.m. *M*A*S*H.* The greatest.

10.15 p.m. *Sportsnight.* Euro middleweight title fight. Minter and some Italian bloke (Matteo Alvemini). Minter looks too normal to be a boxer. Like a bank clerk or something. As usual the most thrilling thing about this will be the theme tune.

Thursday

5.10 p.m. Thursday is *NME* day but I'll sometimes cast an eye over *Blue Peter.*

6.55 p.m. *Tomorrow's World.* In the future all women will look like Anna Karina and will only fancy blokes from Lincolnshire. Not really – this was a boring one about plants that don't need roots. No tinfoil outfits or lasers in sight.

7.20 p.m. *Top of the Pops.* Boring Kelly Marie 'Feels Like I'm In Love' has pipped The Jam's Beatles rip-off 'Start' to number one. It's identical to 'Taxman', the first track on *Revolver.* This is Rob's favourite album, possibly because there's a track on it called 'Dr Robert'. Sadly, there aren't any Beatles songs with Tim in the title.

    Bandy: What about 'The Fool On The Hill'?

    Tim: Grrr...

7.55 p.m. *Blankety Blank* Once or twice a week we get to go round to Gran's to watch telly as she has a colour TV. She likes the company and likes to make comments and interact with the show.

    'He's got nice hands.'

    'I don't like him.'

    Her sitting room is on the top floor of our house, with her flat sort of tacked onto it. *Blankety Blank* is one of her favourites. It could be that Terry Wogan is up there with Kenneth Williams as a comedy genius. Her favourite telly programme is probably *The Good Old Days*, the music-hall variety show. As soon as the master of ceremonies starts off with his long-worded intros, Gran will be laughing. We just look at each other, wondering what's going on, or we might copy Gran and laugh to get in with her. Soon, Gran will be laughing until the tears are rolling down her cheeks and you think she's stopped breathing and is going to die. Whenever Gran tells a joke the same thing happens. She starts crying with laughter and can never finish and I think, That's it – she's going to pop her clogs. Gran only has one joke, about a man who loses his beret in a field full of cow pats. No-one has ever heard the punchline because Gran always gets paralysed with laughter halfway through. To be honest, Dad is no better. He only has one joke as well, about a bear and a squirrel going to do a shit in the woods. He gets very close to the punchline, before he too breaks down in tears. We are a crap joke family. Literally, in fact. I take after Mum – I just don't remember jokes after I've heard them.

Friday
7 p.m. *It's a Knockout* (*Jeux Sans Frontieres*). I tell everyone I don't approve of nationalism and yet I'm nervous to the point of feeling sick whenever I watch *Jeux Sans Frontieres* and I'm rooting for our British lads and lasses from places like Aldershot, Cleethorpes, Chipping Norton, Aylesbury. This is how all wars should be fought – with giant comedy rubber body suits, water guns and lots of flour.

Then it's over to Bandy's to doss about, make drinks with his ace SodaStream and try and maybe nick some of his mum's booze without her ever finding out...

(Artistic licence was, ahem, applied to this chapter.)

33. Love, Chaos and 50cc Motorbikes

Heavy metal was the sound of the disenfranchised working-class kids from rural villages. It was macho and beery, with an undercurrent of violence (and, in the case of Black Sabbath, possibly black magic and budgie eating). But to live this dream you couldn't take public transport or get a lift from your mum. Ha, no way. You needed your own wheels, otherwise you were a wimpy punky New Waver. And so you had the phenomenon of gangs of youths on small motorcycles, with the silencers taken off so they made more noise, that would come buzzing into

Rocker →

↖ Yammy Fizz

town on a Saturday night, a two-stroke metallic posse, hoping to beat up some some punky New Wave wimps.

For any of the kids our age – in other words still sixteen – their bike of choice was the Yamaha FS1-E, or Yammy Fizz as everyone referred to it. You need to be seventeen to drive a car or ride a motorbike but there existed a piece of legislation from the early 70s that allowed sixteen-year-olds to ride mopeds. What was meant by this, however, was the old-fashioned push-bikes with a small engine attached – MOtor-assisted PEDal-cycles. However Yamaha brought out the FS1-E which was 50cc and could do nearly 50mph. (By the late 70s, however, the loop-hole had been changed so that the bikes could no longer go faster than 30mph.) We liked to laugh at the kids who at sixteen started riding these bikes. After all, they weren't proper motor-bikes, they were mopeds. But with the silencers off they made one hell of a racket around the town, not like the restrained little Puch mopeds the kids rode in France. In actuality, the Fizzy was a small motorbike but it had pushbike pedals added (which were also the footrests) so that it conformed to the law. And, just to make sure, I enquired with my mum as to the possibility of acquiring a Yammy Fizz when I was sixteen. Not to ride with the gang, you understand, but purely as a cheaper alternative to driv-ing a car. After all, the Fizzy did 95mpg. Not to be sniffed at.

Of course, said Mum, we'll buy you one for your sixteenth birthday. And just to make sure you really enjoy the experience, Dad will buy you a top-of-the-range leather jacket so you look really cool.

Thanks, Parallel-Universe-Mum, I said.

(Of course, I was told to think again and never mention it any more. No way would I be riding a motorbike. 'Far too dangerous.')

According to the local vernacular, the sound the bikes made was *ying*.

Onlooker: What's your new motorbike like?

Biker: It's ying, beast.

Onlooker: Really? What does that mean?

Biker: The ying is beast. Got beast ying. Beast.

Some of the lads in our year left us behind and moved onto a higher plane, the Temple of Ying. Not allowed to own a Fizzy, and stuck in the slow lane of cycling or walking, Bandy and I could console ourselves that we'd written 'Ying Down Churchill Avenue', a rock 'n' roll-style song that was a tribute to these high-pitched kings of the road.

34. I Drink, Therefore I Am

I was trying to escape from Market Rasen and, because I couldn't yet escape physically, I had to try other ways. At the age of fourteen, I had discovered that alcohol gave me a ready-made escape pod to a more exciting place in my head.

Reality seemed more vivid when I had had a couple of beers. Alcohol suggested that the hard edges of our concrete world were more fuzzy than they appeared, and I seemed to appreciate nature more when I was drunk and walking back from a pub or a party, taking in everything more intensely. After one event at Tealby Village Hall during the big freeze of 1981, I walked the four miles back to my house in a state of high excitement and awareness, wearing just a T-shirt and jumper, observing the dark hedges, the dark shape of Walesby Wood, a sky of stars, Orion's Belt. Thank God Mum didn't catch me.

Like many teenagers, I felt more outgoing when I had a drink. It seemed as though I was listened to more. Or maybe I didn't care so much. I was certainly funnier, in my own mind at least. Everyone was funny when they had had a drink. More importantly, it was as if I could understand the nature of Lincolnshire when I was drunk. When sober I was an outsider, an interloper. Always observing. When pissed, I didn't feel trapped any more. I belonged.

As under-age drinkers, we would be bought a pint by some kindly soul. We were always careful to put the pint in the middle of the table, at arm's length, and have soft drinks in front of us in case of a visit by the local police. At any given time in any pub there would be at least six or seven fourteen- or fifteen-year-olds. During festive periods I listed, Bridget Jones-style, the drinks I was knocking back and giving myself marks out of ten. Ten being no drink at all and zero being completely rat-arsed.

My parents kept me on a long leash. I think they had resigned themselves to me going off the rails for a bit and hoped it would come far enough away from exams so as not to matter. I would soon discover, however, that I had a desire to test the limits of my drinking endurance and so occasionally my drinking could get out of hand. There was the odd time when I would be so out of it that I could remember nothing the next day – one occasion in Lincoln involved me running into different pubs then escaping out of the toilet windows, chased by my anxious friends.

In Rasen there was a constant shifting of pub fashion. There would always be one that was full of the young crowd and this changed every six months or so.

Key

Was once best pub

Good beer

Hardos

Underage drinkers

Fights likely

Massive rubber johnny machine

Good music

Girls

Farmers

Farmers' daughters

Darts

Grannies

Drunkards

The Red Lion

A top pub for a while, in 1979, and my first drinking venue.
There was a public bar with jukebox and pool table that was
always absolutely rammed with young folk and a smarter saloon
bar with patterned carpet, chairs and tables and nice pictures
on the wall – this was for the older (i.e. over twenty-two)
crowd. The bar was usually filled with a cacophony of noise,
shouts, laughter and music – T-Rex, Sabbath, Motown, punk.
I'll never know how we all managed to fit in. As a novice you
had to be really careful near the bar because if you nudged
anyone's pint then you were for it. Kenny Groswin and Adey

Whitehead ruled the
pool table and the
pool cues were always
getting in the way.
The beer was soapily
foamy and bitter, and
made the top of my
head feel light.

The Chase

With a big plush lounge, plush velveteen seats, plush velveteen
wall and a plush barmaid, everything about The Chase shouted
classy in a classic 70s plush style. In a typical idiotic move of the
time, an ancient fifteenth-century inn had been demolished to
make way for this facsimile of an olde English pub. Dad remembered drinking in the old Grey-
hound with its ancient stone
floors and low ceiling. What I'd
give to have had a beer in there.
What did its modern incarna-
tion have to offer? Well, it had
the most gargantuan condom
machine in the East Midlands

(and I used to wince whenever I looked at the little illustration they had for French Tickler). Still, during its brief heyday at the top in 1980-81, The Chase was the place to be seen.

The King's Head

For a brief period in 1981, the tatty old King's Head, right on the main street. on the eastern edge of the town, suddenly became the trendiest pub in town. Although it had lovely old glass panels, a characterful bar and various little rooms and cubby holes, I think it was the dartboard in the main bar that swung it, darts being a big sport thanks to Jocky Wilson and Eric Bristow. Then, just as mysteriously, everyone moved on. Why, I will never know.

The Gordon Arms

A grand old eighteenth-century hotel near the market place. This was where my gran and her old ladies could be found eating curry on a Friday lunchtime, or having a G&T on Saturday before the races. Market Rasen's racecourse is a pretty little course and used to appear regularly on the ITV Seven so we used to have the bizarre experience of seeing our town on telly. Gran would go to every meeting and drink and smoke to abandon. In The Gordon they were untouchable – cue steely-eyed glares and 'Did you knock over my Dubonet and

THE GORDON ARMS HOTEL

lemonade, sonny?' For a brief period in the early 80s it became the pub to go to, mainly because people loved going in and out of its 1930s-style revolving door when they were drunk.

The Aston Arms

The Aston Arms at the back of the market place was the biggest pub in town and always attracted a serious crowd. It only made it as top pub towards the end of my time in Rasen, but it's kept that crown for a quarter of a century since. This was the place everyone went to on Christmas Eve and New Year's Eve, to see and be seen, and for serious snogging in hidden corners. It was once a series of tiny rooms but in the late 70s was

knocked through into one cavernous space. Circular pool table, loads of beers. Dad used to lodge here in his early twenties and cooked midnight steaks for hungry farmers.

The White Swan

An old-fashioned, no-frills, hard-bitten boozer, the 'Mucky Duck' was never much liked but always the most likely to be half full of sullen hardos. If you wanted a scrap this was the place

to go. We only went along there for our football club nights and even then it was a bit scary. But it's not true that we went to the loo in pairs.

The George

An ancient pub on a side street with an old sign depicting George IV looking like George Lazenby. Where the wild things (young farmers) went. Although it was in the town it felt like it was really in a little village off a quiet farm track. It seemed as though every man had a beard, and every woman had the jolly pink cheeks of a farmer's daughter. The toilets were outside in a cobbled courtyard, which could be a bit sobering in the winter.

35. Saturday Night's Alright for Fighting

There is a clipping on the wall of The Aston Arms about Elton John's 'Saturday Night's Alright For Fighting', which claims that the song was about local boy Bernie Taupin's weekend drinking sessions in the pub when he was a teenager. A photo of The Aston Arms appears on the inner sleeve of Elton John's 1975 album *Captain Fantastic and the Brown Dirt Cowboy*.

> *Well they're packed pretty tight in here tonight*
> *I'm looking for a dolly who'll see me right*
> *I may use a little muscle to get what I need*
> *I may sink a little drink and shout out 'she's with me!'*
>
> *A couple of the sounds that I really like*
> *Are the sounds of a switchblade and a motorbike*
> *I'm a juvenile product of the working class*
> *Whose best friend floats in the bottom of a glass*

In the track, I'm pleased Taupin refers to that most quintessential of Lincolnshire sounds, the motorbike. And he's been quite smart in that he's taken out any reference to Market Rasen or The Aston Arms from his final draft, in order to make it appeal to a wider audience. Maybe that's the mistake some of the local bands made when they decided to write songs about specific individuals (local councillors, teachers, bullies or girls they fancied).

The late 70s and early 80s saw regular violence on the streets of Market Rasen. It felt a bit like a mini-Dark Ages at that time, with various marauding groups intent on doing physical damage to the indigenous population. Often the cause was the inter-town rivalry and long-simmering vendettas between Market Rasen and its nearest rival, Caistor, nearly ten miles away.

Caistor was always the rival town. Starting life as a Roman settlement, at that time the most Market Rasen had been was a tile-making settlement, an imbalance that caused underlying tensions to the present day. Caistor was neater – it often won the Tidy (Yet Boring) Lincolnshire Town title – and it was regarded as being prettier. It also claimed to have a better school because they still had a 'grammar'. But when it came to fighting, we had Waterman.

Why was Waterman the toughest bloke of Market Rasen? It was all done on reputation. Waterman wasn't that big, but he must have done something to make us all scared of him. In a small town, reputation is all. If you can convince enough people that you are incredibly tough and hard then, that's it, you are made. No-one is likely to take you on. However, just as in feudal societies, the knights were called upon to defend the lord's lands, so Waterman would now and then be wheeled out to fight for the town's honour against the hard-nuts from another town.

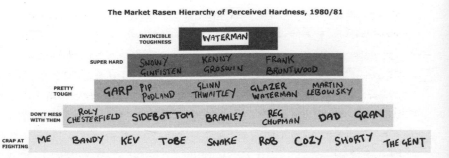

The Market Rasen Hierarchy of Perceived Hardness, 1980/81

Waterman was a local hard-case, a spotty bowl-cut late 70s East Midlands version of the mythical warrior Cuchulain. If there was trouble in the town with the Caistor crew, the cry would go up, 'Send for Waterman!' He had to be roused from his usual spot, propping up the bar at The Red Lion – Achilles in his tent. Sometimes he would ignore the call and carry on drinking and putting Rod Stewart songs on the jukebox. But if he did show, you could guarantee he would batter those Caistor hard-nuts back to their attractive market town, then be

carried shoulder high back to The Red Lion as the people of Market Rasen sang in unison some kind of Lionel Bart big vocal/dance number about provincial violence.

Part of me wondered how there could be hope for the world when working-class teenagers, rather than seeing what they had in common, decide to knock seven bells of shit out of each other for recreation just because they were from a different town. (The other part of me thought, Scrap!! Go on, Waterman!)

Whenever we played Caistor at any kind of sport, they usually won. They had some amazing cricketers over the years and some pretty good footballers too. (See the way I've written the preceding sentences, there's a bit of needle there, a bit of envy. It's that kind of attitude that, blown up and carried on over, what, centuries, produces vendettas of Mafia-like proportions.)

Largely it was to do with that scourge of bored teenage boys – face. If you're in your late teens, what are you supposed to do when your status is threatened? In a small town you have to fight for your honour.

Love triangles cannot happen in a small town without fisticuffs taking place. In 1981 someone I knew was attacked at a party at The Red Lion after going outside and snogging someone he shouldn't have snogged. He was seen and a group followed him:

Are you snogging Paula?

Yeah, I'm snogging Paula.

You can't snog Paula, I snog Paula.

Fig. 1

Well, I'm snogging Paula.

You'd think this kind of incident was so commonplace that everyone would have forgotten it by Monday morning, but because it appeared on the front page of the local paper ('Snog Fight In The Red Lion Car Park'), everyone then knows about it until the end of time.

A more typical Rasen-Caistor turf war would be one that took place along more subtle lines (but with a less subtle outcome): for example, the desired volume of a television set in a local public hostelry. So, some Rasen lads would be sitting in a pub and minding their own business (perhaps one or two of the party might have been sporting ostentatiously bushy moustaches which can upset the easily provoked, but that would have been no different from any small provincial town in the early 80s). They would simply be playing pool and watching *Match of the Day* on the telly. Some lads from Caistor might come in and after a bit of general 'rowdiness', one of the new crowd might turn the sound down. Silencing Jimmy Hill and his mates? Oh dear. A Rasen lad, let's call him Gaz, would then walk over to the TV and turn the sound back up. So a Caistor lad would then turn the sound down. This would go on like a strange dance for a while until Gaz snaps and, of course, a pool cue is acquired for non-pool-playing purposes.

When it came to fighting I wasn't that enthused. Fighting was for losers. As punky New Wavers we were not supposed to fight, though I'd heard stories of punks getting beaten up by people who were scared of change or who just hated anyone who looked different. Perhaps the same would happen to me and Bandy. Then I had to remind myself that we didn't actually look anything like punks. In my imagination of that time, I look like Paul Simeon of The Clash. But the reality was that even when I was posing with the guitar, I still looked like a skinny blond schoolboy with a crap haircut in a donkey jacket.

Nat Fleischer's *Illustrated History of Boxing*

While the threat of violence was a constant, I never actually got hit during my time in Rasen (that all came later). Although I wasn't very tough at school I always felt confident because I was the only kid in the neighbourhood with a copy of Nat Fleischer's *Illustrated History of Boxing*. It was a massive hardback volume with a bright yellow cover. You could knock somebody out in seconds with that book. Consequently I learned a few things about boxing, such as the classic Marquis of Queensberry stance that suggested you knew how to handle yourself. But also made you look like a bit of a knob.

Although it seemed that the technical boxers were usually the most successful, I always liked the more flamboyant, emotional street fighters.

One of my favourites was Harry Greb, a great middleweight from the inter-war years. He ended up blind in one eye and half blind in the other and died from complications related to his detached retina problem while having another eye operation.

But, deep down, I hated fighting and thought about the possibility of becoming a pacifist which, in my idealised view, meant that people would generally leave you alone. But my disinclination to fight made me question how I might have fared in any kind of war situation. Why were some people good at fighting and others really crap? Jeremy Paxman once famously remarked how he felt bad, or even guilty, that he hadn't experienced a war situation. Blimey, I'm fucking delighted!

I talked to my friend Kev about all this. Kev was a real punk. He walked the walk. In other words, someone who didn't know him would presume he was a punk. He had the mad clothes, the earrings, the hair dyed vegetable-water green. Kev was a real pacifist. This meant that if

Fig. 2

he was attacked he tended to roll up in a ball like a hedgehog and take the beating. He never fought back. I remember once him talking about how hard it was not hitting someone who was intent on kicking the shit out of him. But it posed another dilemma. If Kev's friends saw him being attacked, what should we do? If we fought off his attackers, would his rescue be tainted by the fact that we hadn't done it in a pacifist way? About a year later there was an incident at a party a few miles away in a little village hall where we knew that some of the local rocker bullies were after Kev. It concerned me, but not as much as cavorting about like a donkey-jacketed Lord Byron trying to impress some unattainable girl. So I partied hard, like most teenagers, and ended up oblivious to the macabre dance that was going on between Kev and his attacker. Kev got a shellacking on the dancefloor, kicked in the head and ribs. He got his revenge in a different way, though, in the time-honoured fashion of the court and the local paper. Kev pressed charges and King Rocker was found guilty, even though he had the temerity to say to the court that he would never kick a man when he's down: 'That's the lowest of the low.' Ha ha, good one.

Just as the threat from the 1979 era of mods and disco psychos from Cleethorpes, Lincoln and Caistor began to fade away, so peace-loving punky New Wave teenagers like me faced a new threat, this time closer to home. Older Blokes Tanked Up On Snakebite. These older blokes, some with cars and some without, were lower down the food chain than the Older Blokes With Cars and were paranoid that you might be staring at their girlfriend. Or staring at a girlfriend they would like to have. Or sometimes simply just staring.

By the early 80s in Market Rasen, even though the local comprehensive school had been in existence for six or seven years, there was a cultural antagonism from the old days of grammar and secondary modern schools. So stuff went on at school that might carry on in the town at the weekend, involving brainy kids who hated fighting versus not so brainy kids who liked fighting. It was stories straight out of Dennis the Menace and The Bash Street Kids.

While not exactly Cambridge University material, Bandy and I were firmly in the swots camp. To celebrate the bonehead culture of the town, Heart Attack brought out an album called *Local Hards*, with songs about most of the town's teenage hardcases. Adey Whitehead, Mike Mangle, Pip Podland, Kenny Groswin and Martin Lebowsky all had songs about them. OK, when I say 'brought out an album', I mean thought up some funny song titles and that was about it. It was a concept album, a musical version of the *Hardo Mag* of a couple of years earlier. We butchered an old LP cover (*Fantastic Original Hits* by T- Rex/Procol Harum/Move/Joe Cocker) – I did the main artwork and Bandy did the inner sleeve pictures. It was hilarious, a work of genius, and of course could never be shown to the hardos or we'd be beaten to a pulp.

Rob came round one day and saw the album and thought it was dead funny. Could he borrow it? I said yes, but he was under strict instructions not to show it to anyone else. Then a week or so later Rob informed me that somehow the contents of the album had been sort-of-accidentally reported to Kenny Groswin and Mike Mangle. Kenny Groswin tracked Bandy down at a barn dance and put out the message that he was for it. Keen to avoid any conflict (involving me), I advised Bandy to go home. 'Hang on a minute,' said an aggrieved Bandy, hoping for some solidarity, 'you drew that sleeve too!' It was a good point, and might have stood up in a court of law, though he was overlooking the realpolitik of pre-fight face-offs. Anyway, Bandy refused to go home, incredulous at the injustice of it all, and nothing happened. Word came at some point late in the evening that Kenny Groswin was going to let Bandy off. Bandy, unbowed, said, 'Wow, what a generous favour, I'm so blessed.' By the end of the night Kenny was far too busy being a local hard-case to remember what the album was about or who we were. It helped to be invisible sometimes.

The Radio Keeps Churning Out the Hits: 1981

The Jacksons 'Can You Feel It'

Talking Heads 'Once In A Lifetime'

Imagination 'Body Talk'

Kraftwerk 'The Model'

The Specials 'Ghost Town'

Odyssey 'Going Back To My Roots'

Japan 'Quiet Life'

Human League 'Don't You Want Me'

Scritti Politti 'The Sweetest Girl'

Spandau Ballet 'Chant No. 1 (I Don't Need This Pressure On)'

Tom Tom Club 'Wordy Rappinghood'

36. The Rise of Synth Pop

While I was concentrating on my small world of records and girls, there was change in the air. The post-punk musical landscape that had been dominated by Gang of Four and Joy Division was now shifting with the upsurge of synthesiser pop bands. Whereas punk had taken over two years to reach the outer fringes of Lincolnshire, the latest wave – New Romantics, futurists, posers, call it what you will – had taken a mere twelve months (I suppose that's because this latest craze travelled using futuristic technology or something). Yet the members of Spandau Ballet looked like Rupert Brooke wearing old carpet offcuts on a shooting weekend in the Highlands. Steve Strange looked like a depressed clown. Ultravox looked like depressed bank clerks. It wasn't an inspiring movement, except for the fact that they weren't quite as old as the punks.

And a few months earlier we'd had the surprising arrival of Ant Music. How did the arrival of Ant Music affect the citizens of Market Rasen? Where once we had been content to live out our disco existence in small polarised groups, this new music would cause problems for the various factions. This was, after all, pop music and therefore met with the approval of many of the girls. Yet as nerdy New Wavers, we knew that the origin of Adam and the

Ants lay in punk music, so could happily dance to this knowing that we had not transgressed some secret code. Even the rockers were confused. The double drum rhythm section of the Ants reminded them of classic rock drumming of Cozy Powell or Ian Paice. And although the guitar sounds were too far down in the mix for many of the denim brigade to be able to relax fully on the dance floor, it certainly created confusion.

I didn't know any true Ant People. For a start, the look was very expensive to put together. Obviously you would have to scour charity shops to piece together the eclectic bandsman/highwayman/pirate chic look. Our Oxfam was stuffed to the gills with the suits of dead grandads. If one were to put together an Ant look from the contents of Market Rasen's Oxfam, one would look more like a drunken pensioner at a 1960s funeral.

And as pop music pulled away from punk it became less macho. I stopped wearing my donkey jacket and DMs, which in a way had always signified that I was up for a ruck – or at least willing to work on the docks or the roads – and started wearing Grandad's old trousers, Dad's old trenchcoat, old grandad shirts, Dad's old brogues. It was, according to Kev, the 'twat look'. As we got bigger and a bit more confident socially, we began to be aware of the dichotomy between more orthodox macho stuff versus stuff that girls will like – the desire to look good against the desire to not get beaten up.

After the end of 1981 I spent more and more time either playing synths or bass in other people's bands. The track that really got me into electronic music was Cabaret Voltaire's *The Voice of America* that Scooter had taped for me. It sounded like the drum machine from a home organ rewired through the gearbox of an Austin 1800. And the lyrics were well catchy.

Northern electronic music seemed like the perfect soundtrack to the rural suburbs. Yes, I know I said that about punk music, too.

*

Back in the late 70s my brother Tobe, anxious to replicate my LP-and-single-gathering trip to Auntie Hazel's house in 1977, got himself a visit. This was when Hazel and her family ran a bakery and, after two weeks, Tobe returned with an extra coating of lard, particularly under his chin. Dad and I responded in the only way we knew how, by taking the mickey out of his new-found chubbiness. He was re-christened Wattle Man. Strangely his bulk gave him extra gravitas, and around the summer of 1981, when Bandy, Tobe and I started a new music club in the town, we called it The Wattle Club in his honour. Well, when I say 'in the town', it was actually at our house. But it *was* a music venue. We planned to put on a variety of local acts, as long as they were still schoolkids – no old duffers were allowed. The trouble was we needed new gear. My little 5v practise amp was too small.

Later that summer I acquired some new equipment. Scooter had sold me his old RSC Bass Major valve amplifier, which looked like it had come over with Bill Haley and the Comets in the mid 50s (and had been second- or third-hand even then). It had originally belonged to Warlock, one of the area's older prog-rock bands. Bandy and I gazed on the amp like it was some precious booty from an ancient Egyptian tomb. A little square box with some old dials and a rocker switch, connected to a three-and-a-half-foot tall, ten-inch-wide speaker stack. It had a bright sparkly sound and no poncey effects features. For the first time I could hear the notes I was playing on the guitar. Almost from day one my playing style changed. I began to pick out the notes, find tunes where before I had, out of lack of confidence, just thrashed all the chords. The amp was the symbol of the end of punk for Bandy and me. It had worked for Scooter's band, worked for Warlock, even (maybe) worked for Bill Haley and the Comets and now it would work for us. Bandy said he could remember as a small child listening to Warlock practise a few doors down from where he used to live and the amp took on an almost mythic feel for him, a reconnection to young childhood dreams and happy days.

With all my cash gone on the old amp and my vinyl addiction, it wasn't possible for me to buy all the musical equipment I needed. Luckily I had friends and family to do that. Bandy bought a nice and crystal-clear Casio MT-45 keyboard, which was like a futuristic version of the old organ they'd had in the dining room. Then I discovered that Tobe had somehow managed to amass a hefty £150 in savings, which he'd been accumulating for many years while I had been spending my cash on plastic dinosaurs, Action Man outfits, Monty Python books and Clash albums. Tobe planned to spend his money on a new musical instrument. He was already becoming a really good guitarist and with that amount of money he could buy a nice second-hand Gibson or Fender, or even a saxophone, which is what he really wanted. Once again we went to the big music shop in Bingley, near where my grandparents lived, and somehow I persuaded him to buy a Korg MS-10 synthesiser. It was a great, rather Germanic-looking monophonic (as in you can only play one note at a time) keyboard with two and a half octaves plus loads of dials, switches and input plugs. It was the kind of late-70s synth used by Tangerine Dream, Brian Eno, Robert Fripp. It was just what I needed in my bid to become musical supremo and soundtracker of the East Midlands rural townships.

So Tobe came home with his Korg MS-10 and it didn't really occur to me that he might not have been delighted with this purchase. He probably got in the door and thought to himself, Fuck it, what have I done? In recent years he's indicated to me that he didn't really want a Korg MS-10 and really it was me that bought it, using his money. How was this allowed to happen? I feel bad now, but at the time it was fantastic and I knew recording sessions would never be the same again. And at least Tobe had managed to buy his way into our band (of

Korg MS-10

course, he was a much better musician than either me or Bandy). For instance, there's really only one way of making the sound of wind and that's with a Korg MS-10. In fact, if you recorded the sound of real wind and played it, after listening to the wind sound of the Korg MS-10 you would think that the Korg sound was the real thing. But this fantastic old synthesiser is not just for making wind-type effects (even though, as I've already stated, it's fantastic at that). It's also great for doing a handclap sound if you can't get hold of enough people in the studio to make good syncopated 'real' handclaps. But there's even more to it than that, of course. I mean, your brother wouldn't spend £150 on a synth, at your behest, simply to make wind and handclap noises. You may need to replicate the sound of a jet engine taking off but you're miles from the nearest airport. No worries, the Korg MS-10 can do that too. And if someone knocks on your door and says, glumly, 'Shite, I need to get a bass synth sound just like Deutsch-Amerikanische Freundschaft used. Any ideas?' you simply smile and hand them your Korg MS-10. Just for a lend, of course.

On the same tape as *The Voice of America* Scooter had put four or five tracks from his band Easy Listening. It was synth pop with lots of echo on the vocals. How did they do that? Did they record in their downstairs loo? Incredibly, it was obvious that Easy Listening practised each song before they recorded it, which seemed like cheating. I'm not proud to say I was equally impressed and sick with jealousy at the quality of the tape. Easy Listening seemed to be way ahead of us. I consoled myself with the fact that Scooter and keyboard player Francis Finn were a couple of years older and that they had better equipment. And were better organised. The thing I refused to admit to myself was that they were better musicians. But they were. Scooter could play the guitar better than me. Francis could play the piano better than me. Scooter could sing better than Bandy.

Interestingly, Bandy appeared unimpressed by Easy Listening and not the slightest bit alarmed by the possibility that he and I might not be in The Best Band In Market Rasen. Scooter, though, seemed to have a real world view when it came to his band. He'd called it Easy Listening so 'in a record shop we'd have our own section'. I thought this was a brilliant idea. Bandy scowled. Heart Attack – a name that smacked of a *Not the Nine O'Clock News*-style parody – had shifted with the times and we now had a new, even crappier name – Boys At Their Worst, a rather lame play on Girls At Our Best, a short-lived girl indie-pop group, dooming us to continued comedy-band status. We didn't take ourselves seriously enough, that was the problem. Or rather we wished we could take ourselves seriously but appearing a bit daft was a good insurance against us possibly being really shite. Whereas Easy Listening sang about mortality, depression, love, alienation and the pressures of adolescence, Heart Attack/Boys At Their Worst wrote songs about fourth-year girls we fancied, large-breasted home economics teachers with nuclear bunkers, cricket matches, fag-smoking hardos and running in 100m races to impress the chicks.

In the winter of 1981 Easy Listening played a gig at Tealby Memorial Hall. As usual we had our bottles of cider chilling in the beck. Scooter was out front in his white shirt and suit trousers, exuberant and charismatic, while Francis was at the back looking serious and muso-like, as was the style at that time. In my memory there was dry ice and a light show but I think

I'm mixing it up with a proper gig. As usual with a Lincolnshire audience there was polite applause mixed with a somewhat mocking attitude (and Bandy scowling, of course); the terror that other people had got up to do something different. At times there was laughter when Scooter did a little dance. I think I was a bit fanboyish and danced around at the front singing along to some of the lyrics. As far as Bandy was concerned, it was as if we were a couple and I was flirting with another girl right in front of him.

I think it was that night that Scooter asked if I'd like to audition for their band. They needed a guitarist because he didn't want to play guitar any more, he said. I tried to play it cool though I'm sure inside I was jumping up and down and clapping my hands like a little kid. I went for an audition on a Sunday morning at Middle Rasen Village Hall (I probably phoned Bandy and said, 'I'm just going out for a pint of milk'). Kids were playing on the swings outside and there was a football match going on at the far end of the field. It was a bitter, damp day. Scooter and Francis were already there, surrounded by lots of amps, wires, effects, boxes, etc. I was excited at the dreamlike nature of this encounter. I took my guitar out of its case. Actually, I couldn't have done, because it never had a case. I must have just walked through Middle Rasen with it slung over my shoulder. The Les Paul seemed a bit out of place and hard-rockish all of a sudden.

They played some of their songs and I tried to strum along in my cack-handed, Andy Gill-funk-style mixed with Chic and a bit of Haircut 100 thrown in. I had a serious expression on my face, like I was really concentrating. Because I was really concentrating, probably as hard as I'd ever done in my life. I wanted so much to be in that band. I tried like hell to make my rubbish farmer's fingers do what they were told.

It didn't go very well but they seemed reasonably happy. Scooter was a natural polemic lyricist and their songs had catchy

tunes. I felt a bit of a fraud with my limited playing. In later years I could never really understand why I kept being asked to play in bands by everybody when I was really such a limited musician.

'What's that?' I asked, pointing to a black box that looked like the supercomputers on old *Dr Who* episodes.

'It's a WEM Copicat,' said Scooter. 'An echo box. Listen.'

He plugged a guitar in and played a chord, then pressed a couple of the rocker switches. Weam wam wam wam wam wam wam. 'Whoa. Bloody hell!' The sound reverberated through the little hall, then out of an open window and down through the village towards Lincoln, where it dissipated in a large treeless field. At the time this was one of the most amazing pieces of equipment I'd ever encountered. A group of tape heads with a great big circle of tape looping round and round. Three buttons selected the type of sustain (halo, repeat, echo). We could now replicate the experience of a really bad magic mushroom trip, without having to ingest anything more dangerous than Cup-a-Soups.

But I was in Easy Listening. Every Sunday afternoon, after playing rugby in the morning, I'd troop down to Middle Rasen to practise with the band. I didn't get to write much new material, but I did get to play some keyboards as well (yes, second keyboardist if you must know). And still my sessions with Bandy had to be squeezed in somehow. We often had to practise in the evenings after school. This development did not go down well with Bandy, who began to systematically take the piss out of Easy Listening for being rubbish and unlistenable. To smooth this hiatus, we followed good business practice and rebranded ourselves. Boys At Their Worst became the Brezhnev Brothers. And Bandy and I started to write new material, in preparation for the opening of The Wattle Club. The idea was that to publicise it, we would record a cassette of different local bands (most of which I appeared in).

The opening of The Wattle Club was a momentous occasion, with the Brezhnev Brothers (me, Bandy, Tobe), Gang of Rob, The Disturbed (Kev's new punk band), the Sean Nevis Band and local punk poet DJ Adams all playing a small set. The audience was made up mainly of people in bands and, in true Market Rasen style, everyone slagged everyone else's group off. Gang of Rob thought we were futurist rubbish. We thought Gang of Rob were derivative shite. Everyone loved DJ Adams (apart from Rob). Maggie Jefferson came too, with her dad, and entered into the spirit of the event by loudly voicing her opinions as to the musical quality. It was like *The X-Factor*, except more cruel.

The legendary Wattle compilation cassette would a couple of years later fall into the hands of Snake who, for some unfathomable reason, taped over it with a recording of Michael Jackson's *Thriller*. I suppose in a way he could say he was still supporting the local music scene – after all, *Thriller*'s title track was written by Rod Temperton.

37. Girls Girls Girls (Girls) 5: Lincolnshire Love Rectangle

Everyone who was there will say that the most exciting time of their life was the winter of 1981, the end of the first term in the lower sixth form. This was a relaxing time of no uniform and little responsibility, with 'A' levels a year and a half away. We had a whole twelve months to try on our new roles before the dreaded final year of revision and then departures – of which I dreamed often and told anyone who'd listen that I couldn't wait, though in my heart I wasn't so sure.

For a lazy shite, I had done OK in my 'O' levels – A in art, English language, B in history, passed most of the others, even the sciences and maths. The big disappointment was geography, where I'd been top in the mocks, but had done disastrously in the exam. I wondered if it might have been due to the game that Bandy and I played while sitting at the back of the class – writing down any song lyrics that came up in the speech of the teacher Mr Wulfsten, such as, 'Let's look at the geology of the Rhone Valley' ('Into The Valley'), 'The mistral is formed by the difference in high and low pressure areas' ('Under Pressure') and drawing little goofy-toothed faces next to each one. In the exam all I could do was scan the questions looking for song titles like a brainwashed lab rat. Mum couldn't understand how I'd failed. I feigned surprise. Gratifyingly, Bandy failed too.

I'd also failed French, which I couldn't quite believe as I'd just had a summer of great drunken conversations with various members of Alain's extended family, about politics (les politiques), rugby (le rugby) and pop music (le pop musique). For God's sake, I'd even fallen in love in French a few years back – what more could they want? Sadly, 'O' level was more than just trying to charm the oral examiner into going out for a beer with you. You had to know verbs, vocabulary and grammar too, stuff I had no interest in whatsoever. I was a red wine, parrot linguist. It was surely more important to be able to communicate with people from that country than analyse how their sentences were structured, I argued (usually to my mum who was, naturally, sympathetic).

Loads of new students had started in the lower sixth in September, kids from other comprehensives around Lincoln that didn't have sixth forms. Most intriguingly there were some good-

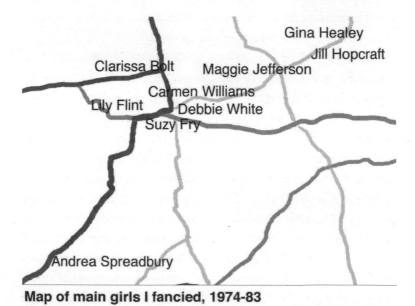

Map of main girls I fancied, 1974-83

looking girls – Andrea Spreadbury, Tracey Duckham, Lizzie Miles. Annoyingly there were also mirrors of our gang, like kids from a parallel universe. My twin was called Patrick Redman, except he was blonder, cooler and trendier that me. It was quite disconcerting at first, but we all got used to it. There were even a couple of bands, the Sean Nevis Band and Marquee.

I was nearly seventeen and waiting for the right Lincolnshire Girl to come along. My friends and I were faced with a dilemma. The things that had seemed cool to girls when I was fourteen – being in a band, being a bit of an idiot, being mad and creative – now seemed uncool. Now we were in the sixth form, the girls all seemed to be going for the reliable jock sportsman type, as if they were pre-programmed for a life of early suburban marriage.

By now everybody was in love with someone, but usually that someone was in love with someone else (who in turn was in love with someone else). Very much like a Dostoyevsky novel, though at that time I would know it more as very much like Woody Allen's *Love and Death* (which did actually reference great Russian literature but seeing as I hadn't read any I didn't realise this at the time).

Here is a brief précis of events. Shorty Blackwell was in love with Jill Hopcraft, who I think fancied Hinesy. Hinesy fancied both Brenda Beamish and Siân Cobner but they were going out with other lads, though Siân fancied Tobe. Tobe always played his cards close to his chest so who knew what he was up to. I can't remember who Sidebottom or The Gent fancied but they weren't having much success. Kev's forays into sartorial experiment were beginning to pay off and he started to attract girls who liked the bohemian look. However, Kev was really into one of the new girls, Tracey Duckham, but hadn't actually spoken to her yet and she didn't know he existed.

Bandy, after a long time being smitten with Edwina Flint, a striking redhead who lived just down the road, was now in love with a girl who lived a few doors up from him. Martina Jeavons was like a young Geraldine James; aristocratic bearing, big shoulders, built like a javelin thrower. Sadly for Bandy, she fancied me. I had absolutely no interest in Martina Jeavons, and anyway I was playing by the unofficial Beatles Rule. The Beatles Rule is based on the fact that, apparently, The Beatles never moved in on each other's girlfriends. They also never tried it on with women that the others had broken up with. Ethics, honour and the strength of the collective and all that – a strangely old-fashioned, un-60s attitude. Actually, the Beatles Rule worked because The Beatles were so different that they were genuinely attracted by different kinds of women. We were all a bit like that. Most of the time...

At discos, we all sort of forgot about any kind of Beatles Rule, though. Discos were a free-for-all environment where all of us went out on our own, thinking only of our own self-interest. It was survival of the fittest.

I had struck lucky by finally (and all too briefly) getting to go out with Carmen Williams, after fancying her for ages. Carmen was like an unearthly pale-skinned, black-haired, blue-eyed beauty from a 1940s Irish butter advert. Everybody wanted her (whatever 'want' means when you're sixteen – a mixture of reality-based snoggy fumbles and fantasy moments involving amazing rough and tumble in sophisticated James Bond-like locations). I most definitely had her on my pencil case for what seemed like ages, the word Carmen written in blue biro, partly obscured by other profound sayings such as Fire Engines Rule OK, and Tories Out! (until Bandy discovered it one day in the cloakrooms and told everyone, as was the norm as far as 'fancying people' went: you were a wuss if you didn't laugh and tell everyone).

Carmen and I definitely went steady for about two or three weeks. Usually this involved us walking hand in hand in the dark over the top field on Mount Pleasant towards her house, having a quick snog then me scarpering in case her dad was watching using some kind of SAS-style infrared night goggles.

It seemed to me that Carmen, a year younger, preferred older boys. On the plus side, I was an older boy as far as Carmen was concerned. On the minus side, her dad had an axe (she said) and was prepared to use it. Carmen had been at my sixteenth birthday party and I had somehow managed to wangle my way upstairs with her, ostensibly to show her some old family photographs or something. I was on the verge of

Carmen's boyfriends

planning a route towards her bra when suddenly the image of her father sharpening his axe (while wearing his infrared night goggles, like Dennis Hopper in *Blue Velvet*) struck me, and in my moment of hesitation Carmen had wriggled away downstairs.

You never really knew where you stood with Carmen, which to a sixteen-year-old boy was a huge attraction. Carmen once travelled with us on the coach to watch our youth football team, Rasen Wanderers, play a match on the other side of Lincoln. On the way there she was a hundred per cent going out with me, as much as Carmen ever 'went out' with anyone, but whatever happened at the game (it's quite likely she watched me playing and decided that she shouldn't be seen with this hard-working, slightly dirty and limited right-back), on the way back I had a feeling she was probably going out with Hinesy. I think I was in such a state of shock at this news that I acted as if nothing untoward had happened. Maybe I would have done the same thing in his shoes. Maybe not. Remember, she looked like an unearthly country beauty from a 1940s Irish butter advert.

Hinesy wasn't deeply committed to Carmen like I was – he was interested mainly because he could get her, and so did. It never lasted long, though. Carmen was curious then would lose interest and Hinesy would go back to what he was doing before – pining for Brenda Beamish. Then out of the blue Hinesy started going out with Brenda and we were all dumbfounded. How did he do it? She was in the upper sixth! My theory was that the sporty Brenda was into Hinesy because Hinesy had recently run 11.1 seconds for the 100m and his status had sky-rocketed. Hinesy's sprinting technique was to imagine The Jam were playing live and there was only one ticket left. It was a cause for celebration for this was the first time someone in our gang had broken through the Older Girl glass ceiling. It was short-lived, and not long afterwards Hinesy was going out with a girl in the year below us.

At some point in the autumn term of 1981, I got off with Maggie Jefferson again at a party. In the last year Maggie had really come out of her shell, which is a euphemism for she had loads of lads chasing after her. She'd gone from being still quite a young kid with daft Deirdre Barlow specs to a real beauty, like a dark-haired version of Debbie Harry, I thought. Afterwards I became so confused at this turn of events that I proceeded to virtually ignore her for a few weeks. Maggie wasn't impressed.

Then things went off at a tangent for a while. It was in art lesson one day, while I was doing an illustration for a piece of text from *The Grapes of Wrath*, that Hinesy, who was scribbling away beside me, whispered, 'You know that Andrea Spread-bury? She really fancies you.' Then he got back to drawing as if nothing had happened. I wasn't interested. I was interested in Maggie. So why suddenly was my stomach churning and I was coming out in a cold sweat?

Andrea Spreadbury was the best-looking girl of the new crowd who'd come that September. I'd seen her around – in fact I saw her most mornings – but hadn't ever really spoken to her. I always thought she was out of my league. But after Hinesy's intervention, in early December I did ask her out and, for the first time ever, barring a disaster, it looked like I would have a girlfriend for Christmas.

38. Here in My Car

Motorbikes are cool. Cars are cool.

The shift from sixteen to seventeen marks the end of an era in terms of being a kid. At sixteen you regard yourself, and are still regarded by others, as an adolescent with adolescent motivations and needs. Once you become seventeen everything changes: the way you see your universe, your past and the future. You become aware that you are on the verge of adulthood and that very soon your life will change for ever. You perceive the melancholy of that existential moment when suddenly you can look both ways in time and understand the fragile nature of reality.

OK. Let's just be honest about it – at seventeen you're allowed to drive a car. You can get into a four-wheeled metal vehicle, put your hand on the steering wheel and drive really fast while shouting, 'Wahhaaaayyyyy!!!'

I'd always presumed that I'd want to drive a car and had loved cars from the moment I was conscious. During motorway trips I used to name the different models and makes of cars to my mum, who was no doubt looking forward to the time in the future that I'd appear on *University Challenge*.

Bamber Gascoigne: And here's a starter for ten... a picture of a car... what is it? Bradford, University of Finsbury Park.

Bradford, University of Finsbury Park: A Ford Anglia.

Bamber Gascoigne: Correct.

Cars meant sex, at least in films. And if you were good at driving you must be good at sex. I thought driving must be a piece of piss but I didn't really fancy it yet. After getting gently dumped by Andrea Spreadbury just a few weeks into our passionate affair, I decided that I couldn't be bothered to make the effort to be a four-wheeled Casanova. I made the decision on my seventeenth birthday at the start of 1982 to forego the driving lessons offered by my parents and instead take the money to upgrade my musical equipment.

I was still using the early 50s radiogram but I was starting to get worried that the ancient stylus was having a bad effect on my beloved albums. Whereas mates such as Sidebottom, Tony Hopkins and Chris Hines were taking driving lessons and starting to talk about Escorts, Cortinas and Vivas, I was off down to Rhodes' Electrical Shop to buy a Sony amplifier, turntable and speakers.

Maggie was going out with Gary Haddock, an Older Bloke With A Car. He had a Triumph TR7. I had a second-hand three-gear racer with no mudguards. I pretended not to care about what Maggie got up to but it ate me up inside. Gary was four years older than her and I found

Public transport is for losers!

myself becoming morally indignant about this, rather like an angry *Daily Mail* reader. I tried not to imagine what they got up to in his car. All I could offer her was a lift on the front of my pushbike.

I'd laugh at Gary Haddock and crack the usual comment that his sports car was just overcompensation for a small penis, yet sadly no-one would have said of a seventeen-year-old with a second-hand, three-gear racer with no mudguards:, 'Wow, he must have a massive willy,' due to undercompensating.

At the end of the spring term of '82 Hinesy hit us with a bombshell. This kid who was once a drummer and bassist in a punk band (admittedly short-lived), was giving up everything – including his 'A' levels – to go and work in a bank for £50 a week. Now, £50 a week was not to be sniffed at. Fifty quid a week was a massive amount of money. In a month you'd have enough to buy a second-hand Fender guitar and get a few new albums as well. But the question was, would it be enough to keep his new girlfriend happy? We knew he was under pressure to be a proper town boyfriend instead of a schoolkid boyfriend, though the pressure was probably in his own head because loads of Older Blokes With Cars fancied her. The rest of us were pretty merciless in our analysis of the situation. 'Next stop Bognor Regis then, Chris!' I said, Bognor Regis obviously representing in my mind the place where all the boring people ended up. In my diary that night I drew a picture of him in a new pinstripe suit, clutching a briefcase. And it dawned on me that, all of a sudden, he looked grown up, at least compared to the rest of us. He would be driving a car, going out with a girl when sober, talking to members of the public without putting on a silly voice or calling them a fascist bastard. Taking home fifty pounds every week. £10 a day. Phew. But on the other hand, no longer would he be creating made-up albums in art lessons, running 11.1 seconds for the 100m in PE or whacking in goals for the school team. He'd be sorting out your current account and sending you a new cheque book.

So what if Chris was giving up all his dreams just to keep some woman happy? We wished him well and in our quieter moments it made us think about the point of any of our school-work. If any of us fell in love with a woman – properly fell in love – we might well be prepared to jack in European history 1630 to 1745.

At the back of my mind was the question, 'Is this what it's all about?' For, unlike me, Chris had questioned his destiny and changed course. Whatever happened to him, it would be different from the future envisaged by his parents, his teachers and his friends. But it made me wonder what it was all for, this onward quest for success and learning. Was it all, perhaps, just to make people love you? For me, all this love, adoration and providing-for was way off in the future, at some unspecified time when

I'd have a job and a girlfriend. At the moment it didn't seem as if I'd ever have a long-term girlfriend, apart from the odd drunken fumble at a party. I looked around and saw people starting to pair off. What did they have that I didn't, those lads who suddenly were driving around with a girl sitting in their passenger seat?

I wanted a girlfriend. But then I didn't want a girlfriend. I wanted someone to love me, to snog me and let me shag them but I suppose I didn't want the hassle of hanging around outside clothes shops in Lincoln on a Saturday, having to buy birthday and Valentines gifts and, of course, having to do that daily walk on Top Field.

39. Grandad Sits On My Shoulder and We Discuss the Falklands War

Although at aged seventeen I usually only really noticed what was right in front of me, the real world hoved into view in 1982 and knocked me from my solipsistic slumbers. This was that dreamlike moment when the UK went to war over the Falkland Isles. I was anti-imperialist and hated Thatcher and it all seemed to me like a nineteenth-century conflict transferred to the present day. The fact that we had to send our task force halfway across the world to defend 'our territory' said it all as far as I was concerned. My cartoons from my 1982 diary show upper-class colonels and posh types revelling in war, while the rank and file soldier is, as usual, the one in the firing line. I hated the war and hated the thought of Argentinian conscript kids – teenage kids like me and Bandy, Kev, Hinesy, Sidebottom, Tobe – kids who were cold and frightened out of their wits, about to face hardened British paras.

And yet when they showed the task force sailing across the Atlantic, something stirred in me. The eager eight-year-old model-building boy in me felt proud, but I killed that feeling straightaway. I didn't want to feel proud. That boy, with a knowledge of ships and gun sizes and naval history and regiment names, would have loved something like this (eight or ten years earlier). I'd already forgotten that kid; he'd got left behind in the rush to be cool and rebellious. He'd want to find out all about the techie side of war, the machinery: the exact trajectory of an Exocet missile, the size of the shells fired from British destroyers, the top speed of a Harrier Jump Jet.

As well as recognising the silhouettes of battle cruisers, another thing eight-year-olds are better at than seventeen-year- olds is appreciating and spending time with their family. That spring my beloved Yorkshire grandad died suddenly and I wondered why I hadn't been sitting with him every day for the last few years, soaking up his wisdom and listening to his stories. I had been so busy doing – what? – and now he was gone. He was eighty but had seemed in pretty good health (I thought). The funeral was in a crematorium with taped organ music, and was completely soulless. Now there was just the two grans left.

I had a brief resurgence of religious feeling at this time, solely for the purpose of grieving, and hoping that Yorkshire Grandad had gone to a good place. This was a really vague idea and part of my need to try and create some kind of order in the face of events. Well, in the face of death. I also started to toy with the idea that there was some greater power observing our every move – a feeling shared by some of the greatest of mankind's texts such as *The Bible*, *1984*, *The Matrix* and *The Truman Show*. I imagined Grandad sitting on my shoulder and I'd ask him what could be done to sort out major conflicts, specifically the Iran-Iraq war and the Falklands War. For some reason this usually happened while I was listening to *Sextet* by A Certain Ratio. Of course, Grandad didn't know how to sort out the world's problems. He might have suggested they take up woodcarving. Or gardening. Or spending time in a shed, making stuff. I'll never forget the sound of my mum straining in the snow trying to pull me and Tobe on the heavy steel and wood sledge Yorkshire Grandad had made for us. According to Yorkshire Grandad, if it wasn't metal, it wasn't quality. No-one could ever steal anything from my Yorkshire gran and grandad's house because all their belongings were either made from reinforced steel or pig iron, or had had steel injected into them at a later date

In my mind the 'good' place Grandad might have gone to, if it existed, was a bit like Spen Victoria Bowling Club, which was just at the back of Granny and Grandad's house in Yorkshire. Waiting for him there would be my great grandad (his father-in-law), who'd died two years earlier. Whereas Grandad was gentle and laidback, Great-Grandad was feisty and competitive:

Great-Grandad: (Sitting on a massive pile of dominoes so he's the same height as his son-in-law): Eighty!? What kind of an age do you call that?

Yorkshire Grandad: It's not bad. Better than the three score years and ten.

GG: I made it to eighty-nine. So I win.

YG: (Sighs): Yes, I suppose you do.

GG: (Looks around) Fancy a game of bowls then?

YG: Alright.

40. 'I Thought You Loved Me but It Seems You Don't Care'

Those of you who have stuck with me until now might be thinking that I come over as a bit clueless in many things, especially with girls. But that's nothing compared to the events of the midsummer of 1982. My renewed love/lust for Maggie was getting so intense that by the end of June it was affecting everything I did and genuinely addling my brain. Then, on June 29th (after going to the off licence for Strongbow and beer rations, then to watch England and West Germany fight out a turgid 0-0 draw round at Bandy's house – Rummenigge hit the bar with a long shot and Sidebottom spilt some cider on the carpet, that was about it), we walked up to Top Farm at the north eastern edge of Middle Rasen for the biggest barn dance of the summer. I planned to finally tell Maggie everything, get off with her, start sleeping with her and finally become a man, *anything*. This was the first night of the rest of my life. And it was all driving me crazy. I couldn't concentrate on anything else.

Although a huge structure, the noise inside the big barn was incredible, a different kind of music experience to the dark, claustrophobic ambience of the Fezzy. For a start everyone was in much better humour than they were at the normal discos. Little pockets of lads and girls were all standing around laughing, enjoying the space and the warmth. The music that I remember was 'No Woman No Cry', 'Geno', 'Too Much Too

Young', 'One Step Beyond', 'So Lonely', 'Jimmy Mack', 'Going Underground'. Maggie was there with her best friend Clementine Fieldhouse. Maggie wasn't going out with anyone, which gave more hope to my plan.

Naturally the first part of my brilliant strategy was as follows: get mildly bladdered, hang around with my mates in a little huddle and have a laugh, slag off most of the music, dance to anything good (and good meant that it met rigorous quality rules, as set down by the committee, i.e. us) – so I hung back when 'Message In A Bottle' came on, one of our staple dance-floor numbers, because I had now decided that The Police were not, in fact, OK, but were uncool and rubbish.

The next stage was to carry on having a laugh and hanging out in a group but, like herding a phalanx of Roman infantry-men, gradually move the gang over to where Maggie was dancing. I couldn't do this too obviously. If I said to them, 'Hey, everyone, I really fancy Maggie. Let's go and hang out near her,' that would obviously have been far too upfront and honest and would have been met with derision and piss-take ammunition for the rest of the evening. So I had to do it by stealth, starting up conversations then moving slowly so that without realising, they followed me where I wanted to go.

The final part of the plan was my tried and tested technique. To wait until the slow numbers came on so that it was officially OK to go and approach a girl, start slow dancing and, nine times out of ten, snogging. The glory of barn dances was that if it went really well you could then continue the entertainment outside in the lanes and fields. The disadvantage of the ortho-dox Slow Dance Approach Manouevre was that it was a big risk – the risk being, someone else might get in for a slow dance before you. Or, a factor that was becoming more common now that many of the girls our age were seventeen and beautiful, older blokes would get in earlier with a devious trick: they would start *talking* to the girls.

Much earlier in the evening they would sidle up to a girl, buy her a drink and then start chatting to her. This shock tactic was regarded as being pretty ungentlemanly in my circles. For a start, if you bought a girl a drink, because of lack of funds you were risking being too sober yourself at the end of the evening. Also, these older blokes were using their own life experience and probably anecdotes from the workplace to impress. Maggie wouldn't be interested if I sidled over to her to chat about what had happened in my latest European history class.

'So anyway we were doing Catherine the Great and Kev said to Haydyn Thomas that she should have concentrated on alliances rather than territorial expansion and Thomas says to him, "Kevin, you are a breath of fresh air in the history world," and we all laughed our arses off. Course you had to be there…'

'I was there, you idiot. I'm in the same history class as you, remember?'

Whereas, say if Gary Haddock sidled over, he could afford to buy her loads of drinks then regale her with stories about filling up people's cars with petrol.

'And then he drove off without putting the petrol cap on…'

Maggie (laughing like a drain): 'Oh Gary, you are so funny. I'm ever so slightly turned on by your wicked sense of humour.'

But, against all odds, my plan seemed to be working. I had manoeuvred the gang (at this stage Bandy, Kev, Sidebottom and Shorty Blackwell) over towards the left-hand side of the bar and we were now all dancing to 'Party Fears Two' (currently one of the greatest songs of all time). Maggie and Clementine were doing their funky handbag jiggly-boobed dancing in the corner of the barn and, thanks to the size of our group, we had effectively cut them off. I was on a high; this was my music and I didn't have to think consciously about dancing. I just inhabited the notes.

Then things slowed down a bit to 'No Woman No Cry'. Maggie was definitely clocking me out of the corner of her eye but was far too canny and stubborn to look at me openly. However, like in sport, this kind of territorial technique is a waiting game. I merely had to keep the group there until the slow dances – we were close to the bar so could refuel easily enough – then I would make my move. It was a timeless part of rural living, like some Thomas Hardyesque seasonal ritual that we didn't fully understand but played out anyway because we were hardwired that way. Maggie was meant for me; I knew it, she knew it, everyone knew it. The birds of midsummer knew it, the fieldmice knew it, the DJ knew it, the farmer knew it, the rockers knew it, my friends knew it, the sheep knew it, the butterflies knew it, the hedgerows knew it (well, they would have done if they hadn't been mostly grubbed up). At that moment, my life was set perfectly. Dancing badly to Bob Marley in a rubbish reggae swingy sidepunch style, cider and beer sloshing around in my system, my friends all around me, the lights in my eyes, the music slightly echoing as my senses became super-aware, time slowed down for a few seconds. Maggie stared at the floor but she was really waiting for me.

Then suddenly everything was normal again. We were all a bit drunk, dancing to Bob Marley and the Wailers and Maggie and Clementine had broken out. EMERGENCY! EMERGENCY! Our left flank had been breached, possibly by a combination of Bandy spontaneously moving into his crazy chicken dance routine (there's a time and place, mate) and Sidebottom and Shorty sleeping on the job and discussing what beer they would drink next (it's going to be lager or bitter, lads – hardly the need for a great debate). Whatever, the girls were free, out in the great grey concrete expanses of the barn floor, out into the middle of the various throngs of dancers, jiggling and bouncing. Like the lass in the Joy Division song, I had lost control.

Then it all becomes a blur. The next thing I know I am outside on High Church Lane. It's warm, though there is a faint breeze. The summer sun has just gone down. There are a few

figures in the shadows near the entrance, people getting a bit of air, a bit of a quiet chat, some snogging. I am further down the lane, off to the side, my feet in the dirt of the field. My arms are round someone, and my hands are holding a lovely round, soft backside while my tongue is wrestling feverishly with another tongue: side to side, trying to disappear down the throat, then back up and around the mouth and teeth; a mouth and teeth that taste of Malibu. Carmen Williams' drink of choice.

I would say to Bandy afterwards, on the way home, part of a defeated retreating army, when he gently but slyly asked if my plan had not gone slightly awry that, 'Look, Bandy, in life NOTHING goes according to plan.'

I can't remember if I waited for the slow dances or if I bought Carmen a drink or, more likely, if I just bumped into her while dancing badly to 'Going Underground'. But, right now, Carmen tastes so good, so exotic and coconutty, her lips are so red, even in the dark, that I have to feel good about it and count the evening as a qualified success. So England didn't beat West Germany, and will probably get knocked out now, and so I didn't tell Maggie everything that was on my mind and didn't get off with her, but maybe this was meant to be.

It's getting late now and people are straggling home. I look up and Maggie is walking past with Clementine, looking at us. She says something but I can't remember what it is – not hurt or upset but funny and gently mocking. Along the lines of, 'Having fun?'

The next few days are spent in a kind of stupor. I start falling asleep in school, in assembly, in lessons and in a big talk we are given by the head of Upper School, who tells us about UCCA, the university clearing system and all the things we need to be aware of next term when the real work starts. But I am just dreaming of Maggie and my parallel life where everything always goes according to plan.

*

Two weeks after the barn dance, I decided to make a definitive move. Once again I had choices, this time two. I could either:

a) Be upfront. Talk to her man to woman and tell Maggie my feelings and explain what happened at the barn dance, say I'm a git and a bit of a tart but that I really love her.

b) Write some kind of cryptic yet inane romantic note quoting ABC lyrics and trying to seem all moody and depressed and interesting.

No contest, really. On a small piece of paper I wrote, 'I thought you loved me but it seems you don't care', a spoken line from ABC's recent hit 'Poison Arrow', and slipped it into a pocket of her blue kagoule (that I had managed to 'borrow'). As a fan of Thomas Hardy I knew this was the kind of thing his characters did all the time, usually with disastrous results – the note would be found years later after the lovers had gone their separate ways, heartbroken. That was the kind of tragic, soulful possibility I liked.

I wrote in my diary, 'Was it worth it? Probably not, and in time I will probably realise this – but it seemed (at the time) the only possible action.'

The 'only possible action'? Oh dear...

Over the next few days I wrote all kinds of sub-poetic, cryptic, tortured and romantic notes in my diary, jotting things down hurriedly in some kind of code as if aware that other people might look at the diary. There are also symbolic pictures like chains breaking, strange sunsets.

'By the way Bandy (or anyone else who might read this), sorry for the poetic philosophies of the last few days – it must make terrible reading.'

'*It's OK,*' writes Bandy, in the margin.

A couple of days later Bramley and I have a tennis match

with Maggie and Lisa Brown. I get a lot of attention from Maggie and my soul is rejuvenated.

Then the next night Maggie gets off with another bloke at a disco and my world comes crashing down as the full force of unrequited love takes hold.

I can feel it eating away at my insides.

I spent the weekend hanging out with the gang and, after a night of seriously brain-numbing, trying-to-forget-it-all drinking at The Red Lion I went back to Sidebottom's place for a long talk on life, girls and what it's all about: whether The Goodies were as funny now that they were on ITV and (the ultimate tragedy of the age) Brazil being knocked out of the World Cup by Italy. I had wanted them to win too much, seeing them as doomed romantics who played with passion and artistry, but in the end they were just not ruthless enough. In football (and maybe life) do we remember those who are winners or those who are brilliant? I had already made my mind up that being successful was overrated.

SOCRATES

41. Supporting Eric Random and the Bedlamites

The last week of July and the summer holidays were here. I lay on my bed and stared at the walls, which were covered in my paintings plus photos and montages I'd made from cuttings of the *NME*. Over my bed I'd taken a head of Mick Jagger and constructed a hangman's noose and little cartoon body, with a bullet hole through his forehead for good measure. This was my rich rejection of the rock 'n' roll grandad generation. Then, jostling for floorspace, was the 1950s/early 60s radiogram, various amplifiers, guitars, the microphone stands, synthesisers and tables strewn with paints and artwork.

Elsewhere in the house there was activity going on. Mum was trying to organise everyone – it was a day of packing as the family got ready for the summer holiday. This year was Wales, but I wasn't going. I had a broken heart to deal with, along with a sculpture to complete as preparation for the last year of the art 'A' level course. It was going to be a head with stuff exploding out of the top of it, ideas and unrequited feelings of love, perhaps. I'd already picked up a load of clay from the school's art room and transferred it to Dad's shed.

Bandy had gone up to Scotland to see his dad. He asked if I wanted to come but I was far too busy being moody and temperamental. What if Maggie found the note and I was in Scotland? I needed to be prepared. Anyway, there was other stuff to do here. Scooter had bought a new RAK tape deck for our recording sessions. He was coming round in a week or so and we were going to record some great new songs. I would forget about Maggie and throw myself into my music and art career.

The week went quickly, with just me and a lump of clay hanging out together. Then at the start of August the family returned from Wales in some excitement, and Snake announced proudly that he had caught a fish for the first time in his life. Not bad going after trying for two years.

With the family back, I retreated to the shed. It was hot and sticky in there. This made me think of Maggie. But I tried to keep my mind focused on small things so as not to think about Maggie. My Maggie. What was she doing now? She'd gone to Greece for a week, so was probably lying topless on a beach, sunbathing and getting lots of attention from local blokes and STOP. I *had* to stop thinking about it. That's when I had to get out of the shed and out into the garden to do some weeding and digging. Great.

Diary entry: Wednesday 11th August
Kev gets a job at Linwood for £7 a day. Lucky bastard!
Kev seems to be working all the time. He is saving up for something big, for sure.
One high point that summer was an article about Easy Listening in the *Rasen Mail* with a big photo of us in front of Scooter's garage, taken by Maggie's dad. As usual I look like a blond twat that most people would like to punch. How did I manage it? All I did was tuck my jumper into my crap grey Bowie trousers:

(To be read in a Pathé newsreel voice)
'Market Rasen band Easy Listening now have a cassette on local independent release entitled 'Six Easy Listening Greats'.

Group members Tim Bradford (left), Nigel Richardson (centre) and Francis Finn are hoping to publicise their tape which is already on sale locally.

The band also plan to look for more gig work for their brand of electronic music.

Tim Bradford and Francis Finn attend De Aston school. Nigel Richardson is a former pupil.'

A tape on sale? On independent release? Well, actually Scooter had made a few copies of the tape alright – we all got one and he sent one to *Electronic and Music Maker* magazine (who said in their review 'it's like a cross between Karlheinz Stockhausen and Kid Creole and the Coconuts') and one to Nottingham's Ad Lib Club in the hope of getting a gig. Bandy had already declared that it was a rip-off of lots of other bands, though he couldn't remember who.

Diary entry: Thursday 12th August
If everything goes according to plan [Quote: 'Look, Bandy, in life NOTHING goes according to plan'] *Easy Listening could be supporting Eric Random and the Bedlamites at Nottingham Ad Lib Club, next Tuesday night.*

Scooter was into Eric Random, a kind of New Wave electronica similar in form and sound to Cabaret Voltaire, with long rhythmic mood pieces and synth textures with echoish guitar. I couldn't actually name any of his songs but had heard him as a kind of background noise. I don't think that mattered.

We recorded half an hour of backing tracks for our best songs. This is basically drum patterns and bass parts, with some sequenced keyboards as well. The idea was that Scooter would sing, I would play guitar/bongoes/melodica/kazoo over the top, and we would go down a storm, and Eric Random would come up to us and either:

a) Say he has to have us supporting him whenever he played from now on.

b) Say we are so good he might as well jack it all in now.

c) Punch me for looking like a blond twat with my jumper tucked into my crap Bowie trousers.

We had also entered a *Daily Mirror* song competition with a local girl singing one of our songs and us backing. I liked the idea of being a backing band to a cool redhead. We were bound to win the *Daily Mirror* competition. We were that good. I had been in Scooter's band for less than eight months and already we were on the verge of greatness. Francis was, all of a sudden, no longer involved for some reason, possibly because he had taken the curious step of getting ready to go to university rather than play plinky-plonk electronic sounds with us. In light of this, we decided to do the 'disbanding then reforming' thing that we all loved so much, and began scouting around for a new name. The shortlist was:

In a Lighter Vein
Daughters of the Late Colonel
Klondyke Pete and the Cereal Gang
Britain's Burglars
Cover-Up
Haig Wins Some Friends
The Buchwalds
Eating Out
The Shining Mandarins
Kulivov
Bottle Party
Golden Idols
Double Life
Tantra
Cafard Dilettante
The Gifted Children

Arthur and the Not Particularly Nice Beige Trousers (my
favourite)
Scooter and the Expensive Equipment (Bandy's, who was
still in Scotland, phoned-in suggestion)

We decided on The Gifted Children because that was Scooter's
favourite choice and he had the casting vote because it was his
band really.

Diary entry: Saturday 14th August
'GUESS WHAT? The concert's off!'

I dealt with this heartbreak by doing what I always did –
pretending it was no big deal. Scooter though had taken it quite
hard and seemed to be seeing it as a sign that good things
weren't meant to happen for us. Eric Random was ill. He'd got
a cold or something. So a snotty nose and a sore throat had
come between us and the big time. I hoped Eric Random felt
really bad about it tomorrow. In fact, he'd probably already
phoned Scooter up and sorted out an alternative date.

Over the weekend we got back into 'the studio' (Scooter's
living room) and tried to get back the old magic. Scooter in his
frustration broke some keys on Francis's really good Yamaha
synth. Francis was going to be really angry when he found out.
A few days ago we were going to be rich and famous and now
we'd probably have to go halves on repairing Francis's synth.
Maybe he'd go to university and forget about it.

The next day, the day we should have been supporting Eric
Random and the Bedlamites at the Ad Lib Club, I needed
cheering up. I phoned up Bandy in Scotland. Then went to
Sidebottom's but he wasn't in. The Gent, Tobe, Kev and I
headed off to Lincoln along with a kid called Mangeworth (the
lad with the pointiest tucker boots in town) for a big record
fair. Kev bought fab records by UK Decay, The Mob and The

Meteors; Tobe got a couple of Clash singles; Mangeworth bought a Japan live rip-off album; The Gent got a rip-off Teardrop Explodes single and a second-hand camera case; and I bought The Associates' 'Tell Me Easter's On Friday' twelve-inch single. And A Certain Ratio's 'Shack Up' twelve inch. We all slagged each other's choices off on the way home.

Kev: The Associates… are shit.

Me: No, The Associates are great. UK Decay are shit.

Kev: Japan are shit.

Mangeworth: No, The Meteors are shit. Japan are ace.

The Gent: The Clash are shit.

Tobe: No, Teardrop Explodes are shit. The Clash are the greatest band in the world.

Me: No, The Clash are shit.

Tobe: I thought you liked The Clash.

Me: I did. But I don't like their new album.

Tobe: OK then can I have your Clash records?

Me: It'll cost you.

Kev: A Certain Ratio are shit.

Me: No, The Mob are shit.

Kev (Pensive): Yeah, The Mob are a bit shit, aren't they?

That afternoon Bandy returned from holiday and gave his opinion on our new purchases.

A Certain Ratio – shit, UK Decay – shit, The Meteors – shit, The Mob – shit, The Clash – shit, Japan – shit, Haircut 100 – shit, camera cases – shit.

He'd obviously had a bad holiday.

By the weekend Eric Random still hadn't got back in touch. And I got a postcard from Maggie. On the front was a photo of a tanned, naked woman, sunbathing. On the back she'd written: 'I am getting brown and even more beautiful.' Then there was boring stuff about the people she was on holiday with.

Great. The note didn't work. Maggie was nude and gorgeous in Europe and I was here and not a famous musician.

There's Always a Radio On Somewhere in the House: 1982

Dollar 'Mirror Mirror'

New Order 'Temptation'

ABC 'Poison Arrow'

Pigbag 'Papa's Got A Brand New Pigbag'

Shalamar 'A Night To Remember'

Marvin Gaye 'Sexual Healing'

Kid Creole & The Coconuts 'Annie I'm Not Your Daddy'

Clannad 'Theme From Harry's Game'

Foreigner 'Waiting For A Girl Like You'

Daryl Hall and John Oates 'I Can't Go For That'

The Associates 'Party Fears Two'

42. Leeds United 'Til I Die (...That Can Be Arranged)

Trying To Find Out How Many Games Mick Bates Played For Leeds in 1972 – Stage 1

The telephone rang – an old friend said he'd pop round for
some tea
With a dog eared Rothman's Yearbook from 1973
As we sat munching custard creams he said 'put in a bid'
And after much hard bargaining, I gave him twenty quid.

I've followed Leeds United since I was a kid. I always tell people that I started supporting them during the 1970 FA Cup Final, but this must be a bit of a fib because in 1970 the only team I supported was Brazil. I watched a few games in the 1970 World Cup and decided I didn't care how England got on – I wanted to become like Rivelino, the moustachioed Brazilian midfield player who single-handedly invented the banana shot. I got Mum to buy me a plastic yellow Brazil ball from the newsagents, then subsequently spent hours in the garden with my dad kicking it about. I insisted on trying to bend it like my hero, using the outside of my foot, much to Dad's annoyance. I still can't kick a ball straight, much to my annoyance.

I've always been amused by the moral logic of football fans. As a well-adjusted adult in the twenty-first century it is perfectly acceptable to change your partner, your religion, your philosophy of life, even your politics, but you're not allowed to change your football team. Changing a football team midstream is like saying 'I am a worthless, shallow puff of wind'. But I did change teams. In 1971, as the memory of the glorious summer was fading, I dumped Brazil.

I had worked out that Leeds hadn't finished out of the top four since they'd got promoted in 1964. It was during their FA Cup run of 1972 that I really became aware of the strength of my love and devotion. It was pragmatic, ruthless, nothing to do with the white shirts. My favourite players were Eddie Gray, a thoroughbred who was usually injured, and a utility player, Paul Madeley, because my mum fancied him. I also particularly liked a player called Mick Bates, who hardly ever played but just kept the subs bench warm. He had a Lincolnshire-sounding name. Then in 1973 I got in my first playground fight before the FA Cup Final and bloodied the nose of a kid who said Leeds would lose to Sunderland. After that game I was in tears on the floor. By 1975, when they had been cheated by the ref out of the 1975 European Cup Final against Bayern Munich, my heartbreak now manifested itself as anguished frustration, which eventually led to scar tissue around the heart and the stoical optimistic pessimism of the true fan.

Everyone hated Leeds. I occasionally meet other Leeds fans the same age as me who all say that at the time admitting to supporting Leeds was almost as bad as admitting you were in the Hitler Youth. I recently got a load of Leeds bubblegum cards from a friend who'd had them when he was a kid. Even at nine years old he hated Leeds and had scribbled Hitler moustaches and fringes onto the Leeds players.

All the kids I knew in the 70s supported a big club. Bandy was Manchester United, Sidebottom and Shorty were Leeds, Kev, Tony Hopkins and Carwyn were Liverpool, and Hinesy and Bramley were Chelsea. But while Tobe and I spent our Saturday afternoons as young kids watching Dad play rugby, most of my mates began to go and see the local football league teams, and so it became acceptable to have a big club while actively supporting a more local side.

We were bang in between Lincoln and Grimsby, so it could go either way, but because Grimsby were the best team for a number of years, only Bandy was a Lincoln supporter in our gang. Everyone else became 'Mariners' through and through, unless Grimsby were playing Liverpool or Chelsea or another of our big sides (as if that was ever likely to happen).

One thing I don't like to talk about was how many times I'd been to see Leeds play. Mum had taken us to Elland Road in 1974 on one of our holiday trips to see the grandparents in Yorkshire, but unfortunately the ground was deserted. They were playing away at West Ham that day. I'll see them some day, I thought. Then in 1982 the unthinkable happened. Leeds United got relegated. The first game of the new season in Division 2 was against a newly promoted side – Grimsby Town. I stood in the Pontoon Stand with Hinesy, Sidebottom and Kev as Leeds booted the ball around to no effect and the game remained scoreless. Then towards the end of the second half, with the cocky, tough Grimsby fans at the back of the stand baiting the Leeds supporters, crowds of Leeds fans began climbing their fences and running onto the pitch. They then jumped onto the fences of the Pontoon, climbing them with ease like terrifying monsters from an old *Doctor Who* episode. They swarmed up the terraces towards us, the lads in the front with eyes of hate and murder, as we backed off. The big tough Grimsby lads who'd been doing the baiting had gone mysteriously quiet. The police waded in and calm of a sort was restored but after the game it was pretty dodgy in the surrounding streets as fists and bottles were flying all over the place. I felt pretty bad that Leeds fans had done it all. Maybe people were right after all: maybe Leeds fans were violent nutcases. I had always loved Leeds, but not in that crazy way that many supporters 'love' their team, which is manifested as hatred of everyone else (but especially local rivals).

My love was passionate, but we were independent souls, me and Leeds. After that I decided I needed some space. We had to lead lives away from each other. I would carry on loving them but we would have separate beds for a while.

Is there someone else?

No, there will never be anyone else.

43. The George Best Condundrum

*'To be really happy, we must throw our hearts over the bar and hope that our bodies will follow.' – Graham Taylor**

The George Best Conundrum probably shouldn't be called The George Best Conundrum. What it describes is the choice many people have to make, at some point in their lives, between the ambition of achieving sporting excellence and that of going to an all-night party with a load of booze and jumping about to crazy punk-jazz-funk music then downing a bottle of rum and then getting off with a good-looking girl. The reason George Best shouldn't really come into it is that he was one of those rare individuals who could do both. If, say for example's sake, George Best had had a best pal – let's call him Bandy – who had decided to organise a big all-night party at his house the night before a big match because his mum was away, George Best would have helped himself to the wine and the women and probably still gone on to play a blinder the next day. And George Best had Matt Busby constantly breathing down his neck, making sure he got a modicum of rest.

Sadly, I had no Matt Busby. It was September 1982 and I had a final trial for the county rugby team coming up on the Saturday morning. Our rugby coach Speed Williamson had been aggrieved that only two of his players had got in the squad

---

* Former Lincoln City and England football manager, born in Scunthorpe.

the year before and felt that politics came into it because a bloke from Spalding (a rival team in the south of the county) had been picking the team. But this didn't stop Speed – he emphasised the importance of focus and concentration. Discipline. Don't give them a chance not to pick you, was his mantra. There was a lot of competition for places. Earlier in the year I had dislocated my collar bone in a Colts rugby match, trying to tackle some massive bloke with a beard (why did they all have beards, how did that work?), which meant that I missed several months of sport. By the time the new season started I was beginning to struggle physically and my worries about my fitness were not helped by the sudden growth spurt of Darren Beamish, a kid in the year below who played in the same position as me. Not only was he younger than me, he was also better at rugby; much bigger, stronger, faster and nastier.

Being comparatively skinny and weedy compared to most forwards in our school team, I needed to be in peak condition to have a chance for the county side. In other words, a plate of Lincolnshire sausages and an early night. (Experts had been telling me for years that I should beef up a bit. Motivational PE teacher Mr Minting had devised a punishing gym schedule which I tried once, felt stiff for a week, then gave up.)

It seems perverse that Bandy would have a party on that night, just before my breakthrough into county-level rugby (and then, naturally, the international scene). But what was he supposed to do? It wasn't every week that his mum went away, and in a clever bit of chicanery, Bandy had already secured an intimate, early evening Chinese takeaway meal in the empty house with his current crush, Siân Cobner. If things went well, with the right atmosphere and music (possibly Cabaret Voltaire and a bit of U.K. Subs and Rip, Rig & Panic), Bandy might be unstoppable. He could be away. And he was six months younger than me! (Good job we weren't competitive about this sort of thing.)

Word was travelling fast about the party. I had heard on the grapevine that Carmen hoped I was going. What did she mean? 'I hope you're going.' Did she mean to the party? Or did she mean to the county rugby trial? Was she going to run me through a few back-row moves in preparation for the trial? And here was my George Best Conundrum – what did I want more, to get off with girls or get into the county rugby team?

I really liked rugby, but I was a normal teenage boy. All of a sudden there was no room in my head for egg-shaped balls, H-shaped posts, boots, shorts, grass, scrums, tackles. Both hemispheres of my brain became locked together in a kind of overdrive situation in which Carmen became my only reason for being.

I got to the party around eight. There were already a few people there, but I couldn't see Siân Cobner. Both Bandy and I had on our Personal Pulling Outfits. For Bandy that meant a headband, a collarless shirt and his burgundy Bowie trousers. For me it meant Dad's suit trousers and my old string vest. Who could resist? Over the next hour the place began to fill up. Word had got around the town of Bandy's Secret Party. Older kids

like Graham Heligore, John Aykbourn, Lily Flint plus Maggie. And it made me feel better that Bramley had come, as he was due at the rugby trial too. About half past nine, Siân Cobner turned up. She'd presumed Bandy was joking about the Chinese meal.

There was a key point in the party that I remember where I was standing in a room, seemingly on my own and with a bottle of Captain Morgan's rum to my lips. In my memory the little picture of the captain turns into Roly Chesterfield, the long-time captain of our rugby team, who says in a salty seadog voice: 'Turn back, Tim. Put the bottle down and run. Go to bed!' I then bellow 'Haaaaaaa!' and down half the bottle.

At around one in the morning, after I'd finished the bottle of Captain Morgan rum and started piling into the Pernod, I found myself heading upstairs with Carmen. It was that moment I'd been waiting for. *Don't give them a chance not to pick you.* I jumped onto the bed but I don't think I landed. Then the room began to swim. I held on tight as the bed did cartwheels. Carmen, as Florence Nightingale, tried to save me but I was beginning to flatline ... it felt like I had nine brains and each brain was thinking about a different thing simultaneously when all I wanted them to do was be quiet so I could have some quality time with Carmen... it would help if I wasn't hanging on to this bed for dear life... *Don't give them a chance not to pick you...* Carmen smelt of vanilla and clotted cream... then we are in a little rowing boat and Carmen was singing softly and rowing us gently along a stream of dark rum, and Captain Morgan appeared in a big galleon and Mr Williamson was there shouting through a megaphone, 'Don't give them the chance not to pick you!' then... the void.

The next morning my first thought was, How far am I from the nearest waste bin? Then I puked up the first of what would be nearing double figures of vomit. I tried to get some breakfast down me but it just came straight back up. I mumbled pathetic apologies to Carmen, who took it all very well, then somehow I got myself together and got to the crossroads in Middle Rasen, where the minibus was waiting. I sat in a daze, concentrating on one thing – not on making tackles, but on trying not to be sick. I couldn't talk. I put on my kit as if in a trance and went out onto the pitch, playing every minute of the trial. There was nothing in my legs. By the end I was ready to die. I ended up at the bottom of a big fat bloke pile-up, and warm bile came oozing out onto the pitch.

I'm sure it was a close-run thing, but I didn't get in the team. But while lying there at the bottom of that prone mound of bodies, at least I could claim some similarity with the life of George Best.

44. A Night Out with The Store Detectives

It was now January 1983, the year it would all change. I wasn't too good at maths but even I could work it out. I was born in 1965 so this was the year I'd leave school. It was preordained. It would be expected. In 1983 I could properly escape.

But first I had to become the bassist in a punk band.

Who were they?

You won't have heard of them.

Go on, try me. I know loads about punk music.

They're quite obscure.

Not to me!

I think so…

Just tell me, will you!!

OK, The Store Detectives.

(Small pause) Never heard of 'em, mate.

The Store Detectives were about the fifth band I had played with in the period that some music historians (i.e. me) now refers to as the Golden Age of the Market Rasen Music Scene. The Store Detectives were a vivid and fast orthodox punk band, like a homemade sports car pieced together from bits of kit and old scrap. The Store Detectives comprised Kev on guitar (his new light brown with a white scratchplate Les Paul copy, the guitar he'd been saving for for ages from his various jobs); Eddie Oates on Johnny-Rotten-style wailing vocals; my cousin Rich on drums (he was still the only drummer in the town); and me on bass.

I'm not a bassist. I kept telling everyone that. I was a rhythm guitarist and Korg MS-10 electronica riff merchant (with farmer's fingers). But The Store Detectives were a lean machine and didn't need two rhythm guitarists and definitely didn't need atmospheric synth textures. Oatesy and Kev knew I could hold down a one-note bass riff after seeing me in the Malcolm Skinner Project the year before. In The Store Detectives I got to play a Fender Jazz Bass. I can't remember who I borrowed it from but it was a class instrument. The idea was that I would play the bass hard with a stiff plectrum: DUM DUM DUM DUM DUM – you get the idea. According to Kev I was on no account to try anything fancy. The trouble was that at this stage I was probably more influenced by funk than punk. I have photos of me rehearsing with The Store Detectives and it's obvious I'm playing crap slap funk bass, Heaven 17 style. In one picture, Oatsey looks like he wants to kill me. There was a fair bit of creative tension between Oatsey and me but it was healthy creative tension.

Oatsey and Kev were real punks, in the sense that they looked like punks, had crap haircuts, pale skin (Oatsey was so committed he would sit in his bedroom with the curtains drawn in case the sun touched his skin, and there was a rumour he used talc on it), and black jackets. Kev's punkness had been turned up a notch or two since the arrival of the Positive Punk movement and the suggestion that Punk Was Actually Not Quite Dead (Actually). The initial motivation for all this had happened a year or so before when Kev, Rich and I listened to an Andy Kershaw interview with Crass on the radio, plugging their latest album. I stuck one of my trusty BASF tapes into the recorder and we hit the phones. Two of us got through – firstly, Rich, who asked if Gang of Rob could support Crass on their next Lincolnshire tour. And said that we were all from Market Rasen. The Crass folk were taken aback and asked, 'Where is Market Rasen?' On being told that it was a sleepy town in a backwater county, they exclaimed, 'Wow, we're getting out a long way!' Then Kev asked Penny Rimbaud, or was it Steve Ignorant, what he meant by 'organised anarchy'.

'Organised anarchy... well, erm... Kropotkin, er... Bakunin... erm...'

A few months later Kev and I had formed a short-lived punk band called Chronic Diarrhoea. We played one gig, in front of nobody, recording a tape of around fifteen songs, none of which lasted more than thirty seconds. Most of the material was inspired by the anarcho-punk of the *Bullshit Detector* album from Crass Records. We also did a couple of Genesis covers, including a ten second version of 'The Lamb Lies Down on Broadway'.

Anarcho-punk singer Steve Ignorant once asked, on BBC radio, the immortal question: "Where is Market Rasen?"

But I was always a bit too clean-cut to pull off the pasty-faced punk look, so usually just wore an old jumper and a pair of grandad trousers in order to vaguely fit in.

It hadn't meant to be like this. I had been in a comedy punk band with Bandy when I was fourteen/fifteen but now I was supposed to be 'making it' in some kind of electronic avante band like the Brezhnev Brothers, not being a member of a punk revival act. But I was along for the ride. And then came the best news: Kev and Oatsey had secured us a real paid gig at a real venue. I'll repeat that because even I find it hard to believe... a real paid gig at a real venue.

According to Kev, Alexandra's in Lincoln was a good place for punk bands and the bloke who ran it did punk nights. We were booked in for a gig on a Sunday night at the end of January, the support act for a band from Lincoln. I can't remember how much we were due to be paid but it was a thrilling new development.

Strangely for a rock gig, the lead singer was also the chauffeur. Oatsey had recently passed his test and on this special occasion his dad let him use the family's brand new silver Ford Escort. (The next day would be the first of the new seatbelt law in England and Wales, but we were punks and couldn't be expected to belt up just because The Man had told us to. Anyway, we lived for today.) On the night, we all went off for some beers and a bite to eat at The Wig and Mitre, an old pub on the hill. A couple of the girls from our school had come along, my old flame Andrea Spreadbury and Kev's girlfriend Tracey Duckham. Sitting in the pub with everyone around felt like we were finally living the dream – beers, girls, music, dosh, notoriety. I could get used to this.

When we arrived at the gig there seemed to be more people with long hair and flares than I would have expected at a punk gig, but maybe the main act had a wide audience. Or they could be roadies. Or parents of the other band. I had made a bit of an effort on the clothes front and was wearing a denim shirt that had had the sleeves ripped off. I would have looked like a backing dancer for Wham! except that for a while now I had been modelling my hairstyle on the introverted lads from A Certain Ratio. Rich, meanwhile, never looked like a punk; in fact, he never bothered with a look. As usual he just had on a crap T-shirt that showed off his muscly arms. Rich's drumming was consistent – he just banged away in a heavy funk style, no matter what the speed or style of song that we were playing.

I knew something wasn't quite right when the place started to fill up a bit more with a mix of Hells Angels and middle-aged hippy metal freaks.

'I thought you said this was a punk venue?' I said to Kev.

'That's what the bloke on the phone said. He said it was a punk night.'

'Funny-looking punks to me.'

We set up our gear while the rockers looked on, I thought, just a little angrily.

The raspy punk thrash chords for the first song 'Stupid War' started up – barre chords A, E, G, D, A, E, G, D, E, then Rich on drums: boom bap bop de boom bish de boom booom bap be biop de boom bish, then me on bass: dum dum dum dum (you get the idea); it all crashing and smashing together at high-speed, and Oatsey stooping over the microphone and screeching in his Lydonesque wail:

You the working class you do what they say
Slog your guts out every day
You end up a victim of a government ploy
In a war you'll be their toy
Not going to be your dogsbody any more
Not going to fight in your stupid war
Not going to get involved in your schemes
Say goodbye to Britain's dreams

and then the instrumental bit A, E, G, D bang boom bip bish crash bass dum dum dum dum (you get the idea).

At the end of the song there was a rather aggressive silence. A couple of our mates clapped but not for long. Whoa, this was not good.

'The next song is called "Killer", said Oatsey, who seemed to be enjoying himself. How many songs did we have? Thankfully not too many more. Rich started with a Tommy Gun-style snare roll – wow, that was good. Kev cheered himself as he started to play the chords. Lots of feedback.

Oatsey's high-pitched banshee wail.

Crusty crunch Big Muff fuzzbox chords: jagged bam pow!

Man destroying man for political gain
shouldn't you feel inhumane

Killer killer killer
You're just a machine
Killer killer killer
You ain't no human being

Big drum solo by Rich: bopbopbopbashbashbashbash.

I thought we had sounded good. Really tight. We looked around at the silent hall – silent apart from the odd comment of 'Fucking shit' – then played a couple more songs that I can't remember. But the atmosphere had gone dark. I just recall thinking we were going to get beaten up by a load of grandad rockers. All these scowling blokes with long hair and flared jeans standing around looking like Disgusted of Tunbridge Wells. And at the end when Kev went up to the manager to ask for the money, he was told to fuck off. As I started to pack up the gear in record time, trying not to catch anyone's eye, a bit of an argument then took place between Oatsey and Kev and this bloke, who was now claiming he didn't know we were a punk band. Various annoyed long-haired middle-aged men looked on.

We felt cheated. Deflated. On the way home I sat in the front and buckled up for the first time, after Oatsey reminded me that the new seatbelt laws came into operation at midnight and it was now about 12.30 a.m. (OK, mate, it's your car, but that's hardly a very punk attitude.)

Driving home from Lincoln, pootling along the A46 like real rock 'n' rollers, as we analysed the gig ('Maybe we need more fuzz on the guitar'), it was pretty icy with the remains of snow around, but Oatsey was a cautious and sensible driver for someone who'd just tried to 'destroy the military-industrial complex'. Then, in the pitch-dark, somewhere near Dunholme Top, a car came from nowhere out of a minor road and, with another car coming in the opposite direction, we had no option but to plough straight into the side of them.

Road travel in Lincolnshire, like being in a punk band, has always been a dangerous business. The county is sparsely populated and there is the typically crazy traffic of a place with lots of scattered nightlife and crap public transport. Most lads who stayed on in the area at some point ended up losing their licences for drink driving (apart from one of the legendary Punk Nigels, the one with the special breathing technique).

I think we all went 'Arrrgghhhh!' at the same time. In my memory we are all rolling around in the car in slow motion, but it didn't really happen like that. Just lightning fast then over.

Thankfully, no-one was injured – although the bass guitar whacked me in the head – but the front of Oatsey's dad's new Ford Escort was completely crumpled. Oatsey was aghast. And Kev spilt some of his cider, which made him really mad.

'Fuck, fuck, fuck, fuck, fuck! What is my dad going to say?' wailed Oatsey as we surveyed the damage to the Y reg car and sucked in the cold night air, thinking about our near-James Dean experience.

After going back to Lincoln police station and much explanation of what happened (luckily they didn't find Oatsey's lyric sheet about smashing the state), we finally all got home around 2.30 with a sense that we probably wouldn't be playing again together for a while. Not exactly kicks on the A46.

45. Being Like Picasso: My Art 'A' Level Triumph

The year I took my Art 'A' level, the school art department had enrolled us in the London Examination Board 'A' levels, believing that the Cambridge Board way of marking was too stuffy. With London you were, apparently, more free to express yourself. The subject I chose was Icarus. I liked Icarus. He was representative of the state of being a Lincolnshire teenager: always wanting to be somewhere else. Unlike the elephant seal, he had found a way to break his bonds. He had escaped.

As an extra layer of confusion I decided to work the theory of flying too close to the sun into the process of painting itself. The teachers had suggested a more realistic approach might be more suitable for an exam – don't fly too close to the sun, *don't give them the chance not to give you a good grade* – but they were Daedelus, the old way, the Lincolnshire way. I was Icarus, eager to try new things for himself (under exam conditions, of course).

I had a vision of a twisted torso muscleman falling to earth, a kind of cross between early period UK Marvel comics – Daredevil falling from a building, say – and Picasso's 'Les Demoiselles d'Avignon'. I persuaded Bramley, the only mate I had with proper muscles (i.e. that you could see), to model for me. We sat in his little study in the boarding house where he lived, listening to Led Zeppelin and Genesis albums played backwards in the hope of hearing some satanic messages (as Bramley claimed), and drinking Pernod, trying to get the Picasso vibe. I did various sketches of him as he held contorted poses. I also did sketches of arms, sinews, hands, expressions. I had covered all the bases. But these sketches were nothing compared to the finished piece.

On the day of the exam I was in a state of calm excitement. I knew what the piece would look like – I had done various colour studies by now – and I had three hours to realise my dream. I had set up in my lucky area of the art studio, and there was a great atmosphere: everyone was doing good work. The Gent was nearby as was Maggie, doing some intricate pencil studies. In those moments I understood school for the first time. I wanted those three hours to go on for ever. At the end of the day I stood proudly by the painting, as everyone came up to congratulate me. Fantastic. I was elated. So elated, I asked Maggie out soon afterwards.

I couldn't *really* tell if the painting was genius or rubbish, mind.

46. A Kind of Kraftwerk-Style Number About Cricket

There was a bit of a problem. The trumpet player, jiggling nervously from foot to foot as if in dire need of a slash, didn't know the first song. It was a kind of Kraftwerk-style number about cricket. He'd only managed to have one rehearsal with us before the gig but we figured that, because the songs were quite simple and mostly all in the same key – who knows what that key was – he'd have no problem, what with being a real trumpet player with a real trumpet.

It was the summer of 1983, just after our 'A' levels, and our band, the Brezhnev Brothers, had over the previous eighteen months morphed from punk/pop to twang/pop electropop to electroindustrialpop. I was not a great believer in trumpets in pop music. It works on Motown stuff and the odd classic like 'Reward' by The Teardrop Explodes, but on the whole it tends to lend an air of the Salvation Army or the Brighouse and Rastrick Town Band, which immediately strips the music of any veneer of sexiness. However, post-ska and with the success of Pigbag and

other funky groups with horn sections like Rip Rig & Panic, the Brezhnev Brothers decided to roll with the times and recruit a horn maestro. Maybe it would jazz things up a bit and we'd get a few more dance-mad female fans as a result.

The Gent had been playing trumpet since he was eleven. He was the only Chinese musician in the area so it was thought to be a bit of a coup that we managed to recruit him – giving us an exotic Eastern feel along with the trumpet playing – plus this meant that other bands, such as our arch rivals Gang of Rob or the Sean Nevis Band, wouldn't be able to nab him. The Gent could also play whatever you told him to play.

This gig was biggest of the year so far for The Brezhnev Brothers. It had come at pretty short notice and word had it the audience would be hard to please. It was Mum who got us the gig. To confess all – it had been our local Akela who had been the one who'd asked us to appear – well, asked my mum, who had arm-twisted me. At first the thought of playing at a local Cub Scout summer jamboree and barbecue had not seemed that appealing. There seemed a possibility that the Cubs – eight- and nine-year-old boys – would not 'get' the music. But what the hell – the Brezhnev Brothers believed in musical democracy. Didn't little kids deserve good music too? Of course, we needed the exposure and weren't getting gigs anywhere else.

The others had been less than enthusiastic at helping out Akela but were persuaded that it would be 'a laugh'. We weren't in a position to turn down gigs and had worked hard, on both the songs and the looks. Bandy was at the height of his burgundy phase – burgundy Bowie trousers with a burgundy top and light-grey soft leather shoes. I'm not sure who were the first purveyors of burgundy in the pop world. It might have been the lead singer of Blancmange. Bandy's burgundiness showed he was classy in a not-trying-too-hard sort of way like, erm, Burgundy wine, I suppose. It actually looked more like a New Romantic school uniform. The Gent had chinos, a white

shirt and gold-framed glasses with his short black hair cut neatly. Everyone rather unoriginally thought he looked like the bloke out of Yellow Magic Orchestra. I was playing a Korg MS-10 synthesiser and looked a bit of a twat in grandad trousers, flipflops and a white vest. Only Tobe, on guitar, showed any sense of perspective or innate understanding of the future of indie rock by dressing in black jeans and T-shirt. The audience shuffled about and eyed us up suspiciously (and not a little aggressively, I thought).

So anyway, it was a Kraftwerk-style number about cricket. We had already performed four completely new tracks we thought might be tailored to our audience, including a song about Henry Moore and a song Tobe wrote about a sparrow. This next song was not *just* about cricket. One of our old tracks from three and a half years earlier, it referenced cricket through-out but the motivation behind the song was a piss-take of a local lad who fancied himself as a bit of a God's gift to women/hard-nut/comedian type. The chorus to our song went:

If you are playing cricket, you'll use him as a wicket,

If you are playing cricket, you'll use him as a wicket.

Then a trumpet bit was supposed to come in going 'parp parp parpity parp' then me and Tobe would come back in on guitar and synth respectively. But The Gent just stood there. We all looked at each other and gradually stopped playing. Just the drum machine carried on for about twenty seconds, then there was a tiny clap of the hand from a middle-aged bloke we knew about fifty yards away who then looked around uncertainly and stopped when no-one else joined in. The rest of the crowd completely ignored us.

'The next song is about the fascist regime in the USA,' shouted Bandy.

'I am an American. I voted Ronnie Reagan,' he wailed. Once again, The Gent had neglected to remember this song and we all started to look at each other nervously again. Bandy did a strange, slightly scary wiggle and shimmy dance (a close, more subtle, relation of his chicken dance), something he would have perceived as lighting the blue sex-touchpaper, to get the crowd going, but no-one noticed.

One problem was that, due to the fact that we were playing in a field, the sound wasn't carrying to all of the crowd. At rock festivals bands utilise highly powered PA systems but the Brezhnev Brothers relied on a 15v Box amp and a little practice amp. At the end of the song no one showed any appreciation, apart from the local Cub Scout leader. She stared at us rather too enthusiastically with a big smile on her face and there was a slight concern that she might have the hots for one of the band. We were all in this to get laid (for the first time) but the thought of copping off with Akela was too scary. If pushed, we would sacrifice Tobe to her.

If you could have surveyed the scene from the other end of the field, it would have appeared quite bizarre. Little Cubs milling around the field playing skittles and running games, with their parents close by clapping the kids and chatting with each other. Then at the far end, near the Scout hut, a tinny drum sound and a tall skinny bloke in burgundy, caterwauling and trying unsuccessfully to dance, with a blond twat on a synth you'd probably like to punch and a Chinese kid holding a trumpet and looking like he needed a wee. What would Baden-Powell have thought?

(It's Just the Same Old Show) On My Radio: 1983

Human League '(Keep Feeling) Fascination'

The Funk Masters 'It's Over'

Yello 'I Love You'

New Order 'Blue Monday'

Style Council 'Long Hot Summer'

Paul Young 'Come Back And Stay'

Wham! 'Club Tropicana'

Bananarama 'Cruel Summer'

Blancmange 'Blind Vision'

Orange Juice 'Rip It Up'

David Bowie 'Let's Dance'

47. Goodbye Small Town

Don't stop to ask
Now you've found a break to make at last
You've got to find a way
Say what you want to say
*Breakout – Corinne Drewery**

The two months between the end of our 'A' levels and the results went too quickly, in a haze of shimmering heat and bright blue skies. Without many of us noticing, the Tories had won another General Election. This time the Bhreznev Brothers formulated a creative rather than political response and wrote a song about the new Tory MP Edward Leigh called 'Ooh, Baby, They Call Him Edward Leigh'.

I was getting into the American cultural scene of the 50s, beat-writing and free jazz. For a few months I'd been reading through Jack Kerouac's back catalogue and had already started to do away with orthodox punctuation in my school essays in a bid to be 'beat' (which might explain the ropey essay marks at this time:

Q: How did the English Civil War affect late seventeeth-century politics in Europe?

---

* From Swing Out Sister's 'Breakout' – Corinne Drewery grew up in Lincolnshire.

A: Charles 1st preening bignose sleepeyed absolutist completist in psychic om chat with God – flint head puritan sweet soul Cromwell's tears of joy at the beauty of a London morning snow frost in plague house wails... etc., etc.

I'd also started flicking through the jazz encyclopedia that my parents had bought me on my thirteenth birthday and which had now gone from being a nerdy book that had to be locked away to an essential guide for regular purchases. I became intrigued by the entry for Ornette Coleman so immediately cycled off to Langfords Records on the off-chance they would have a copy. Down at the back, past the copy of Roxy Music's *Country Life* still gathering dust – pause, just to check it out for old time's sake – was *The Art of the Improvisers*.

So free jazz entered my universe. Bandy, Scooter and I even started an imaginary free jazz group called the Free Association. It was great – it meant you could play stuff without having to practise – until I discovered that Edward Leigh was, actually, in real life part of a right-wing libertarian group called The Freedom Association.

I got a job for a week or two picking wild oats out near the backroad villages. We'd get collected in a van in the early hours to go out to the big fields of North Lincolnshire to pick wild oats out of cornfields. We earned £1 an hour. I knew it was good work because Kev was involved. Every day there was a blazing sun and most people were using the usual local suntan technique: you get as red as possible, all your skin peels off and underneath there'll be a real long-lasting, healthy 'proper' tan. I found the work hard, brain-numbing and couldn't get into it. But while working the fields I had an epiphany of sorts, thinking what the hell am I doing with my time here? I would soon be leaving and realised that I wanted to be with Maggie. It was Love, pure and simple. (At least for the three months before we went off to college.)

As if stung by the very real possibility that, rather than sowing my wild oats in this never-ending summer, I was merely picking them for £1 an hour, the next morning I got on my bike and rode off to Maggie's house to have a cup of tea and somehow persuade her to sleep with me.

My plan worked.

Jesus H. Christ.

Maggie had been waiting for me for a long time. I now had a proper girlfriend. And I had had sex. Soon that searching need for escape and desire to impress that had motivated me all these years, started to dissipate. Maggie and I were nearly the same age my parents had been when they'd first met. People settle down with less than this, I thought.

I went to Scotland for a fortnight with Bandy and Bramley. We played football, climbed mountains, went drinking, lay out at night and watched shooting stars, talked shite long into the night. I listened to Coltrane's *A Love Supreme* a lot and read Sartre and Gide, while making copious notes in my journal about what it was like to be in love, all in preparation for what I thought university life might be like: three years of listening to jazz and discussing existentialism and writing novels. Of course.

I had only received a couple of college offers, from UEA in Norwich or Loughborough University, which was rumoured to have the highest proportion of women to men in the country. Tough choice. Then the results came in. Nearly everyone had got the grades they wanted, except for Bramley, who would have to retake history if he wanted to get onto his Course For People With Big Muscles Who Are Good At Football And Rugby And All Other Sports at Loughborough Uni. And me. I got an E in art. My guts did a swoop worthy of Icarus – I no longer had the grades I needed for UEA. At first I refused to accept it and even asked for a recount, like a losing candidate gasping for air while knowing he's beaten.

Johnny Sidebottom was going to Coventry Poly (cues of 'Ha ha ha ha ha – Sidebottom's been sent to Coventry! Ha ha ha ha' at least 6,000 times), Kev to Trent Poly, The Gent to Middlesex Poly, Scooter to LSE, Eddie Oates to North London Poly, Bandy to Birmingham University, Shorty to UEA. Bramley was going back to school for a year. There was just Hinesy, working away at the bank, and me. I would be put into some kind of clearing system and end up God knows where. I spent the last four weeks of the summer walking or biking the four miles to Maggie's. It was the end times as far as we were all concerned. I had been focused on the moment of departure for so long that I'd forgotten to remember how amazing life as a teenager really was.

One afternoon in September, when people had already started to drift away to their new lives, the phone rang. Snake answered it and started chatting away to someone. Then he said it was for me. It was a woman from the UEA admissions office. They would let me have a place, but doing History rather than English Studies and Film. (I could then sleep with one of my tutors and after a week or so I'd be able to change, if I wanted.)

A few weeks later, Mum and Dad were driving me to Norwich, with me in a kind of trance, finally leaving it all behind. Like most eighteen-year-olds in those days, I would never go back to live where I was brought up. It was like a dream. Did I dream my childhood? Did I really lose Dad's old marbles to Kid Jimmy McKay? Did Bandy really scribble on the back of a limited edition Sex Pistols single? Did I really see a ghost on the landing? Did my girlfriend (when I was eleven) *really* move to Scunthorpe?

48. Being Like Picasso's Dad

It's 2009. I still have a lot of baggage in my life. Except this is proper baggage, i.e. bagged-up in black bin liners, up in the loft. All the old band tapes, my old vinyl singles and albums, an old turntable, my electric guitar. Some of it's in boxes. It's my memory hard disk to help free up my brain for the important day-to-day tasks of life, but after I'm dead people will be able to piece bits of my life together using the baggage (should they so want to, of course). And when the time is right, I will give the kids the guitar, just as my dad gave me his cardboard Subbuteo set (which I destroyed), and his father gave him his WW1 telescope (which I destroyed) and his father gave him – actually, Victorian dads didn't give their sons anything, apart from a clip round the ear, a genetic predisposition for alcohol and a belief that dying for one's country was the right thing to do. But, happily, I now feel part of the chain, the great chain of giving.

I've decided to pass on my old LPs and singles to my children as well, so I bring them down in piles from the attic.

'Dad, are these… RECORDS?' My daughter, C, is jumping up and down.

I nod.

'Mum, we've got records!'

C kneels down and excitedly flicks through the first pile of albums: Swell Maps, Joy Division, Miles Davis, The Clash. I leave her riffling through it while I go upstairs to get the turntable.

'Oh MY GOD!! Is that a record player, Dad? Mum, MUM! Dad's got an old-fashioned record player.'

C moves on to my box of singles.

'So do you need a mini record player to play these, Dad?'

'No, you just change the speed.'

(Doesn't know what I'm on about.) 'Oh.'

'Dad, what do old records sound like?'

I mean for her to find out soon. But nothing is simple any more. After setting up the turntable and connecting it to the amp, I discover that the stylus is broken. The next day I go to the only hi-fi shops I know in North London but neither of them had my particular stylus. So for a few days the records sit there as reminders of old technology ways.

I know people who sold all their guitars years ago for quick cash, mates who spent months working and saving for their instruments then, when they were older and more sensible, got back a few quid to spend down the pub or take their kids to Alton Towers for the day. Now they surely regret it. But I'd held onto the guitar, even though I no longer played it.

If I get rid of the guitar, in many ways that will be it for me. My adolescent dreams of freedom, creativity and excitement will have finally gone. By holding onto the guitar perhaps I'm refusing to let go of the powerfully optimistic teenage me. If I sell it I might be able to fully enter the adult world.

But no. I caress the still-smooth back of the guitar, then smell it. It still smells of 1979. I put the guitar on a stand in the corner of the room and stare at it for a while. It's hard to believe that this was once my weapon of escape and free expression.

In my mid-teens, the thought of me still being interested in my teenage life in the town in general would have seemed preposterous. I became a teenager over thirty years ago. The teenager me would have been disappointed at the idea that the fourty-four-year-old me might still be scrabbling around writing about our small town.

*

Like a lot of men my age I have suffered in adult life, career-wise, because I was on an economic blacklist. The economic blacklist was, of course, a self-imposed one. The rules of this blacklist stated that Thou Shalt Not Sell Out The Ideals Of Punk (And The General New Wave Scene) Lest Thou Be Thought Of As A, Erm, Sell-Out (a job with a suit was seen as a sell-out job). I have been stressing myself a bit about this concept of selling out my teenage self. He was an opinionated arrogant git a lot of the time but I do miss his energy and enthusiasm. When I look at my reflection now he sometimes looks back at me, but usually it's as a quieter, more cautious bloke with lines around his eyes and forehead.

When I lived in the rural suburban hinterland I just wanted to get out. It had felt suffocating and too safe. But now I wonder whether the boredom and frustration teenagers feel in those situations is actually the rocket fuel that ultimately takes them where they want to go. But it's time for me to let go of my own teenager. It's not about *me* any more.

I used to want to be like my heroes, whether it be Picasso, Kerouac, Jack B. Yeats, Joe Strummer, Terry Gilliam. But that's all changed. Now I feel more of an affinity with the fathers of some of my heroes. Yeats's father, John Butler Yeats, a sporadically successful portrait painter; Picasso's dad, José Ruiz y Blasco, also an artist. They did OK but didn't tear up any trees and were far outstripped by their offspring. Terry Gilliam's dad? Hmm, I haven't done my research on that one.

I'm married with three kids and work as an illustrator (for a football mag called *When Saturday Comes* and the *Guardian*). We all recently spent a year and a half living out on the edge of a village in rural Ireland; no traffic, quiet most of the time. More and more I seem to value silence these days. In Market Rasen I was scared by the silence so was always making noise; John Peel's radio show on too loud, records on too loud, anything to stop the buzzing-in-my-head emptiness of day-to-day life.

Lincolnshire was *quiet*. There was the occasional scream of a jet fighter or rasp of a motorbike but it didn't have the constant background hum that makes Londoners feel so safe and secure – whooshing coffee machines, building sites, radios, the rumble of cars, people making smalltalk, people shouting, sirens in the background, helicopters hovering overhead on match days. Ireland was great and we seriously thought of permanently giving up our urban existence for a life out in the sticks, to give the kids that combination of space, fresh air and boredom, but, in the end, the pull of coffee machines and police helicopters was too strong.

'Are you famous, Daddy?'

The words make me feel strange. Simultaneously amused and appalled. What on earth does she mean by that?

'Well,' I laugh, momentarily forgetting that I'm talking to a ten-year-old. 'What does "famous" actually mean?'

'It means that everybody knows your name.'

'Hmm.'

'So are you?'

'What?'

'Famous.'

'No.'

So there comes a time in every man's life when he decides it's time to give up on his dream. At last, I have decided I'm not going to bring out a critically acclaimed album, not going to play a storming electro-acoustic gig with the surviving members of The Velvet Underground (though not Doug Yule) at the Royal Albert Hall, not going to tour the USA in a great big shiny bus with my wife on keyboards, not going to get a snog out of Emmylou Harris, not going to use my fame as a musician to set up an acoustic guitar charity that aims to make everyone in the world a sensitive singer-songwriter.

I'm going to do none of those things.

The awful truth – well, it's awful as far as I'm concerned – is that the nearest I came to fulfilling my dream of musical and creative glory was thirty years ago when I jumped up and down doing pretend guitar on my dad's Bullworker while Bandy shrieked and wailed about flick-knives and VD and fourth-year girls. I still have most of those cassette tapes, in an old cardboard box. Most people would have chucked out this old rubbish years ago, but my mum knew it would be important some day and kept it. After all, as she had said after listening to one of our bedroom music sessions, 'Your stuff is better than most of the stuff you see on *Top of the Pops*.' She also said, 'Your tea is ready. Why are your ears so dirty?' but the history books won't be interested in that.

The cassette labels are covered in a strange indecipherable script, the hurried handwriting of a teenage boy. It's with a mixture of excitement and embarassment that I put them one by one into a tape player. What comes out – frenzied fuzzbox ballads with Bandy's squeaky-voiced singing – is pure time travel and immediately sends me hurtling back to my youth.

Looking back I still wonder why so many of us came together at that time to form bands. In the days before the internet, twenty-four-hour TV or computer games there was a gap in the lives of teenagers – an exquisite boredom – that had to be filled by creative energy. Maybe there was something in the local water – or more likely, the beer. After all, there had already been two songwriting trailblazers from the area – Taupin and Temperton – who'd actually made it in music. Well, not really 'made it' so much as become hugely successful and world famous with swimming pools, lobster thermidore on tap and great big entourages.

But I think in a way my old friends and I, the kids of the rural suburbs, never really thought in our hearts that we would 'make it' at anything. We were somehow made to feel that doing OK was as much as you could expect coming from Lincolnshire. Always falling short, then giving up with a shrug. Whether it was rugby, music, getting girls, being next in line for the throne, supporting rubbish teams, not being tough, not being cool, not being especially brainy. It ties in with my feeling that it was right to not collect the whole set of football stickers.

Our low expectations sometimes made us laugh at the idea of endeavour and taking anything at all seriously. Bandy and I thrived on a celebration of the crapness of things; not wanting to win. What was holding us back? Maybe it was the feeling that we were stuck out in the country and no one would see us no matter how good we were at anything.

And that's where I am once again, with the small-town view of the world, though now it seems like a good thing. At this stage I'm never going to learn anything new on the guitar so really, like Picasso's dad and Yeats's dad, I should try to pass on what little I do know to the next generation before it all disappears and my long-term memory tanks become marooned from the rest of my brain. We bought our daughter a guitar for Christmas. You see, I want her to be in a band and make it big and say 'it was all down to my dad' and… er, I mean, I want her to enjoy the creative expression that the guitar offers and the possibilities for personal redemption inherent in the singer-songwriter idiom.

Controversially I have decided to teach her myself. Some are already questioning this decision. Do you want her to play the guitar like you? they ask. Why don't you get a guitar teacher to do it?

But I'm happy. At last I have something tangible that I can pass on.

There is a learning DVD that came with C's guitar. It's got all the basics but I think that it's such a cop-out way of learning. Far too technical and the student misses out on the frustration that they will eventually feel for the teacher. C is going to learn how I learned. With The Clash songbook. And don't worry, it's not as bad as it sounds. I don't mean the *Give 'Em Enough Rope* era songbook. That would be crazy and I don't want to mess with her mind. I'm talking about the seminal text, the bible of the punk grandad generation. The Clash songbook with guitar tabs from The Clash's *The Clash* and the early singles like 'Clash City Rockers' and 'Capital Radio'.

C's new guitar is smaller than mine. It's a cheap three-quarter size nylon string model from Argos. The rite of passage of guitar buying is not what it was. I went into the shop, wrote down a catalogue number and in seconds a guitar-shaped box was puked up from a doorway and plonked on the counter by a chubby teenager with spots. No magic, no old hippies smelling of dope, no teenagers playing 'Smoke On The Water', no sense of danger or rebellion.

49. Goodbye Maggie

You're probably wondering, Hold on a minute, this is the end of the book – what happened to Tim and Maggie Jefferson?

By the end of 1983 (the middle of my first term at university), Maggie had moved to Norwich to be with me. She was supposed to have been going to drama school to study choreography, wearing leg warmers and leotards and prancing about to disco music like the kids from Fame. I spent the rest of that term hanging out with her and not going to lectures, thinking I was some kind of glamorous Jack Kerouac-type figure (translation: 'Hey, look at me – I have a girlfriend'). It was all a bit of a novelty. At the start of 1984, I narrowly avoided being kicked out of the university, then got my head down and started frequenting the library (thankfully, no penis book graffiti artists) and attending seminars. Then Maggie and I got a flat together. And played at being grown-ups.

It was a good time but also strange being settled down so young. We split up three years or so later and did that awkward thing of staying friends and continuing to live together for several months afterwards – 'you crazy kids, run, run to the hills (or, at least, to separate living accommodation)', I find myself shouting at the twenty-one-year-old me from the comfy vantage point of twenty-three years into the future, but he can't hear me. But if I could build a time machine, what would I have done differently?

And then it ended, finally, one winter evening, when I disappeared off to London on the train, with my 1940s typewriter and my guitar strapped to my body for safekeeping.

Maggie and I hadn't been in contact for a long, long time, until out of the blue towards the end of 2008 she sent me an e-mail asking how much my old 'A' level painting of Icarus might be worth. She had come across some of my artwork online and I guess she thought I might want the painting back. It had been sitting in her loft for years.

Normally I might be a bit cautious at the idea of meeting up with an ex-girlfriend but I am a little curious – who wouldn't be? So we agree, after some intermittent correspondence lasting several months, to meet up in London, where she comes now and then for work meetings, so she could hand over the painting.

When I tell my wife I'm meeting Maggie she gives me a funny look and goes a bit quiet.

'What do you need to meet for?'

'I want to get my painting back,' I say.

'Can't she post it?'

We'd arranged to meet under the announcement board at King's Cross station. And when she suddenly appears it hits me how long ago all this was. She is now married with a seventeen-year-old daughter who is on the verge of taking her 'A' levels and I have three kids, one on the verge of becoming a teenager. We are over a generation on from those early 80s days.

By some sort of catastrophe of progress, the pub at King's Cross Station is no longer open, so we go to an O'Neill's pub on Euston Road. I get a coffee and Maggie has a glass of water. We're both awkward but gradually we loosen up a bit and have a laugh about old times and people we knew. Maggie finally hands over the painting, in a cardboard tube, and I take it out. 'Is it genius or crap?' I say and she laughs (though doesn't answer the question).

After half an hour we walk back to the station, say our goodbyes and walk out of each other's lives again, probably for ever this time. I watch Maggie go and with her walks a ghostly young teenage version of myself, dressed in crap Bowie trousers, trying to put his arm round her but being too shy, as she climbs the steps to the mainline station and I head for the Piccadilly line home.

50. Being Like Phil Lynott's Dad

The new stylus, a Shure V15 Type IV, has arrived, from a warehouse somewhere in 1979. I fix it up, check the speakers and amp are connected properly, then ask the kids to pick a record. With over hundreds to choose from they plump quite quickly for *The Jungle Book* album. The kids are not used to being able to see the technology in action. They watch, fascinated, as the needle comes down; there's that scratchy sound that now seems alien yet so comfortingly familiar, then the room is full of music.

'Dad, how does it work?'

'Well, erm, the music comes off the record, it comes down the needle then into the amp, then down the wire to the speakers, then out into the room.'

'Wow.'

After they've jumped around the room to various bebop dance numbers sung by animals, I ask them to choose another LP. This time by a 'proper band'. They go through the pile slowly, frowning, unable to read some of the titles. The Clash's first album is rejected. As is *Instant Replay* by The Monkees. They don't even dwell on *Sextet* by A Certain Ratio or *Entertainment!* by Gang of Four. The trouble is they don't recognise any of these artists. Then, suddenly, C pulls out a double album with a cry of recognition.

'It's Thin Lizzy!'

Yes, it's Thin Lizzy's *Live and Dangerous*. Slightly disappointed, I take the first disc out of the sleeve. Due to it having been hidden away in my wardrobe for many years, this is in near mint condition. The needle comes down. The opening fuzzed overdrive guitar chords to 'Jailbreak' smash out of the speakers. It is actually really good. The kids start bouncing around the room doing air guitar, their eyes closed in concentration as one long era finally ends and I once again have to resign myself to the way things have turned out.

I am the father of heavy rockers.

Postscript 1

After much searching I finally unearth the truth about the Dickens quote in an old journal he wrote called *Household Words*. Market Rasen was in fact merely *joint top* in the 'horribly dull' stakes with Shepton Mallet. Which puts a whole new spin on things.

(*Household Words, A Weekly Journal*. Vol. 13, 1856. Page 176)

Postscript 2

As John Lennon once remarked, 'Whoo, Yoko, that atonal synth wail overload really works on this track.'

No, not that one. (Flicks through cheap book of John Lennon quotes.)

It's 'life happens while you're busy making plans'.

Acknowledgements

I have a reasonable memory, but there were certain chunks of the 1978-83 period of which I had virtually no recollection at all. My erratically filled-in diaries helped me during these sections, but I also have had to rely on my good friend Ian Plenderleith, whose memory is a spectacularly efficient database of facts, anecdotes, football scores and mundane events. So spectacular, in fact, that I now suspect he employed a secretary during our school years and dictated the day's events to her each evening in his oak-panelled study. I also have to thank him for early draft thoughts and advice.

Thanks to David Smith, my music-loving agent, for all his hard work; Andrew Goodfellow and Ali Nightingale, my editors at Ebury, for guiding me through and for helping tease out the stories. Thanks too to the three famous Lincolnshire songwriters Bernie Taupin, Rod Temperton and Corinne Drewery, for being good sports. Also thanks to inspiring teachers Jane, Julie, Richard and Robin; to those who read early drafts, gave their blessing, helped free up time, helped with research, gave me home made cider – George and Simone, Paul and Hilary, Michael, Sarah, DJ, Ian C, Maxine, Denise, Tim B. and Nicola, plus The Market Rasen Mail and De Aston School for letting me in to reminisce.

Thanks to my folks, Tony and Rhona, for everything; to my brothers Toby and Matthew, for their support and their expensive musical instruments; Tim, Noreen, Rob and Rich, for too many great stories and times to mention here. And all my old friends from Lincolnshire without whom I couldn't have written this, especially Neil Ruane, Richard Scott, Kev Coleman, Andy Hayes, Mark Longden, Derek Yau and Bon Halpenny.

And thanks to Cindy, for her love, proofing, cups of tea and oaties. And to Cathleen, Seán and Tommy for helping me with their great creative ideas and for not getting too cross when I disappear off to write things down. Finished now.

To Mum and Dad.
Thanks for letting us draw on the walls.

Local Hards

Credits

The author and publisher would like to thank the following for permission to reproduce material: EMI Music Publishing for permission to quote from 'Poison Arrow' by ABC, written by White, Fry, Singleton, Lickley; Bernie Taupin for permission to quote from 'Saturday Night's Alright for Fighting'; Corinne Drewery for permission to quote from 'Breakout' by Swing Out Sister; Kevin Coleman for permission to quote from 'Stupid War' and 'Killer' by The Store Detectives, written by Coleman/Hall; Ian Plenderleith for lyrics to various Heart Attack numbers; Rod Temperton for permission to quote from 'Boogie Nights' written by Rod Temperton. Published by Rodsongs/Chrysalis Music Ltd (c) 1976. Used by permission. All rights reserved.

We have made every attempt to find the copyright holders of quotes material, apologise for any omissions and are happy to receive emendations from copyright holders.

Illustration credits
'The Bertillons' by F Chalaud (From *Le Francais d'Aujourd 'hui*, Hodder & Stoughton 1966)
'Dick and Dora' by William Semple (From Happy Venture Readers: Introductory Book) pub Oliver & Boyd Ltd 1958

Photo credits
'Audreys Hairdressers' advert and 'Miss Chamber of Trade competitors,1970'
The Market Rasen Mail

Tim in front of the NME wall, Tim on the A46
By Ian Plenderleith